Advances in Systemic Linguistics

Open Linguistics Series

The *Open Linguistics Series*, to which this book makes a significant contribution, is 'open' in two senses. First, it provides an open forum for works associated with any school of linguistics or with none. Linguistics has now emerged from a period in which many (but never all) of the most lively minds in the subject seemed to assume that transformational-generative grammar — or at least something fairly closely derived from it — would provide the main theoretical framework for linguistics for the foreseeable future. In Kuhn's terms, linguistics had appeared to some to have reached the 'paradigm' stage. Reality today is very different. More and more scholars are working to improve and expand theories that were formerly scorned for not accepting as central the particular set of concerns highlighted in the Chomskyan approach — such as Halliday's systemic theory (as exemplified in this book) Lamb's stratificational model and Pike's tagmemics — while others are developing new theories. The series is open to all approaches, then — including work in the generativist-formalist tradition.

The second sense in which the series is 'open' is that it encourages works that open out 'core' linguistics in various ways: to encompass discourse and the description of natural texts; to explore the relationship between linguistics and its neighbouring disciplines such as psychology, sociology, philosophy, artificial intelligence, and cultural and literary studies; and to apply it in fields such as education and language pathology.

Open Linguistics Series Editor
Robin F. Fawcett, University of Wales College of Cardiff

Modal Expressions in English, Michael R. Perkins
Text and Tagmeme, Kenneth L. Pike and Evelyn G. Pike
The Semiotics of Culture and Language, eds: Robin P. Fawcett, M.A.K. Halliday, Sydney M. Lamb and Adam Makkai
Into the Mother Tongue: A Case Study in Early Language Development, Clare Painter
Language and the Nuclear Arms Debate: Nukespeak Today, ed: Paul Chilton
The Structure of Social Interaction: A Systemic Approach to the Semiotics of Service Encounters, Eija Ventola
Grammar in the Construction of Texts, ed.: James Monaghan
On Meaning, A.J. Griemas, trans. by Paul Perron and Frank Collins
Biological Metaphor and Cladistic Classification: An Interdisciplinary Approach, eds: Henry M. Hoenigswald and Linda F. Wiener
New Developments in Systemic Linguistics, Volume 1: Theory and Description, eds: M.A. Halliday and Robin P. Fawcett
Volume 2: Theory and Application, eds: Robin P. Fawcett and David Young
Eloquence and Power: The Rise of Language Standards and Standard Language, John Earl Joseph
Functions of Style, eds: David Birch and Michael O'Toole
Registers of Written English: Situational Factors and Linguistic Features, ed.: Mohsen Ghadessy
Pragmatics, Discourse and Text ed.: Erich H. Steiner and Robert Veltman
The Communicative Syallabus, Robin Melrose

ADVANCES IN SYSTEMIC LINGUISTICS

Recent Theory and Practice

Edited by
MARTIN DAVIES
and
LOUISE RAVELLI

Pinter Publishers
London and New York

© Martin Davies and Louise Ravelli and contributors, 1992

First published in Great Britain in 1992 by
Pinter Publishers Limited
25 Floral Street, London WC2E 9DS

British Library Cataloguing in Publication Data

A CIP catalogue record for this book is available from the British Library

ISBN 0 86187 070 0

Library of Congress Cataloging in Publication Data

A CIP catalog record for this book is available from the Library of Congress

Typeset by Mayhew Typesetting, Rhayader, Powys
Printed and bound in Great Britain by Biddles Ltd, Guildford and King's Lynn

Contents

List of figures

List of tables

1 Introduction

We present here reports of recent work in systemic functional linguistics which exemplify advances in current theory and practice. While they derive from papers given at the 17th International Systemic Congress (ISC), held at Stirling in July 1990, each incorporates significant further developments.[1]

Our selection presents five areas of systemic linguistics within which there is much current discussion. This is not and could not be a comprehensive representation of all current systemic work: the papers are only a selective exemplification, and not a summary of systemic functional linguistics as a whole, or even of any single part of it. Within the covers of a book of this size, gaps are inevitable, and several areas of considerable interest to systemicists are not well represented. Had the congress been held in Australia, for example, there would have been a strong emphasis on educational linguistics. Further, other areas which have recently been very productive, such as exchange structure, genre, and computational linguistics, while strongly represented at the congress, have only limited representation here.

In common with other systemicists, and despite some of the implications which might have been drawn from our title, we do not use the distinctions often made between 'pure' and 'applied' linguistics, or between 'theoretical' and 'practical' discussion. Rather, the papers try to meet Firth's requirement that we should maintain 'renewal of connection', with theory informing our studies of text and our studies of text informing the development of the theory. So the writers of papers which may appear to be predominantly theoretical are always very much concerned, whether explicitly or not, with what text tells us about language and how it is to be described; and equally the papers which are primarily concerned with practical description have implications for theory, whether or not these are made explicit.

Nevertheless, the first group of papers is distinguished from later ones by taking a very broad view of systemic issues. Sinclair's paper, which opened the congress, similarly opens our collection. He presents a strong challenge to systemics as a whole, and indeed to linguistics as a whole, drawing challenging conclusions from ongoing work with the Birmingham Cobuild corpora: he suggests both that the nature of the evidence used in linguistic theory must be queried and that new models of discourse must be developed. After this, Halliday's plenary paper, attacking a central theoretical matter at a different angle, addresses one of the most central issues in system theory: the task of clarifying how experience is construed as meaning.

The second group of papers is more specifically concerned with developing our understanding of two of the three metafunctions posited within the theory. Interestingly, this section goes some way towards redressing an imbalance in previous thinking about metafunctions, which has tended to concentrate on the ideational. Matthiessen offers a fundamental contribution to the theory of textual meaning, considering not only how it may be interpreted but also its implications for modelling and its relations with the other metafunctions. Interpersonal meaning is explored by Lemke, who argues that, to account for this metafunction in discourse, its role in the social system must be viewed more broadly, and the use of the linguistic system to express this aspect of meaning must be examined more closely.

At the 1987 ISC, at the University of Sydney, Halliday made a plea – in the light of all the ongoing developments in semiotics – that the lexicogrammar should not be forgotten. Davidse provides a sophisticated example of traditional systemic argumentation in tackling an intricate problem in this area – the interaction between transitivity and ergativity. In a different vein, McGregor's provocative paper suggests controversial alterations to orthodox practice, challenging basic systemic assumptions about the way to handle adverbials and providing solutions which will certainly lead to further debate. Tucker, on the other hand, shows the implications of computational modelling for the lexicogrammar. Dealing with comparatives, a long-vexed area of grammatical controversy, he sheds new light on them, while usefully demonstrating again that the computational approach forces grammatical statements to be much more explicit.

The fourth group reflects the great current interest in the text-building function of Theme, which generated large discussion groups both at Stirling and at the preceding Helsinki congress in 1989 (see Ventola forthcoming). Discussion continued at the Nottingham conference held shortly after Helsinki and devoted solely to Theme, and the English Department at Nottingham subsequently hosted another conference devoted to Rheme the following year. A third – at which further substantial discussion of Theme and Rheme took place – was held in 1991. The first paper included here is a most useful summary of Firbas's present thinking in the related approach of Functional Sentence Perspective. It was work in this field thirty years ago that provided one of the starting points from which Halliday (1967–68) separated Theme from Given and specified their respective roles in the creation of text. Moreover, Firbas's paper gives a most useful summary of Firbas (forthcoming) while providing among other things an alternative perspective on the nature of Topical Theme. This is a problematical area that has been discussed in a number of papers presented

at recent systemic conferences, including that of Rashidi. Equally important, her paper contributes to the all too sparse literature on Theme in
languages other than English. We hope this will stimulate further discussion of Theme in other languages.

In one sense the final group of papers – at least at first glance – is the
least abstract: they are all in some way concerned with studies of particular
texts, or at least of substantial passages of texts. But to the systemic mind,
which has always based developments in textual studies on theoretical
developments and developments in theory on studies of text, their position
at the end of this collection is in no sense a reflection of minor theoretical
interest, still less of minor status: it is, rather, a culmination of the New,
though in the text rather than in the Information Group. Here, theory is
illuminating our understanding of text and – at the same time – the theory
is being refined by being tested against text: a dual process which in our
view is what systemic linguistics is all about. First, Benson and Greaves
build on Australian work (Wignell *et al.* 1987) to explore the ways in which
the grammatical relation of Token to Value in identifying clauses is used
to express technicality, in this case in the register of Bridge. This extends
earlier work by J. R. Martin and his colleagues at the University of
Sydney on technicality and abstraction in education. Narrative is the focus
of Emmott's paper, and it is used as a springboard for a novel approach
to one aspect of cohesion – the examination of how referential ties are
actually made in text. She invokes a notion proposed here for the first
time, so far as we know: that of 'narrative enactors'. Finally, the group
is completed by a second study in literary stylistics. Kies's paper is a
powerful analysis of the wide range of grammatical devices used by Orwell
to foreground one of his themes in *Nineteen Eighty-Four*; the numbers of
certain types of these devices increased greatly in a principled way when
Orwell revised his manuscript. Kies shows that both the number and the
range of these devices are critical factors in contributing to the expression
of the themes (in the literary sense) of the novel.

Despite the wide range of topics covered in this collection, the papers
share a common universe of discourse. However, it is not the case that
there is no controversy here, nor even that every paper is an example of
'centrally systemic' thinking. This deliberately reflects the nature of recent
systemic congresses. The main relevant aspect of this is that healthy debate
frequently arises between 'mainstream' papers and papers which overtly or
covertly challenge basic systemic assumptions. It is only necessary to
compare Sinclair's, Davidse's and McGregor's handling of evidence to see
that this is so. But, secondly, congresses in the past few years have tended
to attract new participants many of whom come from other approaches to
language, and the growing number of these represents a dilemma for
speakers: how to interest the systemic old hand while at the same time
interesting and informing the newcomer. This collection does not solve the
problem, but it draws on the situation positively by including papers which
do not necessarily fully accept systemic thinking. For example, while
Emmott's work is related to – and in large part grows out of – systemic

theory, she goes beyond conventional systemic terminology and concepts in presenting her arguments.

So a significant number of the challenges facing systemic linguistics are addressed here, though many questions of course remain, particularly with respect to those coming from pragmatics (Butler 1989). But the atmosphere at Stirling, as usually at systemic meetings, was not only challenging but friendly, and we now offer these papers to a wider audience in the hope that – as was suggested by Halliday and Fawcett (1987: 1–2) – they will contribute to the advance of our understanding of language as a resource for meaning, doing so by vigorous co-operation rather than by polemic or confrontation.

M.D.
L.R.

NOTE

1. All the papers have been subject to a process of selection in which the role of anonymous referees has been critical. We are extremely grateful for the speed and thoroughness with which they responded to our requests for evaluation, as it has helped to make a difficult process much easier. Regrettably, not all the papers they recommended – or which we wanted – could be included.

REFERENCES

Butler, C.S. (1989), 'Systemic models: unity, diversity and change', in *Word* 40.1–2, April–August, 1–35.

Firbas, J. (forthcoming), *Functional Sentence Perspective in Written and Spoken Communications* (submitted for publication to Cambridge University Press).

Gregory, M. (1985), 'Phasal analysis within communication linguistics: two contrastive discourses', in J. Copeland (ed.), *Proceedings of the Second Rice University Symposium on Linguistics and Semantics: Text Semantics and Discourse Semantics*, Chicago, University of Chicago Press.

Firth, J.R. (1957), *Papers in Linguistics, 1934–1951*, London, Oxford University Press.

Halliday, M.A.K. (1967–68), 'Notes on Transitivity and Theme', *Journal of Linguistics*, 3.1, 37–81; 3.2, 199–244; 4.2, 179–215.

Halliday, M.A.K., and Fawcett, R.P. (1987), *New Developments in Linguistics*, 1, London, Pinter.

Ventola, E. (ed.) (forthcoming), *Recent Systemic and other Functional Views on Language*, Berlin, Mouton de Gruyter.

Wignell, P., Martin, J.R., and Eggins, S. (1987), 'The discourse of geography: ordering and explaining the experiential world', in S. Eggins, J.R. Martin and P. Wignell, *Writing Project Report*, Working Papers in Linguistics 5, University of Sydney Linguistics Department.

Part I. Framework

1 Trust the text
John McH. Sinclair

By way of a sub-title to this paper, I should like to quote a short sentence from a recent article in *The European*, by Randolph Quirk.

The implications are daunting.

I shall refer to the discourse function of this sentence from time to time, but at present I would like to draw attention to its ominous tone. The implications of trusting the text are for me extremely daunting, but also very exciting and thought-provoking.

The argument that I would like to put forward is that linguistics has been formed and shaped on inadequate evidence and in a famous phrase 'degenerate data'. There has been a distinct shortage of information and evidence available to linguists, and this gives rise to a particular balance between speculation and fact in the way in which we talk about our subject. In linguistics up till now we have been relying very heavily on speculation.

This is not a criticism; it is a fact of life. The physical facts of language are notoriously difficult to remember. Some of you will remember the days before tape recorders and will agree that it is extremely difficult to remember details of speech that has just been uttered. Now that there is so much language available on record, particularly written language in electronic form, but also substantial quantities of spoken language, our theory and descriptions should be re-examined to make sure they are appropriate. We have experienced not only a quantitative change in the amount of language data available for study, but a consequent qualitative change in the relation between data and hypothesis. In the first part of this paper I hope to raise a point about description based on the appreciation of this fairly fundamental appraisal.

Apart from the strong tradition of instrumental phonetics we have only recently devised even the most rudimentary techniques for making and managing the recording of language, and even less for the analysis of it. In particular we should be suspicious of projecting techniques that are suitable for some areas of language patterning on to others.

This is my first point. Until recently linguistics has been able to develop fairly steadily. Each new position in the major schools has arisen fairly naturally out of the previous one. However, the change in the availability of information which we now enjoy makes it prudent for us to be less confident about reusing accepted techniques.

My second main point is that we should strive to be open to the patterns observable in language in quantity as we now have it. The growing evidence that we have suggests that there is to be found a wealth of meaningful patterns that, with current perspectives, we are not led to expect. We must gratefully adjust to this new situation and rebuild a picture of language and meaning which is not only consistent with the evidence but exploits it to the full. This will take some time, and the first stage should be an attempt to inspect the data with as little attention as possible to theory.

It is impossible to study patterned data without some theory, however primitive. The advantage of a robust and popular theory is that it is well tried against previous evidence and offers a quick route to sophisticated observation and insight. The main disadvantage is that, by prioritizing some patterns, it obscures others. I believe that linguists should consciously strive to reduce this effect, until the situation stabilizes.

The first of my points takes us into the present state of the analysis of discourse which is now some twenty years old and worth an overhaul; the second plunges us into corpus linguistics, which, although even more venerable, has been rather furtively studied until becoming suddenly popular quite recently. They might seem to have very little in common, but for me they are the twin pillars of language research.

What unites them is:

(a) They both encourage the formulation of radically new hypotheses. Although they can be got to fit existing models, that is only because of our limited vision at present.
(b) The dimensions of pattern that they deal with are, on the whole, larger than linguistics is accustomed to. Both to manage the evidence required, and even to find some of it in the first place, there is a need to harness the power of modern computers.

The most important development in linguistic description in my generation has been the attempt from many different quarters to describe structures above the sentence and to incorporate the descriptions in linguistic models. The study of text, of discourse, including speech acts and pragmatics, is now central in linguistics. Since the early 1950s a number of approaches have been devised that attempt to account for larger patterns of language. Although large-scale patterns are clearly affected by, for example, sociological variables, they still lie firmly within the orbit of linguistic behaviour for as long as linguistic techniques can be used as the basis of their description.

No doubt we quite often begin a new study by projecting upwards the proven techniques of well described areas of language. To give an example, consider distributional techniques of description which began in phonology. These led in the early 1950s to attempts by, for example, Zellig Harris, to describe written text using essentially the same methods, by looking for repeated words and phrases which would form a basis for classifying the words and phrases that occur next to them. This is just the way in which phonemes were identified and distinguished from allophones: the basis of the famous 'complementary distribution'. Now there are only a relatively small number of phonemes in any language, numbered in tens, and there are a relatively large number of words, numbered in tens of thousands. The circumstances are quite different, and in the pre-computer era this kind of research faced very serious problems. The unlikelihood of finding exactly repeated phrases led Harris to the idea that stretches of language which, though physically different, were systematically related, could be regarded as essentially the same. This was articulated as grammatical transformation. It is an object lesson in what can go wrong if you project your techniques upwards into other areas without careful monitoring and adaptation. In the event, transformations provided the key feature with which Chomsky (1957) launched a wave of cognitive, non-textual linguistics.

Discourse study took off when speech acts (Austin 1962) were identified in philosophy. It took a development in a discipline outside linguistics to offer a reconceptualization of the function of the larger units of language. However, much of the description of discourse since then has been the upward projection of models, worked out originally for areas like grammar and phonology. I cheerfully admit *mea culpa* here, in having projected upwards a scale and category model in an attempt to show the structure of spoken interaction (Sinclair *et al.* 1972). It has been a serviceable model, and it is still developing, along lines which are now suitable for capturing the general structure of interactive discourse. Recent work on conversation by Amy Tsui (1986), on topic by Hazadiah Mohd Dahan (forthcoming) and by others incorporating the relations between spoken and written language are continuing within the broad umbrella of that model while making it more convenient as a vehicle for explaining the nature of interaction in language.

Louise Ravelli's study of dynamic grammar (1991) is an interesting exercise in turning the new insights of a theoretical development back on to familiar ground. It is in effect a projection downwards from the insights of discourse into some aspects of language form.

While using familiar tools is a reasonable tactic for getting started, we should also work towards a model of discourse which is special to discourse and which is not based upon the upward projection of descriptive techniques, no matter how similar we perceive the patterns to be. In this case, for the description of discourse, we should build a model which emphasizes the distinctive features of discourse. A special model for discourse will offer an explanation of those features of discourse that are unique to it, or characteristic of it, or prominent in discourse but not elsewhere.

Many of the structural features of discourse are large scale and highly variable. As the units of language description get larger, the identification of meaningful units becomes more problematic. The computer is now available to help in this work.

However, we should not use the computer merely to demonstrate patterns which we predict from other areas of language study. It will labour mightily and apparently with success, but it may also labour in vain. Mechanizations of existing descriptive systems are present in abundance. Many teams of scholars have made excellent, but limited, use of the computer to model a pre-mechanized description of part of language form, and tested the model against data. The computer will expose errors and suggest corrections; it will apply rules indefatigably, and it will continue to tell us largely what we already know.

Instead I would like to suggest that we might devise new hypotheses about the nature of text and discourse and use the computer to test whether they actually work. Computers have not been much used in this way so far in language work; their main role has been checking on detail. Gradually computers are becoming capable of quite complex analysis of language. They are able to apply sophisticated models to indefinitely large stretches of text and they are getting better and better at it. As always in computer studies, the pace is accelerating, and this will soon be commonplace.

I would like to put forward one hypothesis, or perhaps a small related set of hypotheses, which should simplify and strengthen the description of discourse. It is a stronger hypothesis than one normally encounters in discourse, and it is one where the computer can be used in a testing role. It is explicit enough to identify a large number of cases automatically. Where it fails the cases will be interesting to the analyst, because in such cases the hypothesis is either wrong or not properly stated, or the evidence is too vague or idiosyncratic to be covered by general statement.

This hypothesis draws on something by which I set very great store – the prospective features of spoken discourse. For me the study of discourse began in earnest when I classified initiations in exchanges according to how they pre-classify what follows (Sinclair 1966; quoted in Sinclair and Coulthard 1975: 151; see also 133). This approach broadened into the view that a major central function of language is that it constantly prospects ahead. It cannot determine in most cases what actually will happen, especially not in spoken interaction, but it does mean that whatever does happen has a value that is already established by the discourse at that point. So the scene is set for each next utterance by the utterance that is going on at the moment. Over the years, the more that attention has been focused on the prospective qualities of discourse the more accurate and powerful the description has become.

In contrast much of the analysis of written language as text has concerned retrospective pattern. Patterns of cohesion, of repetition, reference, replacement and so on. Complex patterns emerge, linking parts of a text to each other. Some become very complex indeed, and sample texts have many lines drawn from one part of the text to another to indicate ties, links, chains etc. I accept, as I am sure most scholars do, that written and spoken language are different in many particulars, but are they as different as the styles of analysis suggest? Is it really true that we mainly find prospection in the spoken language and retrospection in the written language? That would suggest that they are very different indeed.

Of course there are backward references in conversation. But why are they not apparently as important to the analyst as they are in the written language? Vice versa there are prospections that can be identified in the written language, as Winter (1977) and Tadros (1985) have shown.

People do not remember the spoken language exactly and so they cannot refer back to it in quite the simple way that they can with the written language. Because we have written text in front of us to check on it is apparently easy to rely on retrospective reference. But do we really in the normal course of reading actually check back pronominal reference and so on? I doubt it. The point could no doubt be checked by doing studies of eye movements but I doubt if many researchers would consider it viable enough to require checking.

Informal experiments which colleagues and I did many years ago supported the commonsense view which is that in general people forget the actual language but remember the message. And so the question that I would like to ask is 'Do we actually need all the linguistic detail of backward reference that we find in text description?' Text is often described as a long string of sentences, and this encourages the practice of drawing links from one bit of the text to another. I would like to suggest, as an alternative, that the most important thing is what is happening in the current sentence. The meaning of any word is got from the state of the discourse and not from where it came from. A word of reference like a pronoun should be interpreted exactly like a proper name or a noun phrase. The reader should find a value for it in the immediate state of the text, and not have to retrieve it from previous text unless the text is problematic at that point.

The state of the discourse is identified with the sentence which is currently being processed. No other sentence is presumed to be available. The previous text is part of the immediately previous experience of the reader or listener, and is no different from any other, non-linguistic experience. It will normally have lost the features which were used to organize the meaning to shape the text into a unique communicative instrument.

From this perspective, there is no advantage to be gained in tracing the references back in the text. The information thus gleaned will not be relevant to the current state of the discourse because previous states of the text are of no interest to the present state of the text; nor is it important how the present state of the text was arrived at.

I reiterate this point because, although it is straightforward, it is not an orthodox position and yet it is central to my argument. There are minor qualifications to be made, but nothing should disturb the main point. The conceptual difficulty arises, I believe, from the fact that the previous text is always present and available to the analyst, and the temptation to make use of it is too strong.

The notion of *primed frames* in Emmott (Chapter 11 below) is promising. Some form of mental representation of the text so far, the state of the text, must be building up in the mind of a competent reader, and must be available for interpreting the text at any particular point. It would be a digression in this argument to discuss positions concerning mental representations, because my concern is to explain how the text operates DISCOURSALLY – while someone is experiencing its meaning. Very roughly we can understand it as the previous sentence minus its interactive elements – whatever enabled it to be an interaction at a previous stage in the text – plus the inferences that have been used in order to interpret the text at this particular point.

Let us take as a starting position the view that 'the text' is the sentence that is being processed at any time and only that. The text is the sentence that IS in front of us when an act of reading is in progress. Each sentence then is a new beginning to the text. Each sentence organizes language and the world for that particular location in the text, not dependent on anything else. (No wonder, by the way, that we have had such problems in the past about the definition of a sentence, if it is indeed synonymous with the definition of a text. The paradox of the structure which represents a 'complete thought', but which is often verbalized in a form that is clearly part of a larger organization, is resolved.)

The relation between a sentence and the previous text is as follows: each sentence contains one connection with other states of the text preceding it. That is to say it contains a single act of reference which encapsulates the whole of the previous text and simultaneously removes its interactive potential. The occurrence of the next sentence pensions off the previous one, replaces it and becomes the text. The whole text is present in each sentence. The meaning of each previous sentence is represented simply as part of the shared knowledge that one is bringing to bear in the interpretation of a text at any point.

My position, then, is that the previous states of the text up to the one that is being processed are present in the current sentence in so far as they are needed. Previous sentences are not available in their textual form, but in a coherent text there is no need to have them. The same interpretive mechanism that we use to identify proper names, or other references from the text into our experience of the world, is suitable for processing that part of our experience which has been produced by previous text.

If this view is accepted, the way is clear to concentrate in description on the communicative function of each sentence and not to worry about what its textual antecedents might have been.

I now return to my original text, *The implications are daunting*. This text is obviously an act of reference to the whole of the preceding sentence, because the phrase *the implications* does not carry within itself a clear indication of what it refers to. The word *the* says that the reference of the noun group is knowable, and *implications* need to be implications of something. We may assume that the whole of the preceding sentence is whatever has implications. The preceding sentence reads like this:

> The Japanese use western languages not merely to market their goods but to improve their products by studying those of their rivals.

The act of reference works if readers are satisfied that the two sentences can be interpreted in this way.

This sentence also prospects forward to the sentences that we have not yet read. This is one of the ADVANCED LABELLING structures that Tadros (1985) has described in detail. If you mention *implications* in this way, you have to go on to list them; so we may assume that the next sentence or sentences will be understandable as implications. The quoted sentence tells us in advance that what follow are implications. Here is what follows:

> Not merely must the business have personnel with skills in different languages but the particular languages and the degree of skill may vary from person to person according to his or her job within the business. They may also vary from decade to decade as new markets open up in different countries.

These are the implications. So the hypothesis that I am putting forward is that the text at any particular time carries with it everything that a competent reader needs in order to understand the current state of the text. It encapsulates what has gone before in a single act of reference, so that the previous text has exactly the same status as any other piece of shared knowledge. In many cases it also prospects forward and sets the scene for what follows.

The sentence that follows *The implications are daunting*, quoted above, does not contain an act of reference, and so it constitutes a counter-example straight away. The reason is that this sentence is fully prospected by its predecessor. If you think for a moment of spoken discourse, you find that an answer, which is prospected by a question, does not contain an act of reference that encapsulates the question. It would be bizarre if this were the case: the occurrence of the answer is made understandable by the prospection of the question, and yet the answer would encapsulate the question and so cancel its discourse function.

A question can indeed be followed by an utterance that encapsulates it; for example, *That's an interesting question*. Such utterances are called CHALLENGES (Burton 1980) just because they encapsulate the previous utterance and cancel its interactive force.

We therefore conclude that the prospection of a sentence remains pertinent until fulfilled or challenged, although the sentence itself is no longer available in the normal business of talking or writing. Prospected sentences do not contain an act of reference, though they may, of course, themselves prospect. Prospection thus provides a simple variation in text structure. If a sentence is not prospected by its predecessor, it encapsulates it, and by so doing becomes the text.

In this paper it is possible to give only the very broadest outline of this set of hypotheses. There is a lot of detail and a number of qualifications, and it will become much more elaborate as ways are developed of coping with dubious examples. But the basic idea is simple, and probably testable by present techniques. Most acts of reference can be identified by currently available software. The proposal is much simpler than many other models of text, because it selects the features of sentence reference and prospection as being particularly important in structure. If it turns out to be adequate for a starting description of text then it should commend itself because of its simplicity. It also simplifies the business of understanding text structure, in that it points out that each successive sentence is, for a moment, the whole text. This could lead eventually to a really operational definition of a sentence.

So my first main point is a double-edged one. I put forward some proposals for text structure as illustrations of strong and testable hypotheses. I suggest we should use the ability that we now have to perceive the higher structures of language and the powerful computing tools that we now have and that we should find out how reliable and how useful our hypotheses are.

Much of the description of the higher organization of language has remained at the stage of patterns and labels. Little has been done to describe restrictions or to explain the reasons for the patterns, i.e. to make a proper structural description. Similarly, many investigations in language, particularly in areas like stylistics, have remained at a relatively modest level of achievement for a very long time, simply because of the technical problems involved in validating statements. Very detailed and careful analysis is required in stylistics, and it is still usually done by hand (though see the *Journal of Literary and Linguistic Computing, passim*). We are now in a position to be bold, to look for testable hypotheses which may simplify and clarify the nature of text and discourse. It is not enough that a particular description of language can actually provide a set of boxes into which text can be apportioned. We must look for models which help the text to reveal itself to us.

If we are going to take advantage of the computer's ability to test hypotheses over large stretches of text, there is a price to pay, but the opportunity is worth paying for. The price is the requirement of precision of statement, which will add pressure to move linguistics towards scientific rigour; the opportunity is the freedom to speculate and get fairly quick feedback from the computers about the accuracy and potential of the speculations. Far from restricting the theorist, the computers will actually encourage hunch-playing and speculation at the creative stage. The wealth of data and the ease of access will however encourage the compilation of statements which are firmly compatible with the data.

The relationship between the student of language and the data is thus changing. My other point is that we as linguists should train ourselves specifically to be open to the evidence of long text. This is quite different from using the computer to be our servant in trying out our ideas; it is making good use of some essential differences between computers and people. A computer has a relatively crude and simple ability to search and retrieve exhaustively from text any patterns which can be precisely stated in its terms. Now of course we cannot look with totally unbiased eyes at these patterns, but I believe that we have to cultivate a new relationship between the ideas we have and the evidence that is in front of us. We are so used to interpreting very scant evidence that we are not in a good mental state to appreciate the opposite situation. With the new evidence the main difficulty is controlling and organizing it rather than getting it. There is likely to be too much rather than too little and there is a danger that we find only what we are looking for.

I would like to summarize the kinds of observations which are already emerging from such studies, the kinds of studies that have been done in Cobuild and elsewhere. Sometimes they cast doubt on some fairly well established areas of conventional language description.

I shall begin at the lowest level of abstraction, the first step up from the string of characters, where word forms are distinguished by spaces. It has been known for some time that the different forms of a lemma may have very different frequencies. (The forms of a lemma differ from each other only by inflections.) We generally assume that all the forms of a lemma share the same meanings, but we are now beginning to discover that in some cases, if they did not share similar spelling, we might not wish to regard them as being instances of the same lemma. For example, take the lemma *move*. The forms *moving* and *moved* share some meanings with *move*, but each form has a very distinctive pattern of meaning. Some of the meanings found elsewhere in the lemma will be realized, and some will not. In the word *moving* for example there is the meaning of emotional affection, which is quite prominent.

This kind of observation makes us realize that lemmatization is not a simple operation; it is in fact a procedure which a computer has great difficulty with. Of course, with evidence like this it is quite difficult to persuade the computer that lemmatization is a sensible activity. The difference between *move* and *movement* is not noticeably more extreme, yet *movement*, being a derived form, would be expected to constitute a diffferent lemma from *move*.

Such complexities have also been found in several other European languages in a project sponsored by the Council of Europe. When you think of a language like Italian, blessed with a multiplicity of verb forms, and of the prospect that in principle each of those could be a different semantic unit, and also of the fact that there is evidence in many cases that this is so, then you can see the kind of problem that lies ahead. Bilingual dictionaries may soon grow in size substantially as the blithe assumption of a stable lemma is challenged.

Second, a word which can be used in more than one word class is likely to have meanings associated specifically with each word class. Just to give one example, the word *combat* as a noun is concerned with the physical side of combat, and as a verb is concerned with the social side. There is an exception: in the phrase 'locked in combat', *combat* is used in the social meaning although it is a noun. The exception draws attention to another useful point – that the correlations of meaning and word class break down when the words form part of some idiomatic phrase or technical term.

We have not yet made estimates of the proportion of the vocabulary which is subject to this phenomenon, but in the compiling of the Cobuild dictionary (Sinclair *et al.* 1987) we tried to identify the predominant word class of each meaning of each word. We were pretty flexible in judgement and kept the detail to a minimum. Even so if you look at a few pages of the dictionary you will get the strong impression that meaning correlates with word class.

Third, a word may have special privileges of occurrence or restrictions in group structures. For example there is a class of nouns whose members occur characteristically as prepositional objects, and not as subjects or objects of clauses; *lap* as a part of the body is one such. There is a large class of nouns whose members do not occur alone as a group or with only an article; they have to be modified or qualified in some way. I shall not develop this point here because Gillian Francis (forthcoming) gives an excellent account of the phenomenon as applied to nouns. This work is a close relation of valency grammar, which is likely to see an upsurge of interest in the next few years.

Fourth, traditional categories, even major parts of speech, are not as solidly founded as they might appear to be. A recent computational study (Sinclair 1991) of the word *of* revealed that it is misleading to consider it as a preposition. Only occasionally, and in specific collocations with (e.g.) *remind* does it perform a prepositional role. Normally it enables a noun group to extend its pre-head structure, or provide a second head word. In due course the grammatical words of the language will be thoroughly studied, and a new organizational picture is likely to emerge. We must not take for granted the lexical word classes either.

A fifth type of pattern occurs when a word or a phrase carries with it an aura of meaning that is subliminal, in that we only become aware of it when we see a large number of typical instances all together as when we make a selective concordance. An innocent verb like *happen*, for example: if we select the most characteristic examples of it we find that it is nearly always something nasty that has happened or is going to happen. Similarly with the phrasal verb *set in* – it is nasty things like bad weather that set in. This feature associates the item and the environment in a subtle and serious way that is not explained by the mechanism of established models.

As a corollary to this, I must emphasize that a grammar is a grammar of meanings and not of words. Grammars which make statements about undifferentiated words and phrases leave the user with the problem of deciding which of the meanings of the words or phrases are appropriate to the grammatical statement. Most dictionaries give us very little help, and since distinctions in meaning are arrived at without any systematic consideration of grammar (apart from the Cobuild dictionaries) they cannot be used as evidence in this case. Each grammatical feature will probably correlate with just one meaning, unless it is a very common word, or a word of very multifarious meaning, in which case the same grammar may apply to two or three meanings. But the coincidence of distinct environmental patterns with the shades of meaning of a word is remarkable, and is confirmed all the more as we examine the detail in more and more instances.

Sixth and last, and for me the most interesting result of this research concerns the area of shared meaning between words and between phrases; the results of collocation. Put fairly bluntly it seems that words in English do not normally constitute independent selections. I cannot speak with much confidence yet about other languages, with different principles of word construction, except to say that the underlying principle, that of collocation, is certainly to be found operating in languages like German and Italian, and on that basis one can predict with fair confidence that shared meaning will be a feature.

One way of describing collocation is to say that the choice of one word conditions the choice of the next, and of the next again. The item and the environment are ultimately not separable, or certainly not separable by present techniques. Although at this point I risk my own censure about the upward projection of methodology, I find myself more and more drawn to Firth's notion of prosody in phonology to apply to the kind of distribution of meaning that is observed in text when there is a large quantity of organized evidence. Successive meanings can be discerned in the text, and you can associate a meaning or a component of meaning or a shade of meaning with this or that word or phrase that is present in the text. But it is often impossible in the present state of our knowledge to say precisely where the realization of that meaning starts and stops, or exactly which pattern of morphemes is responsible for it. This may be simply an unfortunate stage in the development of the description, but I do not think so. I think that there probably is in language an interesting indeterminacy. Once you accept that in many or most cases of meaningful choice in English the words are not independent selections, but the meanings are shared, then you are in an area of indeterminacy from which I cannot at the moment see any exit. It is no longer possible to imagine a sharp division between one type of patterning which behaves itself and conforms to broadly statable rules, and another which is a long list of individual variations, and then to insist that they both create meaning at the same time.

Now a model which does not take into account this point, is going to represent the language as carrying more information (in the technical sense of information theory) than it actually does. The patterns which are marginalized by our current attitudes include everything from collocation of all kinds, through Firth's colligations, to the conditioned probability of grammatical choices. This is a huge area of syntagmatic prospection. If a model claims to include all such features, but does not explain their effect on conventional grammar and semantics, it will exaggerate the meaning that is given by the choices. That is a fairly serious misrepresentation if the grammar creates more meaning in a set of choices than is mathematically possible.

In the way in which we currently see language text, it is not obvious how each small unit of form prospects the next one. We identify structures like compounds, where the assumption is of a single choice, or idioms, although the precise identification of these is by no means clear-cut. The likelihood is of there being a continuum between occasional quite independent choices and choices which are so heavily dependent on each other that they cannot be separated, and so constitute in practice a single choice.

At present what we detect is a common purpose in the overlapping selection of word on word as if these are the results of choices predetermined at a higher level of abstraction. The choices of conventional grammar and semantics are therefore the realizations of higher level choices. Phrasal verbs are quite an interesting case in point, recently documented in a dictionary that Cobuild has published. Phrasal verbs are difficult to enumerate or identify because there are so many grades and types of co-selection that the relevant criteria are difficult to state and even more difficult to apply. But contrary to what is often claimed, each word of a phrasal verb does contribute something semantically recognizable to the meaning of the whole. In some cases, it is mainly the verb, and in other cases it is mainly the particle.

For instance the particles index in the *Collins Cobuild Dictionary of Phrasal Verbs* (Sinclair *et al.* 1989) shows that the particle can often guide you to the meaning through a semantic analysis of the phrasal verb. A particle like *along* for example combines with common verbs such as *get* or *come* to make a range of linked meanings. From a basic sense of *travel* there is the related meaning *progress* in literal or figurative terms. In parallel to this is the meaning of *accompany*, as found in *tag along*, among others. This develops into the notion of *accept*, and collocation with *with* is strong. We can draw a diagram (Figure 1.1). The phrasal verbs are semantically ordered in this analysis.

The meaning of words chosen together is different from their independent meanings. They are at least partly delexicalized. This is the necessary correlate of co-selection. If you know that selections are not independent, and that one selection depends on another, then there must be a result and

Figure 1.1 Semantic analysis of phrasal verbs with *along*

effect on the meaning which in each individual choice is a delexicalization of one kind or another. It will not have its independent meaning in the full if it is only part of a choice involving one or more words. A good deal of the above evidence leads us to conclude that there is a strong tendency to delexicalization in the normal phraseology of modern English.

Let me try to demonstrate this by looking at the selection of adjectives with nouns. We are given to understand in grammar that adjectives add something to the noun, or restrict the noun or add some features to it. That is no doubt true in some cases, but in the everyday use of adjectives there is often evidence rather of co-selection and shared meaning with the noun. Here are some examples, using recent data from *The Times*, with grateful acknowledgement to the editor and publishers. Classifying adjectives are more prone to show this, but it is common also in qualitative adjectives.

Here are some nouns that are modified by *physical*:

physical assault   *physical confrontation*
physical attack   *physical damage*
physical attributes   *physical proximity*
physical bodies

In these cases the meaning associated with *physical* is duplicated in one facet of the way we would normally understand the noun. The adjective may focus the meaning by mentioning it, but the first meaning of *assault* is surely physical assault. It is not suggested that of all the different kinds of assault this is identified as one particular kind, namely physical assault. This co-selection of noun and adjective does not make a fixed phrase, nor necessarily a significant collocation; it is just one of the ordinary ways in which adjectives and nouns are selected. The selections are not independent; they overlap.

Here are some nouns that occur with *scientific*:

scientific assessment   *scientific analysis*
scientific advances   *scientific study*
scientific experiment

Here *scientific* is fairly seriously delexicalized; all it is doing is dignifying the following word slightly.

Here are some nouns that occur with *full*:

full enquiry   *full range*
full account   *full consultation*
full capacity   *full circle*

These are mainly types of reassurance more than anything else. We would be unlikely to have an announcement of a partial enquiry.

Here are some nouns that occur with *general*:

general trend   *general perception*
general drift   *general opinion*
general consent

In all these cases if the adjective is removed there is no difficulty what-
soever in interpreting the meaning of the noun in exactly the way it was
intended. The adjective is not adding any distinct and clear unit of meaning, but is simply underlining part of the meaning of the noun.

In such ways we can see that many of the word-by-word choices in
language are connected mainly syntagmatically; the paradigmatic element
of their meaning is reduced to the superficial. The same phenomenon
occurs with qualitative adjectives such as *dry* in *dry land, dry bones, dry weight*
(which is perhaps slightly technical), or *loud* in such combinations as *loud
applause, loud bangs, loud cheers.*

The co-selection of adjective and noun is a simple and obvious example.
There are many others. For example, there are in English many phrases
which behave somewhat like idioms; they are built round a slightly
specialized meaning of a word that goes with a specific grammatical
environment. Take, for example, the framework AN . . . OF, one of the
commonest collocations in the language. Consider the words that go in
between those two words, in collocation with the word that immediately
follows. There may be quite a small range: for example, with *an accident
of* there is *an accident of birth, an accident of nature, an accident of society.* The
whole phrase *an accident of* seems to have an idiomatic quality (Renouf and
Sinclair 1991).

These are subliminal idioms which were heralded many years ago
(Sinclair *et al.* 1972). They do not appear in most accounts of the language
and yet they are clearly found in texts. We understand them as centring
on a slightly specialized meaning of a word in a common grammatical
environment and in a regular collocation. This alignment of grammar and
lexis is typical of co-selection.

The subtitle of this paper is *The implications are daunting.* Relating this
sentence to the points I have made, clearly *daunting* is a member of an odd
lemma. There are no finite forms *I daunt, you daunt,* etc. Further, *daunting*
is obviously co-selected with *implications.* I do not know what other things
can be daunting, but the collocation of *implications* and *daunting,* with those
inflections, and in either an attributive or a predicative syntax, illustrates
the shared meaning in that phrase. So the sentence also does duty as an
example of co-selection.

In summary I am advocating that we should trust the text. We should
be open to what it may tell us. We should not impose our ideas on it,
except perhaps just to get started. Until we see what the preliminary
results are, we should apply only frameworks that are loose and flexible,
in order to accommodate the new information that will come from the text.
We should expect to encounter unusual phenomena; we should accept that
a large part of our linguistic behaviour is subliminal, and that therefore we
may find a lot of surprises. We should search for models that are especially

appropriate to the study of texts and discourse.

The study of language is moving into a new era in which the exploitation of modern computers will be at the centre of progress. The machines can be harnessed in order to test our hypotheses, they can show us things that we may not already know and even things which shake our faith quite a bit in established models, and which may cause us to revise our ideas very substantially. In all of this my plea is to trust the text.

REFERENCES

Austin, J.L. (1962), *How to do Things with Words*, Oxford, Oxford University Press.

Burton, D. (1980), *Dialogue and Discourse: the Sociolinguistics of Modern Drama Dialogue and Naturally Occurring Conversation*, London, Routledge.

Chomsky, N. (1957), *Syntactic Structures*, The Hague, Mouton.

Dahan, H.M. (forthcoming 1991), 'The Structure of Conversations in the English of Malaysians', Ph.D. thesis, School of English, University of Birmingham.

Emmot, C. (this volume), 'Splitting the referent: an introduction to narrative enactors'.

Francis, G., (forthcoming) 'Nominal group heads and clause structure', *Word*.

Harris, Zellig (1952), 'Discourse analysis', *Language* 28, 1–30.

Ravelli, L.J. (1991), 'Language from a Dynamic Perspective: Models in General and Grammar in Particular', Ph.D. thesis, School of English, University of Birmingham.

Renouf, A.J., and Sinclair, J.M. (1991), 'Collocational frameworks in English', in *English Corpus Linguistics*, Aijmer, K. and Altenberg, B. (eds), London, Longman.

Sinclair, J.M. (1991), *Corpus Concordance Collocation*, Oxford, Oxford University Press.

Sinclair, J.M., and Coulthard, R.M. (1975), *Towards an Analysis of Discourse*, Oxford, Oxford University Press.

Sinclair, J.M., Jones, S., and Daley, R. (1972), *English Lexical Studies*, report to Office of Scientific and Technical Information.

Sinclair, J.M., Forsyth, I.J., Coulthard, R.M., and Ashby M.C. (1972), *The English used by Teachers and Pupils*, report submitted to the Social Science Research Council.

Sinclair, J.M., *et al.* (1987), *Collins Cobuild English Language Dictionary*, London, Collins.

Sinclair, J.M., Moon, R.E. *et al.* (1989), *Collins Cobuild Dictionary of Phrasal Verbs*, London, Collins.

Tadros, A. (1985), *Prediction in Text*, Discourse Analysis Monograph 10, English Language Research, University of Birmingham.

Tsui, B.M.A. (1986), 'A Linguistic Description of Utterances in Conversation', Ph.D. thesis, School of English, University of Birmingham.

Winter, E.O. (1977), 'A clause relational approach to English texts', *Instructional Science*, 6: 1.

ACKNOWLEDGEMENTS

This paper is edited from the transcript of a talk I gave to the 17th International Systemic Congress at Stirling in July 1990. I would like to thank Kay Baldwin for her excellent transcript. This version has greatly benefited from the plenary and informal discussions at Stirling, and from the comments of two colleagues, Michael Hoey and Louise Ravelli, who kindly read the first written version and made extensive comments.

2 How do you mean?

M.A.K. Halliday

I realize that the title might well prompt someone to ask, 'How do you mean, "How do you mean?"?'. I could have written, 'How are meanings made?' – although I prefer the more personalized version. The question is meant theoretically; but, like so many theoretical questions, it becomes relevant in practice the moment we want to intervene in the processes we are trying to understand. And some processes of meaning are involved in more or less everything we do.

I shall need to talk about two fundamental relationships, those of realization and instantiation; so let me begin by distinguishing these two. Instantiation I take to be the move between the system and the instance; it is an intrastratal relationship – that is, it does not involve a move between strata. The wording *fine words butter no parsnips* is an instance, or an instantiation, of a clause. Realization, on the other hand, is prototypically an interstratal relationship; meanings are realized as wordings, wordings realized as sound (or soundings). We often use the term to refer to any move which constitutes a link in the realizational chain, even one that does not by itself cross a stratal boundary (for example, features realized as structures); but the phenomenon of realization only exists as a property of a stratified system. To anticipate the discussion a little, I shall assume that realization may be formalized as metaredundancy, as this is defined by Jay Lemke. Instantiation I shall define by making reference to the observer; it is variation in the observer's time depth. Firth's concept of exponence is the product of these two relations: his "exponent" is both instantiation and realization.[1]

I shall take it that meaning is not a uniquely human activity; rather, it is part of the experience of at least some other species, obviously including the so-called "higher" mammals. In humans, meaning develops, in the individual, before the stage of language proper; it begins with what I have called "protolanguage". So where does this mammalian experience come from? It probably evolved out of the contradiction between the two primary modes of experience, the material and the conscious. Material processes are experienced as 'out there'; conscious processes are

domain of experience \ form of conscious -ness	action	reflection
1st/2nd person	regulatory	interactional
3rd person	instrumental	personal

Figure 2.1 The protolanguage 'microfunctions'

experienced as 'in here'. We can see in observing the growth of an individual child how he or she construes this contradiction in the form of MEANING. The child constructs a sign, whereby the one mode of experience is projected on to the other. In my own observations this took the form of what I coded as "v.h.p.s." (very high-pitched squeak), Nigel's first sign that he produced at five months old; I glossed it as "what's that? – that's interesting". In other words, Nigel was beginning to construe conceptual order out of perceptual chaos: 'I am curious (conscious) about what's going on (material)'. This impact of the material and the conscious is being transformed into meaning by a process of projection, in which the conscious is the projecting and the material the projected.[2]

But there are two possible modes of such projection – two forms that the consciousness may take: one, that of reflection, 'I think', and the other that of action, 'I want' – one the way things are, and the other the way they ought to be. There are also, as it happens, two domains of the material experience: one, that of 'you and me', and the other that of 'the rest (it, them)'. So, once the process begins (at around eight months, with Nigel), what is construed into meaning is not a single sign but a two-dimensional semiotic space constituting a SIGN SYSTEM (Figure 2.1). We can justifiably refer to such a sign system as a "language", but since it lacks the essential properties of an adult language I preferred to label it more specifically as a protolanguage. The four quadrants of the space I referred to as "microfunctions".[3] In these terms, then, the microfunctional meanings of the protolanguage evolve through the projecting of the material on to the conscious, in a single two-dimensional construction. And this becomes possible because the *conscious* mode of experience is the SOCIAL mode. We have often pointed out that it takes two to mean; but we still tend to refer to consciousness as if it was an individual phenomenon, with the social as an add-on feature. I would prefer the Vygotskyan perspective, whereby consciousness is itself a social mode of being.

In the act of meaning, then, the two modes of experience, through the projection of the one by the other, become fused and transformed into

something that is new and different from either. We can think of this as
creating a 'plane of content' in the Hjelmslevian sense. If we look at this
process dynamically, it is meaning-creating, or semogenic. If we look at it
synoptically, as a relation construed by this process, it is semantic; and it
appears as an interface (our original notion of semantics as "interlevel"
was relevant here),[4] one 'face' being the phenomena of experience. We
often refer to these phenomena collectively as "the material", as if the only
form of experience was what is 'out there'. But this is misleading. Our
experience is at once both material and conscious; and it is the contradiction *between* the material and the conscious that gives these phenomena
their semogenic potential. The other 'face' is the meaning – the signified,
if you prefer the terminology of the sign. Many years ago I did my best
to gloss the child's protolinguistic meanings using 'adult' language as
metalanguage, and found myself forced into using glosses like 'nice to see
you, and let's look at this picture together' for Nigel's protolinguistic [ɑ́ɔ̀
ɑ́ɔ̀ ɑ́ɔ̀]. This was a way of identifying these signs; I then interpreted
them in terms of the microfunctional categories just referred to. But those
categories themselves were not interpreted further. I think they can now be
explained at this somewhat deeper level, as the intersection of the two
modes of projection with the two domains of experience.

But in order for meaning to be created there has also to be a second
interface, a transformation back into the material, or (again, rather) into
the phenomenal – this time in its manifestation in the meaning subject's
own body: as physiological processes of articulation or gesture. This is the
phonetic/kinetic interface; the 'expression plane', in Hjelmslev's terms.
Since there can be no meaning without expression (meaning is *inter*subjective activity, not subjective), the act is 'doubly articulated', in Martinet's
terminology: it is the transduction of the phenomenal back into the
phenomenal via these two interfaces of content and expression. (Transduction not transformation, because as Lamb (1964) pointed out many years
ago in transformation the original is lost, ceases to exist. And again I am
suggesting that we should conceive of it as phenomenal rather than
material, since both the 'outer' faces, that of the content substance on the
one hand and that of the expression substance on the other, embody both
the material and the conscious modes of being.)

What is construed in this way, by this total semogenic process, is an
elastic space defined by the two dimensions given above: the 'inner'
dimension of reflective/active, 'I think' as against 'I want', and the 'outer'
dimension of intersubjective/objective, 'you and me' as against 'he, she,
it'. (Again, there is a naming problem here; we could say that the 'out
there' dimension is that of person/object, provided we remember that
"object" includes those persons 'treated as' object, i.e. third persons.
Instantially, this means any person other than whoever is the interlocutor
at the time; systemically it means any person not forming part of the
subject's (the child's) meaning group.)

This two-dimensional 'elastic space' defines what I have called the
mammalian experience. Obviously I am begging a lot of questions by

calling it mammalian; but I am using this as a way of saying that it is a potential we hold in common with other creatures, which I think is rather important. It is a rich semogenic potential; but it is also constrained in certain critical respects. In our own specifically human history, in both phylogenetic and ontogenetic time, it comes to be deconstructed – or rather deconstrued – and reconstrued as something else, this time in the form of a potential for meaning that is effectively infinite, or at least unbounded (to use an analogue rather than a digital mode of expression). This reconstrual is the explosion into grammar. If we keep to the 'interface' conception, it is the evolution of an interface between the interfaces. If we put it in terms of even more concrete metaphors, what happens is that an entirely non-material (again, better: non-phenomenal) system is slotted in between the two material/non-material (phenomenal/non-phenomenal) systems that are already in place. By means of this critical step, protolanguage evolved into language.

This step of reconstrual could not be taken with an inventory of single signs, but only with a sign SYSTEM – a semiotic that is already (two-)dimensional. It operates not on the terms but on the oppositions, the paradigms that we have been able to identify as reflection/action and person/object (or intersubjective/objective). By 'grammaticalizing' the process of meaning – reconstruing it so that the symbolic organization is freed from direct dependence on the phenomenal, and can develop a structure of its own – the collective human consciousness created a semiotic space which is truly elastic, in that it can expand into any number of dimensions. (We will model this more explicitly in a moment.) The immediate effect is to re-form the reflection/action OPPOSITION into a SIMULTANEITY, such that all acts of meaning embody both – i.e. both reflection and action – not just as components, but as sets of options, each constituting a distinct dimension of choice. In other words they now evolve into the metafunctional categories of ideational and interpersonal. The ideational is the dimension that is primarily reflective (the construction of experience), the interpersonal that which is primarily active (the enactment of social processes[5]). (But note that each engenders the other mode as a secondary motif: the way we CONSTRUE experience (by verbal reflection) disposes us to ACT in certain ways, e.g. as teachers structuring the role relationships in the learning process, while the way we CONSTRUCT our social relations (by verbal action) enables us to REPRESENT – to verbalize – what the resulting social order is like.)

What has made this possible is what I called just now the "explosion into grammar" – an explosion that bursts apart the two facets of the protolinguistic sign. The result is a semiotic of a new kind: a stratified, tristratal system in which meaning is 'twice cooked', thus incorporating a stratum of 'pure' content form. It is natural to represent this, as I have usually done myself, as 'meaning realized by wording, which is in turn realized by sound'. But it is also rather seriously misleading. If we follow Lemke's lead, interpreting language as a dynamic open system, we can arrive at a theoretically more accurate and more powerful account. Here the key concept is Lemke's principle of "metaredundancy".[6]

Consider a minimal semiotic system, such as a protolanguage – a system that is made up of simple signs. This is based on the principle of redundancy. When we say that contents **p**, **q**, **r** are "realized" respectively by expressions **a**, **b**, **c**, what this means is that there is a redundancy relation between them: given meaning **p**, we can predict sound or gesture **a**, and given sound or gesture **a** we can predict meaning **p**. This relationship is symmetrical; "redounds with" is equivalent both to "realizes" and to "is realized by".

Let us now expand this into a non-minimal semiotic, one that is tri- rather than bi-stratal. The expressions **a**, **b**, **c** now realized WORDINGS **l**, **m**, **n**, while the wordings **l**, **m**, **n** realize MEANINGS **p**, **q**, **r**. In terms of redundancy, however, these are not two separate dyadic relationships. Rather, there is a METAredundancy such that **p**, **q**, **r** redounds not with **l**, **m**, **n** but with the redundancy of **l**, **m**, **n** with **a**, **b**, **c**; thus,:

l, m, n ↘ a, b, c   p, q, r ↘ (l, m, n ↘ a, b, c)

Why has it to be like this? Because there is not, in fact, a chain of dyadic relationships running through the system. (If there was, we would not need the extra stratum.) It is not the case, in other words, that **p** ↘ l and l ↘ a. **p**, **q**, **r** is realized by **l**, **m**, **n**; but the system at **l**, **m**, **n** is sorted out again for realization by **a**, **b**, **c**, so that what **p**, **q**, **r** is actually realized by is the realization of **l**, **m**, **n** by **a**, **b**, **c**. This is the fundamental distinction between redundancy and causality. If realization was a causal relation, then it would chain: **l** is caused by **a** and **p** is caused by **l** – it would make no sense to say "**p** is caused by the causing of l by **a**". But realization is not a causal relation; it is a redundancy relation, so that **p** redounds with the redundancy of **l** with **a**. To put it in more familiar terms, it is not that (i) meaning is realized by wording and wording is realized by sound, but that (ii) meaning is realized by the realization of wording in sound.

We can of course reverse the direction, and say that sounding realizes the realization of meaning in wording:

p, q, r ↘ l, m, n   (p, q, r ↘ l, m, n) ↘ a, b, c

For the purpose of phonological theory this is in fact the appropriate perspective. But for the purposes of construing the 'higher' levels, with language as connotative semiotic realizing other semiotic systems of the culture, we need the first perspective. Thus when we extend 'upwards' to the context of situation, we can say that the context of situation **s**, **t**, **u** redounds with the redundancy of the discourse semantics **p**, **q**, **r** with the redundancy of the lexicogrammar **l**, **m**, **n** with the phonology **a**, **b**, **c**. Thus:

s, t, u ↘ (p, q, r ↘ (l, m, n ↘ a, b, c))

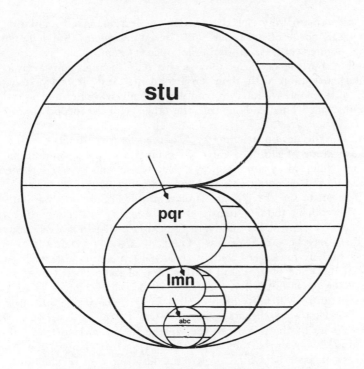

Figure 2.2 Metaredundancy

(cf. Figure 2.2). Once the original protolinguistic redundancy has been transformed into metaredundancy in this way, the relation becomes an iterative one and so opens up the possibilities for construing, not only the context of situation, but also higher levels such as Hasan's symbolic articulation and theme in verbal art, or Martin's strata of genre and ideology.

The metaredundancy notion thus formalizes the stratal principle in semogenesis. What makes meaning indefinitely extendable is the evolutionary change from protolanguage to language – whereby instead of a simple plane with two interfaces to the material (the phenomenal), we have constructed a semiotic SPACE, a three-dimensional (potentially n-dimensional) system in which there is a purely symbolic mode of being between these two interfaces. It is this that we call grammar, or more explicitly lexicogrammar. Without this semiotic space, situated in the transduction from one purely symbolic mode to another, and hence not constrained by the need to interface directly with the phenomenal, we could not have a metafunctional organization in the grammar, and we could not have the phenomenon of grammatical metaphor.[7]

The metaredundancy theory explains the 'stratal' organization of language, and the semiotic principle of realization. It explains them synoptically: by treating realization as a relation. Now, a system of this kind could still remain fully closed: it could be a circular, self-regulating system without any form of exchange with its environment. But a language, as Lemke pointed out, is a dynamic open system; such systems are not autostable, but metastable – they persist only through constantly changing by interpenetration with their environment. And in order to explain a system of this kind we have to complement our synoptic interpretation with a dynamic one. This leads us into the other critical concept, that of instantiation.

Consider the notion of climate. A climate is a reasonably stable system; there are kinds of climate, such as tropical and polar, and these persist, and they differ in systematic ways. Yet we are all very concerned about changes in the climate, and the consequences of global warming. What does it mean to say the climate is changing? Climate is instantiated in the form of weather: today's temperature, humidity, direction and speed of wind, etc., in central Scotland are INSTANCES of climatic phenomena. As such they may be more, or less, TYPICAL: today's maximum is so many degrees higher, or lower, than AVERAGE – meaning the average at this place, at this time of year and at this time of day. The average is a statement of the PROBABILITIES: there is a 70 per cent chance, let us say, that the temperature will fall within such a range. The probability is a feature of the SYSTEM (the climate); but it is no more, and no less, than the pattern set up by the instances (the weather), and each instance, no matter how minutely, perturbs these probabilities and so changes the system (or else keeps it as it is, which is just the limiting case of changing it).

The climate and the weather are not two different phenomena. They are the same phenomenon seen by two different observers, standing at different distances – different time depths. To the climate observer, the weather looks like random unpredictable ripples; to the weather observer, the climate is a vague and unreal outline. So it is also with language:[8] language as system, and language as instance. They are not two different phenomena; they are the same phenomenon as seen by different observers. The system is the pattern formed by the instances; and each instance represents an exchange with the environment – an incursion into the system in which every level of language is involved. The SYSTEM is permeable because each INSTANCE redounds with the context of situation, and so perturbs the system IN INTERACTION WITH THE ENVIRONMENT. Thus both realization and instantiation are involved in the evolution of language as a dynamic open system.

Now the relation of system to instance is in fact a cline, a continuous zoom; and wherever we focus the zoom we can take a look into history. But to know what kind of history, we have to keep a record of which end we started from. To the SYSTEM observer, history takes the form of evolution; the system changes by evolving, with selection (in the sense of 'natural selection') by the material conditions of the environment. This is seen most clearly, perhaps, in the evolution of particular sub-systems, or registers, where features that are functionally well adapted are positively selected for; but it appears also in the history of the system as a whole once

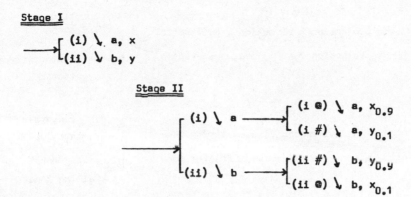

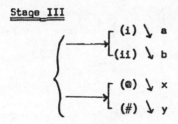

Figure 2.3 A model of semogenesis

we look beyond the superficial clutter of random fluctuations into the grammar's cryptotypic core. To the INSTANCE observer, on the other hand, history is individuation: each text has its own history, and its unique meaning unfolds progressively from the beginning. (Note that the probability of any instance is conditioned both systemically (a register is a resetting of the overall probabilities of the system) and instantially, by the transitional probabilities of the text as a Markoff chain.) Given any particular feature – say grammatical metaphor – we may be able to track it through both these histories, the phylogenetic – its history as it evolves in the system; and what we might call the "logogenetic" – its history as it is built up in the course of the text. There is of course a third kind of history, the ontogenetic, which is different again – the cladistic model here is one of growth. This too is a mode of semogenesis; and we could follow through with the same example, asking how grammatical metaphor comes into being in the developmental history of a child. These are in fact the three modes or dimensions of semohistory – the phylogenetic, the ontogenetic and the logogenetic; in the dynamic perspective, we can ask: how did this meaning evolve, in the system? how did it develop, in the learner? and how did it unfold, in the text?

In all these histories, the meaning potential typically tends to increase. (Where it decreases, this is generally catastrophic: the language dies out, or is creolized; the individual dies, or becomes aphasic; the text comes to

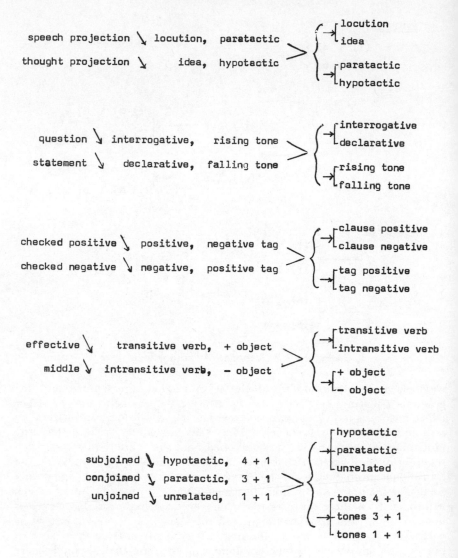

Figure 2.4 Postulated examples of semogenic evolution in relation to some systems of Modern English. (*Note*. Those on the right are labelled merely for identification, not in terms of their systemic features in the grammar.)

an end, or is interrupted.) Now, the mechanism of this increase of meaning potential may be modelled in the most general terms as in Figure 2.3. Nesbitt and Plum (1988; see also Halliday 1991) showed how to do this in a corpus-based study of "direct speech and indirect thought" (the intersection of speech projection and thought projection with the interdependency system of parataxis and hypotaxis). This and other postulated

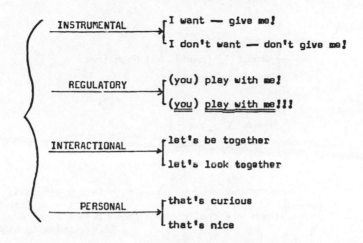

INSTRUMENTAL
⌈ I want — give me!
⌊ I don't want — don't give me!

REGULATORY
⌈ (you) play with me!
⌊ (you) play with me!!!

INTERACTIONAL
⌈ let's be together
⌊ let's look together

PERSONAL
⌈ that's curious
⌊ that's nice

Figure 2.5 Microfunctional systems (Nigel's protolanguage)

examples of evolutionary semogenesis are set out in Figure 2.4. These involve relations between strata (semantics realized in grammar); and they suggest how metaredundancy becomes dynamic – through shifting probabilities, as the values change instance by instance. In other words the permeability of the system depends on the metaredundancy relation: this is the only way it can be nudged along. Thus where a closed system is self-regulating (autostable) and circular, an open system is other-regulated (metastable) and helical. And it is through the combination of these two relations or processes, instantiation on the one hand and realization on the other, that the system exchanges with its environment, creating ORDER in the course of this exchange and so increasing its potential for meaning.

Thus the possibility of meaning – of acting semiotically – arises at the intersection of the material (or phenomenal) with the conscious, as the members of a species learn to construct themselves ('society') in action and to construe their experience in reflection. These two dimensions – *action/reflection*, and *you + me/other* – define a semiotic field. At first this is a plane, a rubber sheet so to speak, elastic but two-dimensional (this is the protolanguage phase); having just two surfaces, interfaces between the conscious and the two facets of the material (content purport and expression purport), such that meaning consists in making the transduction between them. The simple signs of the protolanguage shape themselves into a sign system as they cluster in the four quadrants of this semiotic plane; there is thus already a proto-system network, which we could set up in an idealized form as in Figure 2.5. (I use the variables that emerged from my own Nigel data; this should be compared with studies by Clare Painter and by Jane Oldenburg, where other systemic variables may appear more prominent.[9]) We must leave open the question of what

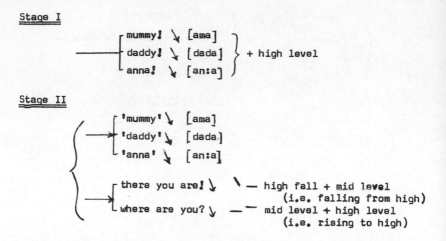

Figure 2.6 Nigel's first stratifications (age one year two months)

variables are the ones in respect of which the protolinguistic system is TYPICALLY construed, but I think it will be a fairly small set. Nigel's seemed to be (1) in instrumental: polarity, (2) in regulatory: intensity, (3) in interactional: mode of being, or process type, relational/behavioral; (4) in personal: mode of consciousness, cognitive/affective.

This two-dimensional plane is then deconstrued and evolves into an *n*-dimensional space, as the activity of meaning becomes dialogically dynamic and metafunctionally complex: that is, it becomes possible to mean more than one thing at once, and to construe meanings into text. I have written elsewhere about how Nigel took the first step in this transformation, using the semogenic strategy already described (combining two functionally distinct variables); it is summarized in Figure 2.6. Here for the first time Nigel is selecting in two systems of meaning at once, and by this token the initial move into grammar has been made. Through the second year of life this new stratified system will gradually replace the protolinguistic one, and all meanings (except for a few protolanguage remnants that persist into adult life like *hi!* and *ah!* and *yum!* and *ouch!*) will come to be stratally and metafunctionally complex. So in Nigel's first exemplar, just cited, we have (i) proto-metafunctions (proto-ideational – different persons; proto-interpersonal – seeking/finding), and (ii) proto-strata, with the meaning 'first' construed as wording (the ideational as contrasting names; the interpersonal as contrasting mood) and 'then' (re)construed as sounding (names as articulation, mood as intonation). At this second interface the child can now combine the segmental and the prosodic choices, in this way both realizing and also iconically symbolizing the two different modes of meaning that are combined at the first interface. The resources for making meaning are now in place.

It is probably not a coincidence that, as the ideational grammar evolved, so in the system of transitivity the field of processes was construed into different process types along precisely the lines that (if my understanding is right) went into the making of meaning in the first place. If meaning arises out of the impact of the conscious and the material, as mutually contradictory forms of experience, then it is not surprising that when experience is construed semantically, these two types of process, the material and the conscious, should come to be systematically distinguished. But there is a further twist. The semogenic process, as we saw, involves setting up a relationship between systems such that one is the realization of the other – that is, they stand to each other in a relation of Token and Value. This Token–Value relationship is set up at both interfaces, and it is also what makes it possible to prise the two apart and wedge in a grammar in between. Here then we find the third of the kinds of process construed by the grammar: the relational process, based on identifying a Token with a Value. The grammar of natural language, in its ideational metafunction, is a theory of human experience; thus it may reasonably be expected to take as its point of departure the very set of contrasts from which its own potential is ultimately derived.

Let me return once again, finally, to the suggestion that meaning is a mode of action engendered at the intersection of the material (or phenomenal) and the conscious, as complementary modes of experience. Now, the effect of this impact is to construe order. By the act of meaning, consciousness imposes order on the phenomena of experience. When protolanguage evolves into language, with the stratal dimension of realization, meaning becomes self-reflexive: and in two senses. On the one hand, it imposes order on itself: the TEXTUAL metafunction, as Christian Matthiessen has shown, construes a reality that is made of meaning (see Chapter 3). On the other hand, we can TALK ABOUT the way we mean, and examine the nature of the order our way of meaning has imposed. As well as a grammar, a theory of experience, we have a GRAMMATICS – a grammar of grammars, a theory of theories of experience, or a metatheory in one sense of this term. At this very general level, we can then examine our own notions of order. Experience now appears as an interplay of order and disorder: analogy and anomaly, in the terms of the ancient Greek debate (begun, like so many other issues in the history of ideas, with arguments about language – in this case arising from regular and irregular morphological patterns) – or order and chaos, in current terminology. Is chaos a feature of the phenomena themselves, or merely a product of the deficiency in our understanding? Are the two merely a function of the observer, so that patterns repeat if we wait for them long enough, probabilities become certainties when we know all that needs to be known? Or to put this in more specifically linguistic terms, will all the various contradictions in the grammar resolve themselves into some higher level of order? – I mean things like transitive and ergative as complementary theories of process, or tense and aspect as complementary theories of time; as well as all the other indeterminacies which arise in our polyelastic semiotic space? (See Chapter 5 below.) I am not of course setting out to

answer these questions; I am merely pointing out that the meaning potential we have evolved for ourselves construes the possibility of asking them.
But I will allow myself one further thought in the closing paragraphs of the
paper.

It is a human failing that we usually try to impose order much too soon.
There are many examples of this in recent linguistics.[10] The attempt fails;
and we then resort to 'theories of chaos', trying to make sense of things
while remaining instance observers – looking for 'une théorie de la parole',
so to speak.[11] Such constructs are ultimately self-contradictory; but they
serve as a way of reformulating the questions and allow us to move back
a bit, to shift our stance. A good example of the overimposition of order
through language is provided by a designed, or semi-designed, system like
the language of science. Having construed a reality that is technological (in
the true sense of this term: a reality constructed not out of *technē* but out
of the *logos*, or discourse, of *technē*), scientists themselves are now finding
their language – that is, their own scientific metalanguages – too rigid and
determinate, and are seeking ways to restore the balance: a discourse with
which to construe experience in terms of indeterminacy, of continuity and
of flux. Now by comparison with the languages of science, the ordinary
evolved language of everyday life HAS many of these properties. It is
oriented towards events rather than objects, and is in many respects fluid
and indeterminate. But it is important to be aware that even our most
unconscious everyday language also imposes an order which we may need
to re-examine and to deconstruct. To return to the weather: we can say
"it's raining" or we can say "it's snowing" – but we have to decide
between them. We may accommodate an intermediate form, "it's
sleeting"; this cuts up the continuum more finely, but still into discrete
parts –'rain or sleet or snow'.[12] (Contrast in this respect the semantics of
sign, such as Auslan, which often allows a more continuous interpretation
of experience – though of course it is constantly being modified under the
influence of spoken language (Johnston 1990).) In other words, while the
order – that is, the particular mix of order and chaos – that our grammar
construes has served us well, and continues to do so, it is not necessarily
the most functional for all times and all circumstances; especially at times
of rapid change like the present, we may need to hold it up to the light
and see how it works.[13] It is easy to remain unaware of the stories our
grammar is telling us.

One thing I have been trying to do, in this paper, is to use the grammar
to think with about itself. Not just in the usual sense, of using language
as its own metalanguage; of course I am doing that, because there is
nothing else I can do. I mean this more specifically in the sense of using
what I have called the grammatics – the concepts that we have developed
in order to interpret the grammar – as a means towards understanding the
nature and evolution of language as a whole. The strategy is that of
treating LANGUAGE as 'other' – as if it was a different kind of semiotic
that the grammar was being used to explore.[14] Thus I have found it
helpful to think of meaning as the way consciousness (that is, mental

processes), by a type of projection, construes a relationship (that is, a Token = Value identity, or a nested series of such identities) between two sets of material processes (those of our experience, at one end, and those of our bodily performance – gesture, articulation – at the other). I do not know how useful anyone else will find this strategy. But at least it is something I can answer with, the next time anyone says to me, "How do you mean?".

NOTES

1 For Firth's concept of "exponence" see especially his 'Synopsis of Linguistic Theory' in Firth (1957).

2 I am speaking here of phylogenesis; but the process is recapitulated in the growth of the individual, where it can be observed in the form of behaviour. A child experiences certain phenomena as 'out there' – as lying beyond the boundary between 'me' and 'non-me': some perturbation seen or heard, like a flock of birds taking off, or a bus going past, or a coloured light flashing. At the same time, he also experiences a phenomenon that is 'in here': his own consciousness of being curious, or pleased, or frightened. At first these two experiences remain detached; but then (perhaps as a result of his success in grasping an object that is in his line of sight – in Trevarthen's terms, when "pre-reaching" becomes reaching, typically at about four months) a spark flies between them by which the material is projected on to the conscious as 'I'm curious about that', 'I like that' and so on. Now, more or less from birth the child has been able to address others and to recognize that he is being addressed (Catherine Bateson's "proto-conversation"). The projection of the material on to the conscious mode of experience maps readily on to this ability to address an other; and the result is an act of meaning – such as Nigel's very high pitched squeak, which he first produced at five months, shortly after he had learnt to reach and grasp.

3 Other microfunctions were added as the protolanguage evolved by degrees into the mother tongue; but these were the original four. See Halliday (1975, 1978).

4 At first labelled, somewhat misleadingly, the level of "context". See the discussion of levels in Halliday et al. (1964). See also Ellis (1966).

5 Based on giving and demanding – that is, on exchange. Initially this meant the exchange of goods-and-services; but eventually, by a remarkable dialectic in which the medium of exchange became itself the commodity exchanged, it extended to giving and demanding information. By this step, meaning evolved from being an ancillary of other activities to being a form of activity in its own right.

6 See the chapters entitled 'Towards a model of the instructional process', 'The formal analysis of instruction' and 'Action, context and meaning' in Lemke (1984).

7 It is impossible to have metaphor in a protolanguage at all, unless one chooses to call "metaphor" (or perhaps "proto-metaphor") what is taking place when, for example, Nigel transfers a particular sign [gᵚɪ gᵚɪ gᵚɪ] from 'I'm sleepy' to 'let's pretend I'm going to sleep'. See Halliday (1975: chapter 2).

8 The analogy should not, of course, be pressed too far. Specifically, while the relation of instantiation holds both for language/speech (langue/parole) and for climate/weather, that of realization does not. It could be said that climate is in

fact modelled as a stratified system (in the semiotic, not the atmospheric sense!); but this would be using "stratified" with a significantly different meaning.

9 See Painter (1984), Oldenburg (1987). For an investigation of Chinese-speaking children see Qui (1985).

10 As pointed out by John Sinclair in Chapter 1 of the present volume.

11 Note that current "chaos theory", as in Gleick's book *Chaos*, is not a theory of chaos in this sense; rather, it is establishing a new kind of principle of order.

12 But note Tigger's defence in *Winnie-the-Pooh*: "You shouldn't bounce so much." "I didn't bounce; I coughed." "You bounced." "Well, I sort of boffed."

13 In a recent paper (Halliday 1990) I suggested that our present grammars are in some respects environmentally unsound.

14 As is done by Michael O'Toole in relation to other semiotics such as art and architecture; see for example O'Toole (in press). Cf. also Theo van Leeuwen (1988).

REFERENCES

Bazell, C.E. *et al.* (eds) (1966), *In Memory of J.R. Firth*, Longmans' Linguistics Library, London, Longman.

Ellis, J.O. (1966), 'On contextual meaning', in Bazell *et al.*

Fawcett, Robin P., and Young, David J. (eds) (1988), *New Developments in Systemic Linguistics 2: Theory and Application*, Open Linguistics series, London and New York, Pinter.

Firth, J.R. (ed.) 1957, *Studies in Linguistic Analysis*, Oxford, Blackwell.

Fries, Peter, and Gregory, Michael (eds) (in press), *Discourse in Society: Functional Perspectives*, Norwood, N.J., Ablex.

Halliday, M.A.K. (1975), *Learning How to Mean: Explorations in the Development of Language*, Explorations in Language Study, London, Edward Arnold.

—————— (1978), 'Meaning and the construction of reality in early childhood', in Pick and Saltzman (1978).

—————— (1990), 'New ways of meaning: a challenge to applied linguistics', Journal of Applied Linguistics (Greek Applied Linguistics Association), 6.

—————— (1991), 'Towards probabilistic interpretations', in Ventola (1991).

Halliday, M.A.K., McIntosh, Angus, and Strevens, Peter (1964), *The Linguistic Sciences and Language Teaching*, Longmans' Linguistics Library, London, Longman.

Johnston, Trevor (1990), 'A Study of the Grammar of Auslan (Australian Sign)', Ph.D. dissertation, University of Sydney.

Lamb, Sydney M. (1964), 'On alternation, transformation, realization and stratification', in Stuart (1964).

Lemke, J.L. (1984), *Semiotics and Education*, Toronto Semiotic Circle Monographs, Working Papers and Prepublications 1984.2, Toronto, Victoria University.

Nesbitt, Christopher, and Plum, Guenter (1988), 'Probabilities in a systemic grammar: the clause complex in English', in Fawcett and Young (1988).

Oldenburg, Jane (1987), 'From Child Tongue to Mother Tongue: a case study of language development in the first two and a half years', Ph.D. dissertation, University of Sydney.

O'Toole, Michael (in press), 'A systemic-functional semiotics of art', in Fries and Gregory (in press).

Painter, Clare (1984), *Into the Mother Tongue: a Case Study in early Language Development*, Open Linguistics Series, London, Pinter.

Pick, Herbert L., Jr, and Saltzman, Elliot (eds) (1978), *Modes of Perceiving and Processing of Information*, Hillsdale, N.J., Lawrence Erlbaum Associates.

Qiu, Shijin (1985), 'Transition period in Chinese language development', *Australian Review of Applied Linguistics* 8.1.

Stuart, C.I.J.M. (1964), *Report of the Fifteenth Annual (First International) Round Table Meeting on Linguistics and Language Study*, Monograph Series in Languages and Linguistics 17, Washington, D.C., Georgetown University Press.

van Leeuwen, Theo (1988), 'Music and ideology: notes towards a socio-semiotics of mass media music', in *Sydney Association for Studies in Society and Culture Working Papers* 2.1/2.

Ventola, Eija (ed.) (1991), *Functional and Systemic Linguistics: Approaches and Uses*, Berlin, Mouton de Gruyter.

Part II. Metafunctions

3 Interpreting the textual metafunction
Christian Matthiessen

3.1 TEXTUAL ISSUES TO BE DISCUSSED

This paper explores the nature of the textual metafunction – the nature of both textual meaning and textual modes of expression; it builds on and expands the discussion of these issues in Halliday (1979) and Matthiessen (1988). It is part of ongoing research on metafunctional modes of meaning and expression, partly inspired by the task of modelling the grammar and its semiotic environment computationally – see, for example, Bateman (1989) on the logical metafunction and Matthiessen (1990b) on all three metafunctions.

Most issues concerning categories within the textual metafunction – issues such as the relationship between Theme and text organization, the boundary between Theme and Rheme, the selection of a Theme from outside the clause in which it operates, the definition of New, the systemic potential of ELLIPSIS, and so on – presuppose the more general question of how to interpret and represent textual categories such as 'Theme', 'New' and 'specific' through notions such as 'point of departure', 'point of a message' and 'swell of information', and it is this fundamental issue I will focus on here.

I will begin by raising the question of how textual categories have been interpreted by linguists in the past: 'MOVEMENT' emerges as common to a number of metaphors that have been used in the interpretation of the textual metafunction (section 3.2). I will then identify three basic properties of this movement – waveshape, second-order character and dynamicity (section 3.3) – and discuss these in some detail in the next three sections (sections 3.4–6). Having explored the properties of 'TEXTUAL MOVEMENT', I will then show how we can begin to model these properties in an explicit account of textual semantics (section 3.7). In conclusion, I will review the discussion and identify misinterpretations of the textual metafunction and the interpretations that are to be preferred (section 3.8).

3.2 THE PROBLEM OF INTERPRETING THE TEXTUAL
METAFUNCTION

Textual categories are perhaps the hardest to interpret and represent
among the three metafunctions. Consequently the textual metafunction
tends to be built into semantic and grammatical theories later than at least
the ideational metafunction and not to be treated in its own terms; but this
also depends on the overall approach to language that is adopted – for
example, whether it is based on words (traditional grammar), autonomous
sentences (formal syntax) or text (functional linguistics). The difficulty in
approaching the textual metafunction arises from the fundamental
difference between this metafunction and the ideational one. The ideational
metafunction embodies a theory of reality; it gives us the resources for
construing the world around us and inside us. We can talk about wholes
and their parts, about processes and their participants, about causes and
their effects, and so on. And we can talk about talk; we can use the ideational metafunction to construe language itself, both in commonsense terms
and in technical linguistic ones.[1] So, using the resources of relational
transitivity, we can discuss what to MEANS, discover that it EXPRESSES
directed location; we can note that it is a preposition, that it SERVES as
Minorprocess and thus is PART of a prepositional phrase, where it
PRECEDES the Minirange; and so on. Now this works reasonably well as
long as we are interpreting that domain of language which has itself
evolved as a construal of reality – that is, the ideational metafunction. We
can turn the ideational metafunction back on itself reasonably successfully
precisely because it is itself concerned with interpretation and representation. There will certainly be difficulties. In particular, grammatical
categories, such as projection, Process and Client are difficult to gloss
lexically, i.e. using lexical categories. But this type of ineffability (Halliday
1984) is primarily a matter of delicacy: grammatical categories are much
more general than lexical ones, so it is impossible to lexicalize them just
as it is impossible to grammaticalize lexical categories (unless the system
itself changes at this point by generalizing an item from lexis to grammar,
as with GOING TO, WILL, ON TOP OF, and so on, in English). That is,
grammatical and lexical ideational meanings are not different in kind, only
in generality.

However, ideational and textual meanings are different in kind (just as
ideational and interpersonal meanings are). The textual metafunction is
not a representational one. Consequently, unlike the ideational metafunction, it cannot be turned back on itself to REPRESENT itself. We cannot
represent the textual category of Theme in textual terms. Textual
categories thus have to be INTERPRETED OUTSIDE THE TEXTUAL
METAFUNCTION ITSELF by means of the ideational metafunction. Since it
is unlike the ideational metafunction, it is also hard to interpret and represent in ideational terms. The way the difficulty is addressed depends on the
nature of the semantic theory employed. I will take note of formal semantics, 'cognitive semantics' and functional semantics.

FORMAL and COGNITIVE SEMANTICS contrast with FUNCTIONAL SEMANTICS in that they interpret meaning in terms of something that is essentially OUTSIDE language, a model of the world (formal semantics) or a mental model (cognitive semantics). They are both essentially concerned with ideational meaning; interpersonal and textual meaning are either largely ignored or assumed to fall within the domain of pragmatics rather than semantics. Textual meaning is sometimes explored within cognitive approaches to language (as in the work of Wallace Chafe); it is interpreted ideationally in terms of some framework of mental states involving degrees of activation, attention, and so on. The nineteenth-century notion of psychological subject belongs here. Formal semantics is, of course, particularly concerned with representational meaning, with the relation between language and the world as it is represented in a model; since the textual metafunction is not part of that world, it is hardly surprising that it falls outside of the domain of formal semantics.

In contrast, FUNCTIONAL SEMANTICS takes meaning as something to be explained in its own right rather than by reference to a model of the material world or the mental world: the dominant mode of interpretation is a social-semiotic one, and neighbouring disciplines are ethnography and rhetoric (cf. Halliday 1977). All three metafunctions fall within the scope of a semantic account; textual meaning is interpreted by reference to its contribution to the development of text (Daneš 1974; Fries 1981, to appear a, b; Martin in press, n.d.; cf. also Mathesius 1975: 81; Halliday 1967/8). Now textual meaning is often articulated in terms of an IDEA- TIONAL METAPHOR involving (motion through) abstract space (a kind of metaphor we also find within cognitive interpretations): topic (from *topos*, 'place'), basis, peg [as a location for meaning], framework, foreground/background, point of departure, transition, in/out of atten- tion/focus, guidepost, stream of narration (Mathesius 1975), [thematic] progression, flow of information (Chafe 1979), swell of information (Halli- day 1982b).[2]

The metaphors employed in functional semantics are often rejected precisely because they are metaphors, and the solution to the problem of characterizing textual categories is then sought in cognitive terms such as degree of activation within a cognitive theory of semantics. This does not really constitute a solution at all. (i) The cognitive terms are often metaphorical themselves (cf. *in and out of attention*, *in focus*, *out of focus*, [*spreading*] *activation*) and are thus in just as much need of grounding as the metaphors employed within functional semantics. More generally, cogni- tion itself can be seen as created by ideational grammar and semantics in the first place; it is certainly construed by mental transitivity (*I think, therefore I am*; *seeing is believing* and so on; cf. D'Andrade 1987: 115–16 on folk and scientific models of the mind, and his discussion of the mental processes and states of which the folk model is composed).

(ii) Metaphor is established as a pervasive strategy for expanding the linguistic resources to allow us to construe various areas of experience that typically fall outside those areas that can be construed congruently. For example, intensity is construed in terms of a vertical orientation in an abstract space (cf. Whorf 1956); and this metaphor is crucial to the field of economics (as is a related one of growth; cf. Halliday 1990a), where various indicators move up and down:

> **Steep declines** in capital spending commitments and building permits, along with a **drop** in the money stock pushed the leading composite **down** for the fifth time in the past 11 months to a **level** of 0·5% **below** its **high** in [month] [year]. Such a **decline** is highly unusual at this stage in an expansion; for example, in the three most recent expansions, the leaders were **rising**, on average, at about a 7% clip at comparable **phases** in the **cycle**. While not signalling an outright **recession**, the current protracted **sluggishness** of the leading indicators appears consistent with our prognosis of **sluggish** real GNP growth over the next few quarters.
>
> [Federal Reserve Board]

We would not reject economics because of the pervasiveness of metaphor but we would ask how the metaphorical system is grounded in a model. Similarly, metaphors such as 'semantic space', 'lexical field', 'closeness in meaning', 'semantic dimensions' have long been accepted and used in linguistics (as have those based on language as organism). It thus seems pointless to reject characterizations of textual categories such as 'point of departure' or 'information flow' simply because they are metaphorical; that would be to dismiss a fundamental strategy for expanding our understanding of 'reality'.

(iii) More important, we are simply transferring the problem of characterizing textual categories to another domain, cognition. That would make sense if cognition was very well understood or could be shown to be something other than meaning. But it is at least perfectly possible that our current notion of cognition is essentially a scientific version of the folk model of thinking embodied in the lexicogrammatical and semantic resources we use to construe experience.

A more interesting alternative is to recognize that the semantic system for interpreting language – or any other phenomenon – is typically expanded by means of ideational metaphors and analogies and then to develop an account that grounds 'point of departure' and other ideational metaphors of abstract space in a model of textual meaning.[3] Let us take the first step towards this in section 3.3.

3.3 TEXTUAL MOVEMENT

The concept of movement through semantic space is at the foundation of most of the metaphors for construing textual organization ('POINT OF DEPARTURE', 'GUIDEPOST', 'STREAM OF NARRATION', 'INFORMATION FLOW', 'SWELL OF INFORMATION'). Figure 3.1 shows its taxonomic

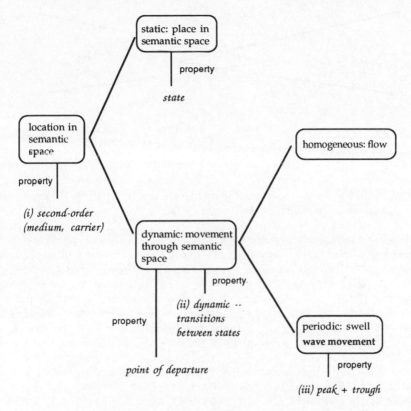

Figure 3.1 Part of the system of spatial metaphors

location in a cluster of spatial metaphors used to construe textual categories; each class in this taxonomy has one or more properties, which are inherited by its sub-classes. Movement through semantic space is a sub-type of the metaphor of textual meaning as a location in semantic space (shown at the taxonomic top of the diagram); the other major sub-type is that of a static place in semantic space. There are different types of movement, most importantly 'FLOW' *v.* 'SWELL'.

If we can develop an account of this movement, we may also be able to 'GROUND' metaphors such as 'point of departure' or 'guidepost'. First we should examine the concept of movement, contrasting the two types recognized in Figure 3.1, FLOW and SWELL. Halliday (1982b) comments on the notion of 'FLOW OF INFORMATION' (cf., e.g., Chafe 1979):

Indeed there is nothing in the exchange of information which generates chunks of discourse. We favour metaphors like flow of information, and this suggests an ongoing process without any clearly definable segments. But the flow of information is not an unstructured flow; it is

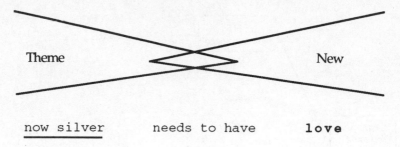

now silver   needs to have   **love**

Figure 3.2 Textual waves of prominence and non-prominence in the clause

characterized by a periodic movement, a wave-like pattern of peaks and troughs. It is perhaps a swell rather than a flow.

Following Halliday's suggestion, we can thus identify one particular type of semantic movement – a movement like a swell consisting of WAVE-LIKE MOVEMENTS through semantic space. The textual mode of expression is a wave or pulse with peaks of prominence and troughs of non-prominence. Halliday (1979; 1985: 316) has shown how the textual wave-like pattern operates within the typical clause, with one peak of thematic prominence followed by one trough of rhematic non-prominence and one trough of given non-prominence followed by a peak of new prominence; see Figure 3.2.

A textual wave movement can be further characterized in terms of three fundamental properties (i) THE SHAPE OF THE MOVEMENT, (ii) THE CARRIER OR MEDIUM OF THE MOVEMENT, and (iii) THE TEMPORAL CHARACTERISTICS OF THE MOVEMENT.

(i) *Shape.* In terms of the type of organization of meaning and expression: the textual metafunction is concerned with creating contrasts between prominence and non-prominence in meaning as an aid in the processing of text. This contrast in prominence tends to engender a wave-like mode of expression, which embodies peaks of prominence against troughs of non-prominence; the result is often periodicity in discourse (as in the alternating use of different reference strategies). (See further section 3.4.)

(ii) *Carrier.* In terms of 'ORDER OF REALITY': the textual metafunction is concerned with enabling the construal of ideational and interpersonal meaning as text in context. That is, if we view the three metafunctions from above the linguistic system, the textual one is set apart as the ENABLING one and the ideational and interpersonal ones group together as EXTRINSIC (Halliday 1978: 131). The latter two orient towards natural and social reality; in contrast, the textual metafunction orients towards SECOND-ORDER, SYMBOLIC REALITY – the reality brought into existence by language itself. This enabling, second-order character of the textual metafunction is reflected in the fact that it employs the modes of organization engendered by the other metafunctions as carriers of textual waves. (See further section 3.5.)

(iii) *Temporal characteristics.* In terms of the distinction between synoptic and dynamic: textual meaning is DYNAMIC, ever-changing (non-identifiable becomes identifiable, new becomes given, and so on), and it requires us to develop dynamic models that can capture the progressive contextualization achieved by the textual metafunction as a text unfolds. (See further section 3.6.)

I will discuss these properties in more detail below (sections 3.4–6). I will begin with the shape of the movement – the textual wave.

3.4 THE SHAPE OF THE TEXTUAL MOVEMENT: WAVES

The wave embodies both peaks of prominence and troughs of non-prominence; sometimes I have used the alternative metaphor of 'PULSE' to capture this characteristic (cf. Matthiessen 1988). Catford's (1977: 85) characterization of pressure pulses at the level of phonetics ('EXPRESSION SUBSTANCE') captures the essential quality we are concerned with in the textual metafunction – and here (at the expression plane) the interpretation is largely congruent:

> In all languages the principal 'CARRIER WAVE' of speech is a pulmonically initiated egressive air-stream. In many, if not in all languages, this main stream of pulmonic egressive air appears to be delivered in more or less rhythmic bursts, or 'quanta'. For instance, in English, it seems clear that the pulmonic initiator operates in a series of pressure pulses each consisting of a single sharp rise in initiator power followed by a slower decline, then a new sharp rise at the beginning of the next pulse and so on.

Catford (1977: 286) illustrates this pulse with the example given in Figure 3.3(i). Alternatively, we can diagram it in the same way as Halliday (1985: 272) does – see Figure 3.3(ii). These pulses or waves realize the phonological system of rhythm; they are expression waves whose function is largely internal to the expression system of English. In other words, there is pulsating variation in prominence in the 'expression' but none in the 'content' (where semantics and lexicogrammar are the two strata of 'content'). In addition to pulmonic air pressure, pitch is also used to create waves or pulses in English expression – tone contours with a (pretonic) build-up to a major (tonic) pitch movement. These pitch waves are not only internal to the phonological system; they also serve to realize the textual system of news management, INFORMATION (cf. further below). In other words, there is pulsating prominence in content as well as in expression: see Figure 3.4. Textual meaning in general is characterized by variation in prominence. This variation in content prominence is quite analogous to the pressure pulses of the expression system; and variation in news prominence is actually realized by pitch pulses.

Pitch pulses construe and express information pulses: they redound with

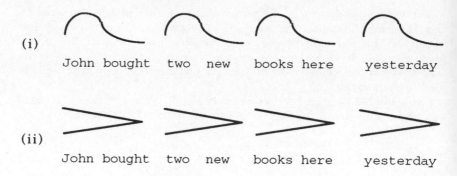

Figure 3.3 Phonetic pulses

one another (cf. Halliday's 1990b discussion of Lemke's 1984 principle of metaredundancy).[4] Any textual pulse or wave constitutes a gradual transition in the contrast between peaks of textual prominence and troughs of non-prominence.

In addition to the waves or pulses within the expression plane of language that realize pulsating prominence within the content, we also find waves whose carriers are patterns of 'content' rather than patterns of 'expression': see further below and section 3.4.3 in particular. In general, we can see that the rhythmic periodicity that results from bursts of prominence followed by declines into non-prominence (or non-prominence building up towards prominence)[5] may serve a textual function.

3.4.1 Carriers of textual waves

First I will show how textual waves can be achieved by means of different carriers. To do this, I have to refer briefly to the other metafunctional modes of organization. The textual wave contrasts with the other metafunctional modes of expression as summarized in Table 3.1 (see Halliday 1979; Matthiessen 1988, 1990b; Matthiessen and Halliday 1990 for more detailed discussions).

Thus, if we look within the clause, we find that experiential selections are realized by constituency configurations of a process, participants and circumstances (transitivity structures), interpersonal selections are realized by pitch contours (a phonological prosody), modal prosodies, negative prosodies and so on, and textual selections are realized by sequential prominence; and if we look beyond the clause, we see that it is expanded logically into complexes through interdependency structure. The experiential, interpersonal and textual modes of expression within the clause are shown in Figure 3.5 (an expansion of Figure 3.2).

We can now return to the carriers of textual waves: the textual metafunction uses the (i) experiential and (ii) interpersonal modes of organization as carriers of textual waves.

(i) The experiential metafunction creates constituency but it does not

Table 3.1 Metafunctional modes of meaning and modes of expression

metafunction	mode of expression
experiential	particulate – constituency configurations
logical	particulate – interdependence (relational)
interpersonal	prodosy
textual	pulse (wave) of prominence/non-prominence

assign any value to the relative order of the constituents; for example, ACTOR + PROCESS ⊢ GOAL and GOAL + PROCESS + ACTOR are experientially the same. Since the expressive potential of ordering the experiential constituents is not taken up by the experiential metafunction, the textual one can draw on this constituency to give textual meaning to the relative ordering of the constituents.

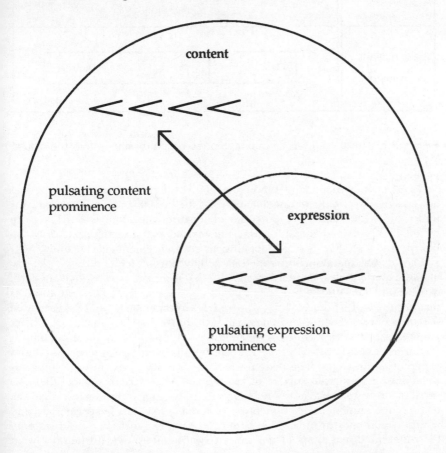

Figure 3.4 Redounding waves of content and expression

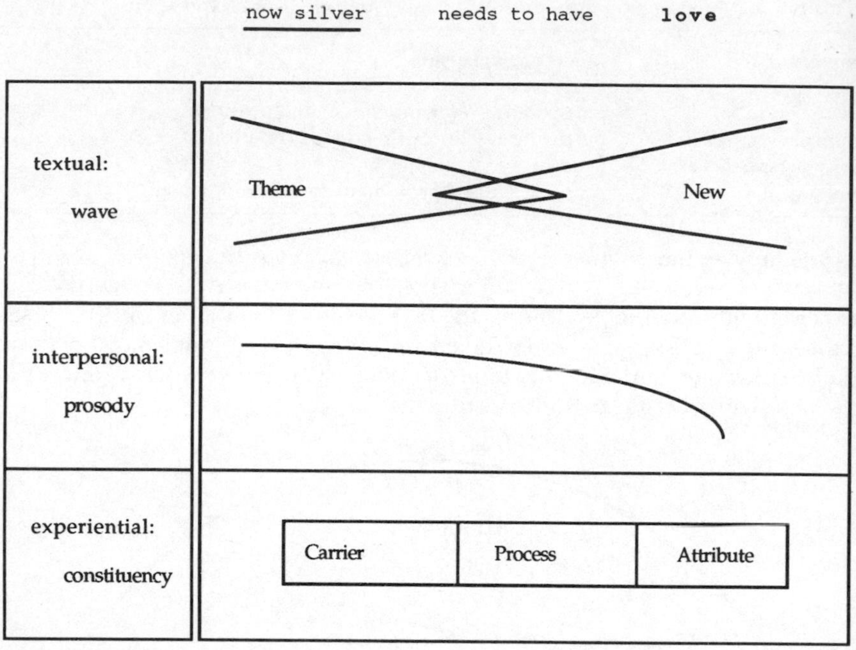

Figure 3.5 The three metafunctional modes of expression within the clause

(ii) The interpersonal metafunction creates a pitch prosody but it does not assign any value to the location of the major pitch movement, the tonic. Since the expressive potential of locating the tonic is not taken up by the interpersonal metafunction, the textual metafunction can draw on this prosody to give textual meaning to the placement of the tonic.

The textual metafunction can thus achieve prominence through the use of the experiential and interpersonal modes to create a wave-like mode of expression 'CARRIED' by constituency and prosody. The situation is diagrammed in Figure 3.6, where the interpersonal and experiential metafunctions are shown as enacting and construing 'REALITIES OUTSIDE' language in the process of semogenesis and the textual metafunction is shown as 'CONSTRUING' semiotic reality – the reality of interpersonal and experiential meaning. The textual metafunction also construes the interpersonal and experiential modes of expression as textual by using them as carriers of textual waves. (The diagram may appear to suggest that the textual metafunction is somehow ordered after the experiential and interpersonal ones in time. This is not the case; the ordering indicates only the different orientations of the three metafunctions: see further below in section 3.5).

The textual metafunction thus gives value to aspects of the expressive

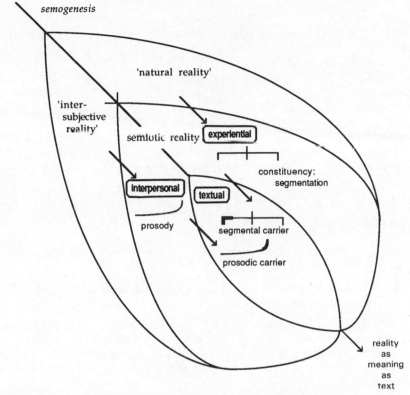

Figure 3.6 The carriers of textual waves

potential that are opened up by the segmental constituency mode of organization of the experiential metafunction and the prosodic mode of organization of the interpersonal metafunction but are not used by these two metafunctions. The textual metafunction co-ordinates the ideational and interpersonal metafunctions in an abstract way: it shows how both these metafunctions can be 'carriers' of textual waves.[6]

Since two non-textual metafunctions operate in the clause, there are two potential carriers for textual waves, as shown in Figure 3.6 – constituency and prosody. Figure 3.2 illustrates the complementarity of the two waves of the typical English clause.[7] (i) The first peak of thematic prominence is realized by sequential prominence – early position in the clause; (ii) the second peak of prominence of newsworthiness is realized by the phonological prominence created by the major pitch movement in a tone group. There are thus two realizational scales of textual prominence – one where the wave is carried by constituency and mapped on to sequence and one where it is carried by prosody and mapped on to the location of pitch movement: see Figure 3.7.

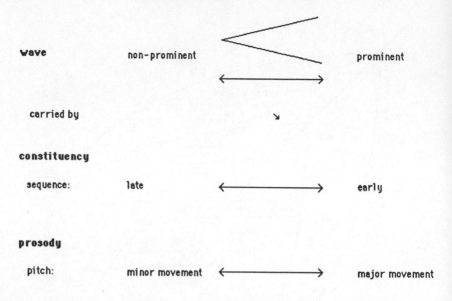

Figure 3.7 Realization of two types of textual prominence

Both sequence and pitch can be used by the textual metafunction to form compound waves. Compound sequence realizes theme substitution – as in *this* is *Bobby's special, **this one*** – and compound pitch movement realizes two points of information (Halliday's tones 13 and 53; cf. Halliday 1967; 1967/8).

Both sequence and intonation are, of course, used to realize non-textual selections as well as textual ones. But this serves to bring out the textual mode of expression more clearly rather than undermine the principle that different metafunctional meanings are realized by different modes of expression. Let us consider (i) intonation and then (ii) sequence inside and outside the textual metafunction. When they are used inside the textual metafunction, they are used as waves; outside the textual metafunction, they are used in accordance with the mode of expression typical of the metafunction within which they realize selections – in particular, they are used prosodically to realize interpersonal selections.

(i) *Intonation.* The different uses of the same realizational category are perhaps most obvious in the case of intonation. As already noted in section 3.3, intonation is used by the interpersonal metafunction as well as the textual one. However, different aspects of the pitch movement are used by the two metafunctions. The textual metafunction employs the PROMINENCE created by the major pitch movement as a realizational category (cf. Figure 3.7); the direction of the pitch movement is not at issue. In contrast, the interpersonal metafunction employs the DIRECTION of the movement (rising *v.* falling; or some combination of the two: rising–falling, falling–rising; neither rising nor falling: level) and this relates to

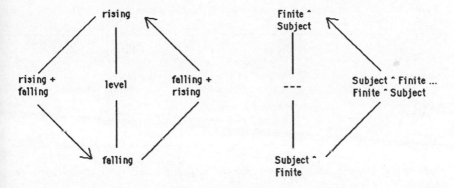

Figure 3.8 Interpersonal 'word order' as prosody

the pitch contour as a whole. In particular, it involves not only the major pitch movement but also minor ones preceding it (within the Pretonic, as an aspect of secondary tone; see Halliday 1967).

(ii) *Sequence.* The situation is very similar with the other realizational category, sequence, or 'WORD ORDER' as it is often called. As already noted, the textual metafunction employs the prominence created by the overall linear sequence of the elements of the clause – the scale from early (thematically prominent) to late (thematically non-prominent) in the clause. In contrast, the interpersonal metafunction employs 'word order' not as a scale of prominence but in order to create a two-term opposition. It gives value not to early (initial) position in the clause but to the relative sequence of Subject and Finite within the Mood element of the clause. Consequently the basic expressive contrast in English is SUBJECT ^ FINITE : FINITE ^ SUBJECT. This is analogous to the interpersonal intonational contrast between falling and rising pitch movement:

SUBJECT ^ FINITE : FINITE ^ SUBJECT ::
FALLING : RISING

There is even an analogy in the expansion of these two basic systemic oppositions, as diagrammed in Figure 3.8, which can be contrasted with the textual analogy between sequence and intonation in Figure 3.7.

FINITE ^ SUBJECT/RISING realizes 'YES/NO-INTERROGATIVE' and SUBJECT ^ FINITE/FALLING realizes 'DECLARATIVE'. The two may combine through the addition of a Mood Tag, SUBJECT ^ FINITE . . . FINITE ^ SUBJECT (cf. the combination of FALLING + RISING TONE, FALLING-RISING), as in *it is . . . isn't it?*; or the Mood element may be absent, as it typically is in an imperative clause (cf. level tone). The point of this excursion into the interpersonal domain is to show that the textual use of 'word order' is different from the interpersonal use of 'word order'; and that they are different precisely along the lines of WAVE *v.* PROSODY just as TONIC PROMINENCE *v.* PITCH MOVEMENT are. The contrast

Table 3.2 Contrast between the wave and prosodic use of sequence and pitch movement

	Sequence	Pitch movement
textual	early (Theme)	major (New)
	late (Rheme)	minor (Given)
interpersonal	Subject ^ Finite/	falling/
	Finite ^ Subject	rising
	+ extensions (both–and; neither–nor).	

between the wave and prosodic use of sequence and pitch movement are summarized in Table 3.2.

We can also note that sequence and pitch movement combine in predictably different ways within the textual and interpersonal metafunctions. In the textual metafunction they combine to form complementary waves: sequential peak followed by intonational peak in the unmarked clause (as in Figure 3.2). In contrast, in the interpersonal metafunction they combine to form a prosody of either SUBJECT ^ FINITE + FALLING or FINITE ^ SUBJECT + RISING. Any approach that just operates with an undifferentiated notion of sequence or 'word order' will not, of course, bring out the fundamental point that it can be employed as wave or as prosody.

3.4.2 Imposing discreteness on wave

The notion of a textual wave or pulse helps us see why representational problems arise in the modelling of the textual area of the linguistic system. Representing a textual wave or pulse motion in constituency terms will obviously create problems. Thus even though textual waves are non-discrete (as suggested by Firbas's notion of Communicative Dynamism) we have to create experiential-like discreteness by drawing constituency boundaries between Theme and Rheme on the one hand and between Given and New on the other; Figure 3.9 illustrates the constituency interpretations of the wave shown in Figure 3.2.

The thematicity wave and news waves have different carriers – constituency and prosody – respectively. The constituency carrier makes it easier to draw a discrete boundary than does the prosodic carrier. Let us consider these two cases in turn.

(i) In the case of THEMATIC PROMINENCE it is comparatively easier to draw the boundary since the carrier of the wave is constituency. (See Halliday 1985: chapter 3 for the principles in interpreting the English thematic wave in constituency terms.) The basic principle is that the boundary can be drawn after the first experiential phase of the thematic peak (which is *silver* in Figure 3.9). However, experiential adjuncts may pile up at the beginning of the clause, and the effect is clearly one of successive thematic contextualization; for example:

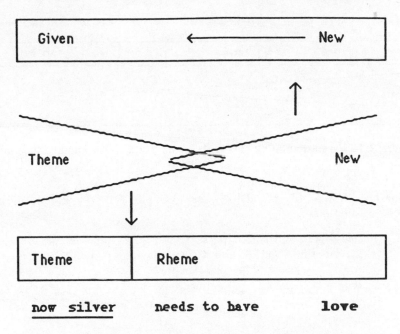

Figure 3.9 Wave continuum interpreted as constituency discreteness

A. 'Do you mean we're overdressed?' said the charming father of the Family.
B. '[Place:] In England, [Time:] at this moment, [Purpose:] for this occasion, [Carrier:] we [Process:] would be [Attribute:] quite over-dressed.

[Muriel Spark]

Similarly:

['Time:] In two or more years, [Place:] both in London to which he went for the season and to pay a round of country house visits in the early autumn, and in Paris, where he had settled down, [Sensor:] he [Process:] knew [Phenomenon:] everyone whom a young American could know.

[Somerset Maugham]

Focusing on the first example, we can see how the thematic prominence of the clause gradually decreases as the clause unfolds; Figure 3.10. Here it is hard to impose a constituency boundary after the Place ('in England') and simply treat the rest as Rheme. But we get the same kind of dimi-nuendo effect even with single marked Themes in declarative clauses, where the Subject still has some thematic prominence, as indicated by the fact that it may relate to the method of development just as when it is the

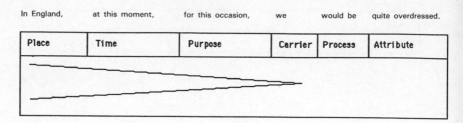

In England,	at this moment,	for this occasion,	we	would be	quite overdressed.
Place	Time	Purpose	Carrier	Process	Attribute

Figure 3.10 From thematic peak to rhematic trough with multiple ideational Themes

unmarked Theme of the clause; for example (Themes italic, marked Themes underlined):

[i] *Autumn* passed and *winter* [passed], and <u>*in the spring*</u> *the Boy* went out to play in the wood. While *he* was playing, two rabbits crept out from the bracken and peeped at him.

[ii] And *he* found that *he* actually had hind legs! <u>*Instead of dingy velveteen*</u> *he* had brown fur, soft and shiny, and *his ears* twitched by themselves.

In example i, there are three successive temporal Themes. The first two are unmarked; they also serve as Subject; but the third is marked – a circumstantial Theme. Yet the Subject still seems to have some thematic value: it introduces *the Boy* as Theme, which is then retained as Theme in the subsequent clause (*while he was playing*) and cancelled in the clause following that one (*two rabbits crept out from the bracken*). In example ii, *he*, the rabbit, arguably retains thematic status throughout even though the second sentence begins with a clause whose Theme is a marked circumstantial one (*instead of dingy velveteen he had brown fur, soft and shiny*). In this clause the Subject still falls within the diminuendo of the thematic wave.

(ii) In the case of NEWS PROMINENCE, it is, quite predictably, comparatively harder to draw the boundary between Given and New, since the carrier of the wave is not constituency but prosody. That is, the carrier does not itself provide a constituency structure and the boundary between Given and New is more indeterminate (Halliday 1985: 275).[8] Following Halliday, this indeterminacy is indicated by means of the left-facing arrow pointing from New, as in Figure 3.9. (Identifying the end of the New is not a problem, since it coincides with the end of the intonational or tonic prominence.)

3.4.3 From grammatical waves to discourse semantic waves

We have seen, then, that grammatical constituency can serve as a carrier of a textual wave (just as prosody can): given a particular configuration of constituents, the textual metafunction assigns thematic prominence to the sequence of unfolding these constituents, from early (thematic peak) to late (thematic trough). Halliday (1985) shows that the same thematic principle as in the clause is at work within the nominal and verbal groups in the grammar of English, as well as within clause complexes. These are still grammatical waves; but in addition we find higher-order waves at the stratum above lexicogrammar, (discourse) semantics.[9] In the semantic organization of text the sequence of semantic elements is textually significant: traditional rhetoric and composition reflect this in the notion of the 'topic sentence' of a paragraph, and this point is taken up in Halliday (1982b) in his comparison of the organization of text (semantics) and clause (grammar). Within systemic linguistics, Fries (e.g. forthcoming) and Martin (in press, n.d.) have followed up Fries's (1981) pioneering work on the relationship between text organization and clausal Theme selection; cf. also the related work on the sequence of dependent clauses relative to the development of text by Thompson (1984) and Longacre (1986). Martin has suggested that we can recognize thematic peaks not only within paragraphs (hyper-themes) but also within larger discourse segments (macro-themes). (Martin also extends this to the textual system of information.) From the point of view of our present concern with the interpretation of the textual metafunction, the most important point is that the 'SCALE' from Theme to Macro-Theme (or even more global Themes in discourse) is on the model of waves within waves, with the bigger ones predicting the smaller ones.

3.5 SECOND ORDER NATURE OF THE TEXTUAL METAFUNCTION

Having considered the notion of the textual wave, let us now focus specifically on the second-order nature of the textual metafunction. The textual metafunction is second-order in the sense that it is oriented towards semiotic reality – towards reality as meaning, brought into existence by the ideational and interpersonal metafunctions, reflecting natural reality and enacting intersubjective reality, respectively (see Figure 3.6). Its function is, as Halliday (1978) puts it, an enabling one. It probably needs emphasizing repeatedly that the enabling, second-order nature of the textual metafunction does not mean that it is less important than the other two metafunctions (see further below). The aspect of context that is specifically related to the textual metafunction, mode, is a second-order category within context; Halliday (1978: 145) writes:

All the categories under this third heading [i.e., mode, CM] are second-order categories, in that they are defined by reference to language and depend for their existence on the prior phenomenon of text. It is in this sense that the textual component in the semantic system was said to have an 'ENABLING' function vis-à-vis the other two: it is only through the encoding of semiotic interaction as text that the ideational and interpersonal components of meaning can become operational in an environment.

Because of its second-order, enabling nature, the textual metafunction operates in terms of the resources brought into existence by the other metafunctions; this is manifested in lexis (lexical cohesions) as well as in grammar (theme, information, ellipsis, etc.). The recognition of this principle helps us explain and deal with representational problems in modelling the textual metafunction, both with respect to systems and with respect to structures. The second-order nature of the textual metafunction is reflected in many ways:

(i) Developmentally (unlike the ideational and interpersonal metafunctions, it is not anticipated in protolanguage; it emerges only as the child moves into adult language),

(ii) The use of sequence once the configurational constituency mode of organization has opened up the possibility; and the use of intonation once the prosodic mode of organization has opened up the possibility,

(iii) The use of interpersonal and ideational structure as a mode of realization in substitution and ellipsis,

(iv) The use of taxonomic movements to achieve lexical cohesion once experiential lexical taxonomy has opened up the possibility,

(v) The use of the resources of identifying relational clauses; and the motivation and use of ideational grammatical metaphor in general.

(i) *Developmental perspective.* The first point emerges from the case studies in Halliday (1975) and Painter (1984). The ideational and interpersonal metafunctions are both anticipated in protolanguage (reflective and active, respectively); but the textual metafunction evolves only as the child has started the transition into adult language and begun to develop discourse. With respect to THEME and INFORMATION, Painter (1984: 243 onwards) observes of Hal, the child whose linguistic development she studied:

One striking difference between the grammar I have described for Hal at 24 months and any adult description of English lies in the absence from the former of any systems relating to the textual metafunction. . . . At clause rank, the systems relating to the textual metafunction in adult are those of THEME and INFORMATION. I have very little to say concerning the former, since up to 2 years Hal did not produce monologues of any lengths which might provide data for considering Thematic choice in text development (see Fries, 1983 [1981]). Nor were his structures long enough or complex enough on the whole to allow for different orderings of elements which might be attributable to marked *v.* unmarked Theme selection. There were a very few cases of variably employed ordered structures . . . However, it would be difficult to demonstrate that such occasional variations were systematic realizations of Thematic choice.

There was, however, clearly a system of INFORMATION established by 24 months. Even before this, there were some examples of the information Focus being placed away from the unmarked final position. . . . It is much easier to observe the operation of Given and New choices in

Mood		Residue
Subject	Finite	Predicator
This kind of multimedia disc	could	exist
but ---	doesn't	---
when it	will	---

| continuity | contrast | continuity |
| (non-prominent) | (prominent) | (non-prominent) |

Figure 3.11 ELLIPSIS carried by modal structure

dialogue than to establish the development of Thematic ones, but perhaps it may anyway prove typical for the former to develop first.

(ii) *Constituency and prosody as carriers*. The use of constituency and prosody as carriers was discussed in section 3.4. This point is related to the developmental perspective at least in so far as intonation seems to be used prosodically before it is used as a wave in language development.

(iii) *Substitution and ellipsis* are resources for assigning textual statuses, just like theme and information; more specifically, they serve to indicate contrast in the context of continuity (see Halliday and Hasan 1976, who show that substitution and ellipsis are essentially the same). The possibilities of ellipsis and substitution depend on the kinds of structures generated by the ideational and interpersonal metafunctions. Thus, once an ideational or interpersonal structure has been established, the textual metafunction can give meaning to the presence and absence of an element of that structure – significantly, the manipulation of presence and absence presupposes the existence of the structure in the first place. For instance, in the following example, ellipsis is used to indicate the continuity of the Residue (non-prominence) against the contrast of the Mood, most specifically the Finite (prominence):

This kind of multimedia disc *could* exist
but [0] *doesn't* [0] –
and nobody seems to know
when it *will* [0].

(Italics on the Finite *could* in original; bold added here to indicate subsequent contrastive Finites.) The example is analysed in Figure 3.11.

This does not constitute a textual STRUCTURE such as the thematic wave or the wave of newsworthiness (see Halliday and Hasan 1976), but the principle of using ideational and interpersonal structure to create a textual differentiation between prominence and non-prominence is the same. And ELLIPSIS and INFORMATION support one another: what is elided is presumed as Given and what is not elided will include the focus of the New information; for instance, the focus of the New in a reading of the example above would most likely be *could – doesn't – will.*[10]

(iv) *Textual lexis* operates in terms of the taxonomic organization of lexis created by the ideational metafunction: textual meanings are made by movements up and down this ideational taxonomy as a text is developed. That is, the ideational taxonomy acts as a 'carrier' for the textual movements along it. For example, one lexical cohesive strategy is to move from a specific lexical item in one mention to a more general one in a subsequent mention, as is illustrated in the following excerpt.

One of the very largest dinosaurs was Brontosaurus (bron-toe-SAWR-us). This giant was about 70 feet and probably weighed as much as 30 tons.

[P. Zallinger, *Dinosaurs*, 1977]

Here the choice of the general term *giant* serves to SUMMARIZE ('distil') the information given about the dinosaur: 'CREATURE + LARGE SIZE'. This illustrates how lexical cohesive strategies operate in terms of the ideational taxonomy of lexis; they use it by moving up and down it, for example, as a text proceeds with successive lexical choices (see also Matthiessen 1991).

(v) *Grammatical metaphor* (Halliday 1985: chapter 10) is a 'second-order' use of the grammatical resources: one grammatical feature or set of features is used as a metaphor for another feature or set of features; and, since features are realized by structures, one grammatical structure comes to stand for another. For instance, an identifying clause may be used to represent a non-identifying one, thereby providing an alternative construal of that other clause as a configuration of IDENTIFIED + PROCESS + IDENTIFIER. Thus the clause *you want this* may be reconfigured as an identifying clause by nominalizing 'the thing that you want' as *what you want*, and identifying it with *this*, either as WHAT YOU WANT IS THIS or as THIS IS WHAT YOU WANT:

and I said 'I am not competent to do it and I wouldn't have me name on the title page to do it' and I said 'I'm bloody sure that Hilary and Gavin aren't competent to do it either' and I said '*if this is what you want*, I would put maximum pressure upon somebody like Derek Brainback to do it' but I said . . .

[*A Corpus of English Conversation*, ed. R. Quirk and R. Svartvik, pp. 802–3]

The two versions of the clause are related in Figure 3.12.

The motivation behind the identifying metaphor is actually textual: the alternative configuration in the identifying clause constitutes a textual alternative way of distributing information in the clause. This is why this clause

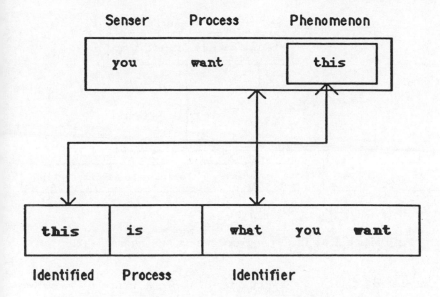

Figure 3.12 Clause construed as identify clause (1)

type is known as thematic equative (Halliday 1985: 41–4). Now the central point in the present context is that the textual organization is realized by the second-order resource of grammatical metaphor. That is, the grammar is turned back on itself to reconstrue itself for textual reasons as diagrammed in Figure 3.13. We can see, then, that experiential grammatical metaphor is a strategy for creating a 'carrier' of textual meanings.

The textual option of theme predication similarly employs the identifying type of clause to achieve a textual distribution of meaning with the added feature of identification. I will again give one example taken from Quirk and Svartvik (Information Focus in **bold** type):

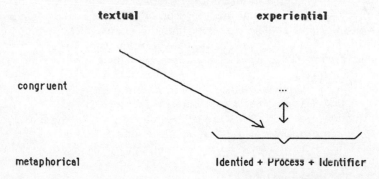

Figure 3.13 Textual organization carried by experiential metaphor

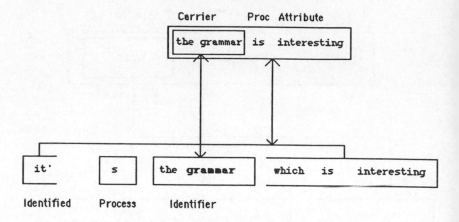

Figure 3.14 Clause construed as identifying clause (2)

A. There's a lot more in grammar than people notice. People always notice the lexis.
B. Yes.
A. Lots has been done about that – but I mean you can only get so far and so much fun out of 'pavement', 'sidewalk', etcetera.
B. Mm.
A. It's the grammar where the fun is.
B. //1 **Yes** //4 it's the **grammar** which is interesting//

[*A Corpus of English Conversation*, p. 255]

Here grammar, 'the thing which is interesting', is identified as grammar rather than lexis; the relationship between *the grammar is interesting* and *it's the grammar which is interesting* is shown in Figure 3.14.

These two identifying clause types – THEMATIC EQUATIVE and THEME PREDICATION – are fully integrated parts of the THEME system in English grammar. But ideational grammatical metaphors in general often have the effect of providing the textual metafunction with an alternative grouping of quanta of information. The principle that the textual metafunction brings metaphor into textual service is quite a general one. Let me just give examples of two further types of ideational metaphor brought into textual service.

(i) Metaphorical mental clauses of perception, such as Halliday's (1985: 324–5) *the fifth day saw them at the summit*, may serve to create two quanta of information, SENSER (THEME) + PHENOMENON (NEW); consider the following example: (Theme underlined in ranking clauses, paragraph 2; seasonal Themes in italics; relevant culmination of the New in bold):

One of Australia's most majestic mountain ranges is one of Sydney's most popular year-round playgrounds. The Blue Mountains to the west of the city have beckoned Sydneysiders to its resorts since the last century, but only after World War I have the pleasures of the Blue Mountains been developed to attract foreign visitors as well. The main town in the mountains is Katoomba, 104 km (62 mi) west of Sydney. *Spring and fall* are the most beautiful times of year here. *In springtime*, millions of wildflowers and trees are in bud, and the many planned gardens in the region start to flourish. *In fall*, the North American species of trees introduced long ago to the region – oak, elm, chestnut, beech, and birch – do the same in the Blue Mountains as they would in the Catskills: turn brilliant reds, oranges, and yellows. *Summer* finds **campers and hikers descending on the mountains in throngs**, *and winter* is the time the mountains are at their quietest and most peaceful, offering perfect solitude for city escapees.

If you're looking for a swinging resort, the Blue Mountains may not be for you. . . .

[*Fodor's Sydney*, p. 115]

Here the metaphorical clause *summer finds campers and hikers descending on the mountains in throngs* is textually motivated in terms of both THEME and INFORMATION. From the point of view of THEME, it provides *summer* as the unmarked Theme of the clause – one instalment in the seasonal method of development. From the point of view of INFORMATION, it groups *campers and hikers descending on the mountains in throngs* as one quantum of information (the Phenomenon of the metaphorical mental clause); contrast the congruent version, which has the same Theme (marked) but a different culmination of the New: '*In summer,* campers and hikers descend on the mountains **in throngs**.'

(ii) In the second type to be exemplified, a clause or clause complex is nominalized as a Medium participant in a clause whose Process simply means 'HAPPEN' (*happen, occur, take place; begin, continue, stop*). The Medium constitutes a thematic quantum of information, as in the following example (information involved in progression in italics; relevant culmination of New in bold):

The speed of light, and of all electromagnetic waves, was given as a constant by Maxwell's equations, and this speed and the existence of the waves themselves was independent of any outside effect. However, Einstein realized that if an observer was travelling alongside a light wave at the same speed as the light wave, *the wave would essentially disappear, as no wave peaks or troughs would pass by the observer. But the disappearance of light waves because of the motion of an observer* should not happen **according to Maxwell**, so Einstein concluded that either Maxwell's equations were wrong or that no observer could move at the speed of light. He preferred the latter explanation for a particular reason.

[M. Shallis, *On Time*, p. 38.]

Here the metaphorical clause makes it possible to summarize the preceding clause complex *the wave would essentially disappear, as no wave peaks or troughs would pass by the observer* as a thematic nominalized participant, *the disappearance of light waves because of the motion of an observer.* Halliday (1988) provides many examples of this kind in scientific English and shows how this type of metaphorical clause has evolved over the past 500 years or so in the history of English.

3.6 DYNAMIC CHARACTER; TRANSITIONS

Having discussed the second-order nature of the textual metafunction, I will now turn to the third major property I identified in section 3.3 – its dynamic character. A textual wave or pulse, like any movement, is inherently dynamic – a TRANSITION from one state to another. This reflects the dynamic character of textual meaning: what was new becomes given, what was rhematic often becomes thematic, what was non-identifiable becomes identifiable, and so on.[11] These all constitute CHANGES IN TEXTUAL STATUS; and they show how the dynamic character of the textual metafunction involves the notion of TEXT or DISCOURSE HISTORY – the past and the future of any given current clause. In particular, this is the history of text development as a semiotic journey.

3.6.1 Thematic progression

We can thus see evidence for the dynamic character of the textual metafunction when we look across clauses in a discourse, taking in both the past and the future of any given present clause. This textual dynamic is embodied in the notion of THEMATIC PROGRESSION (Daneš 1974; Fries 1981) as in the following text:

Rugged Coast to Bleak Desert

[Theme to Theme progression:] This northern strip of Southern California is remarkably varied in its topography, its communities, its weather, the products of the land, both above and below ground, and in the rewards of travel. Along its northern edge, it stretches 240 miles, but in the south the abruptly angling coast cuts the east–west distance to only 150 miles. In length north to south the section is about 100 miles.

   From west to east the character of the land changes, often abruptly. From the Pacific shore – one of the most scenic regions in the West – rise *steep-sloped, wild, inhospitable ranges* [Rheme to Theme progression:] Beyond them is a chain of narrow *valleys*, . . . dotted with a succession of *towns*, . . . linked by *US 101*. Beyond its route rise other tumbled ranges and heavily forested wildernesses, part of the Los Padres National Forest. Further east spreads *the southern end of California's central valley* – hot, wide, and immensely fertile – thanks to irrigation. In the north-central part of the section *low mountains* cut the central valley from forest areas to the south of them, . . . forming the whole eastern third of the section into the vast and inhospitable Mojave Desert.

[*Southern California, Rand McNally Guide*]

The text starts with a series of related Themes (a succession of locations) and then changes to a Rheme-to-Theme type of progression.

A clause occurs at some point in an unfolding discourse; and because of its location in the discourse, it has a certain discourse history (cf. Sinclair, Chapter 1 above). The point at which a clause occurs determines the current DISCOURSE CONTEXT of that clause. It constitutes a point of departure for the clause before it has even been started; but in addition the textual metafunction gives the resources for specifying a LOCAL CONTEXT for the clause itself – its own point of departure or Theme. As the example above illustrates, the Theme is typically chosen in such a way that it relates to the clause's discourse history. At the same time, the clause contains a potential germ of its own future. While the clause often distils its own past (cf. Halliday 1988 on the use of grammatical metaphor to achieve this; Longacre 1986 on the use of thematic dependent clauses within clause complexes to get this effect), it does not predict its own future (cf. Martin, n.d.); but it does provide material for a number of possible futures. Thus *Further east spreads the southern end of California's central valley* harks back to a past reference point already provided; but its future is more open:

Further east spreads the southern end of California's central valley

- In the north-central part of the section low mountains cut . . .
- This section is well known for . . .
- This valley . . .
- Further west spreads . . .
- etc.

3.6.2 Transitions between waves

So far I have focused on the dynamic nature of the peaks of prominence and troughs of non-prominence; but the textual wave itself moves forward. It does so by means of textual transitions: rhetorical (conjunctive) relations for moving from one textual status of prominence to another in the discourse by expanding (elaborating, extending or enhancing) the first stage by the second. There are thus two aspects to this type of movement – transitions, and phases of relative prominence and lack of prominence; see Figure 3.15.

The two aspects of this 'swell of information', textual transitions and textual statuses, are complementary and part of the same picture. The following span of text is a movement in two phases:

Most long-haul flights used to be exactly that. A long haul, with the inevitable refuelling stop en route. The barriers of distance stood in our way. *But now* those barriers have been broken, by the largest, fastest long-haul aircraft in the world. SIA's MEGATOP 747.

[*Time*, March 1989]

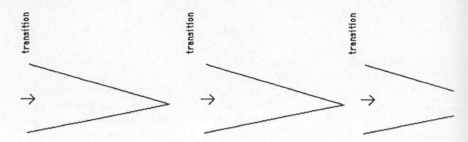

Figure 3.15 The two aspects of textual movement

The textual movement is indicated by *but* as well as by *now*, as shown diagrammatically in Figure 3.16. The relation of contrast can be inferred from the fact that *now* has been given thematic status as one of the points of contrast; but the relation of contrast is also explicitly marked by *but*.

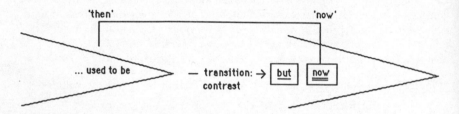

Figure 3.16 Relation and point of contrast in textual movement

In general, transitions may be marked explicitly by conjunctions (Halliday and Hasan 1976; Martin in press). Like other features of the textual metafunction, the transitions that can be marked by conjunctions are oriented either towards the experiential metafunction or towards the interpersonal metafunction – external and internal conjunction, respectively (see Halliday and Hasan 1976); see Figure 3.17. That is, the textual metafunction may draw on either the experiential sequence of processes or the interpersonal sequence of interactive moves to create transitions moving a discourse forward. We can now see that the distinction between external and internal conjunction is not an isolated fact about the textual metafunction but a manifestation of the same basic property of the textual metafunction as we find in its orientation towards interpersonal and experiential carriers of textual waves.

The transitions themselves (whether explicit or implicit) can be characterized by means of Rhetorical Structure Theory (RST; e.g. Mann and Thompson 1987; Mann *et al.* 1989). That is, the transitions constitute rhetorical interdependency relations for moving a text forward – for expanding it temporally, causally, additively, and so on. In fact they embody the method of development of a text. As Fries (1981) has shown, Theme is selected to bring out the method of development of a text (such as the

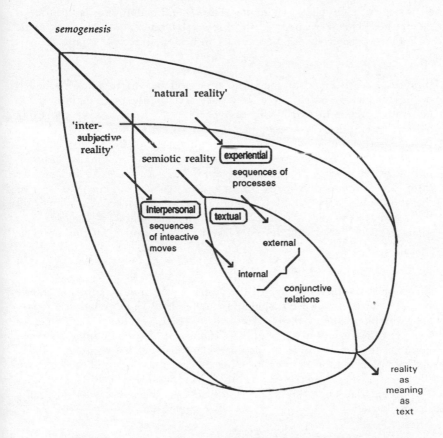

Figure 3.17 Metafunctional orientation of conjunctive relations

spatial method of development of the guidebook text in section 3.6.1 above). This can now be interpreted in terms of rhetorical relations: Themes are selected to bring out the points that enter into a rhetorical relation – the points of sequence (times), points of contrast (as in Figure 3.16), points of elaboration, and so on. The texts analysed in Fries (1981) can be seen to illustrate this point (see further Matthiessen 1990c).[12]

The thematic strategy of creating a marked Theme (typically signalled by *as for*, *as to*, *regarding* in written English but not in spoken English (the so-called left dislocation of formal grammar)) that is related cohesively (typically by reference but sometimes only by lexical cohesion) to the rest of the clause is used specifically to identify a point of elaboration that is picked up after another point has been elaborated (see Matthiessen 1990c; cf. Ochs-Keenan and Schieffelin 1976; Kies 1988 on spoken English). For instance, in the following excerpt, a number of food items are introduced in the 'HYPER-THEMATIC' nucleus of the paragraph and then picked up in the subsequent elaborating segments. The second elaboration is introduced by a marked Theme related to the Subject by referential cohesion (*as for pickles*; the top layer of organization is indicated, internal organization is not):

[nucleus:] Also served at the same time will be vegetables – parboiled or raw – pickles or chutneys and curd. [elaboration 1:] Chutneys are generally prepared with fruit or vegetables, vinegar and something closely resembling Worcestershire sauce. Two of the most delicious varieties are mint and mango chutney; but here again there will be as many varieties as there are 'raw materials' and in as many different guises as the cook cares to dream up. [elaboration 2:] As for pickles they can be made with fruits like mangoes, peaches or limes as well as the more familiar vegetables. [elaboration 3:] The curd has somewhat the same role to play as dhal, i.e. it is very soothing if *your curry* has made a particularly fiery descent. *You* may also find it on the menu as dahi.

[*Fodor's India*, p. 150]

This is just another instance of the general principle that textual transition and thematic status are systematically related. This relationship also helps us explain an interesting feature of Theme in the development of discourse: if it appears in a rhetorically dominant clause (complex), a given thematic element of a clause or thematic clause of a clause complex is likely to extend its semantic domain beyond the grammatical unit it occurs in until it is 'CANCELLED' by another comparable Theme (cf. Fries forthcoming a). Thompson (1984) illustrates this effect for thematic purpose clauses.

3.6.3 Textual statuses and textual transitions

Having identified the two complementary aspects of textual movement – transitions and textual statuses – we can interpret the textual resources of English along the lines shown in Table 3.3. That is, transitional relations moving the discourse forward are realized by the resources of CONJUNCTION within the textual metafunction. This is the type of textual cohesion identified as organic by Hasan (1985); it relates clauses as organic wholes. Alternatively, transitional relations can be 'GRAMMATICALIZED' as relational structures by means of the logical resources for forming clause complexes (cf. Matthiessen and Thompson 1989). Textual statuses are realized by cohesive resources (ELLIPSIS/SUBSTITUTION and REFERENCE) as well as structure-forming ones (THEME and INFORMATION). The value of textual prominence (PROMINENT *v*. NON-PROMINENT) can thus be achieved not only by the wave-like structures of THEME and INFORMATION within units but also by resources that do not create textual structures within grammatical units, ELLIPSIS/SUBSTITUTION and REFERENCE (cf. section 3.5 (iii) above and Figure 3.11).[13]

Table 3.3 Textual transitions and statuses in English

	logical: structural alt. to CONJUNCTION	textual — cohesive: organic	textual — cohesive: componential	structure forming
clause	CLAUSE COMPLEX (expansion/projection)	CONJUNCTION (expansion: elaboration/extension/enhancement)	ELLIPSIS-SUBST. (contrast in continuity: in clause complex, clause, and groups)	THEME (local context: thematic – Theme ^ Rheme) VOICE (unmarked Theme)
group-phrase			REFERENCE (recoverable/ not recov.)	
information unit				INFORMATION (news status – Given + New)
	Transitional relations			Textual statuses

NB. Lexical cohesion

The possibility of interpreting all textual resources as strategies for managing either textual transitions or textual statuses in the 'swell of information' is very important when we ask how to model our interpretation of the textual metafunction: the dichotomy suggests that we need two basic types of mechanism, as outlined in section 3.7.

3.7 MODELLING WAVES

It is now possible to pick up the three characteristics of textual waves first mentioned in section 3.3 and then discussed in more detail in sections 3.4–6 and use them as a way into modelling waves at the level of semantics. One approach is to draw on work that has been done in computational linguistics on knowledge representation, discourse structure, focus and focus shifts (for discussion of this work and its relevance to the textual metafunction see also Bateman and Matthiessen 1991, forthcoming; for discussions of dynamic modelling of systemic theory see also Bateman 1989, and O'Donnell 1990). To draw on this body of work, we have to start with the representation of ideational meaning: this constitutes the first order of representation in terms of which second-order, textual meaning can be specified in the way discussed below.

Various knowledge representation techniques have been developed for representing mostly ideational meaning (for surveys see for example, Scragg 1976; Brachman and Levesque 1985; Sowa 1983a). For present purposes it will suffice to focus on semantic nets or networks (conceptual graphs) and simply to think of ideational meaning as being represented as a large network of nodes linked by various kinds of relations (such as hyponymy and participant relations).[14] When a text is produced, certain nodes in this network are selected for presentation. For a very informal and incomplete example, consider the semantic network in Figure 3.18; the information is drawn only from the short biography included in the Penguin edition of Joseph Conrad's *Nostromo*.

I have drawn this network as a succession of transitivity configurations, with processes (*be born*, *pass*, *be*, etc.) as nodes with participant roles (Medium, Range) and circumstantial roles (Time, Place, Destination, etc.). I have included only information present in the source text;[15] any actual semantic network would include a good deal of information that is not presented in any particular text: producing a text means selecting from the information present in the network. I have organized the diagram in such a way that it is fairly easy to see how one can read it as a text. The vertical axis represents process time, from 1857 onwards. Processes on the same horizontal line are related by some type of logicosemantic relation within a clause complex in the text. The actual Conrad biography reads as follows (clauses not diagrammed in Figure 3.18 are in italics; ideational Themes are underlined and will be discussed presently); note that this is only one possible 'TEXTUAL READING' of the ideational meanings represented in Figure 3.18:

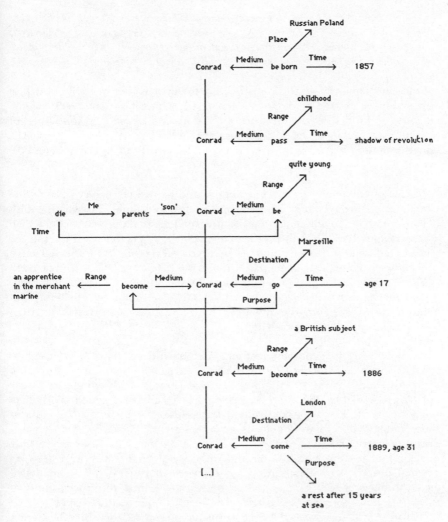

Figure 3.18 Informal example of ideational semantic network

Joseph Conrad (originally Konrad Korzeniowski) was born in Russian Poland in 1857, and . . . passed his childhood in the shadow of revolution. His parents died when he was quite young. At the age of seventeen he went to Marseille to become an apprentice in the merchant marine. *This began a long period of adventure at sea, Conrad having his share of hardship, shipwreck, and other accidents.*

He became a British subject in 1886. In 1889, at the age of thirty-one, he came to London for a rest after fifteen years at sea. *On this short London holiday, he began writing a sea novel, which, after surviving subsequent jungle travel, shipwreck on the Congo, and a railway cloakroom in Berlin, came into the hands of Edward Garnett and through him to a London publisher. The book was 'Almayer's Folly', . . . destined to be the first of a long series of novels and stories, . . . mostly inspired by his experiences of life at sea, which have placed him in the front rank of English literature. He died in 1924.*

Once the semantic network has been defined, it is then possible to define abstractions in terms of it. In particular, it is possible to PARTITION the network – to divide the network into domains or spaces consisting of collections of related nodes and links (see Hendrix 1978, 1979).[16] Partitioned semantic networks are characterized succinctly in Bundy (1986: 110) as follows:

Means of enhancing the organizational and expressive power of semantic nets . . . through the grouping of nodes and links, associated with Hendrix. Nodes and links may figure in one or more 'SPACES', which may themselves be bundled into higher-level 'VISTAS', which can be exploited autonomously and structured hierarchically. The effective encoding of logical statements involving CONNECTIVES and QUANTIFIERS was an important motivation for partitioning, but the partitioning mechanisms involved are sufficiently well-founded, general and powerful to support the dynamic representation of a wide range of language and world knowledge.

As noted in this characterization, such partitions have been used to represent various kinds of information; of particular interest here is the use of partitioned spaces to represent textual states of prominence. Grosz (1978) presents the idea of representing focus as a partitioned space in a semantic network – what she calls a focus space. A focus space 'contains those items that are in the focus of attention of the dialog participants during a particular part of the dialog' (p. 233). Since focus is really only one kind of textual status of prominence, we need to generalize Grosz's original proposal: textual states of prominence in general can be modelled as partitioned spaces in a semantic network. Against the background of this, it is now possible to suggest very briefly how textual waves can be modelled; I will start with the first two wave properties identified in section 3.3 above:

(i) The second-order character of a textual wave is captured by defining it in terms of the already existing ideational semantic network (the first-order representation, such as the fragment shown in Figure 3.18). This is clearly only a first approximation: as I showed in section 3.5, the textual metafunction may in fact motivate ideational organization as a means of 'carrying' textual organization.

(ii) The peaks of prominence of a wave constituting textual statuses can then be modelled as partitioned textual spaces of the semantic network. As already noted, this is a generalization of Grosz's notion of focus spaces to include thematic spaces, new spaces, identifiability spaces, and so on. This is clearly only a first approximation: textual prominence is a matter of

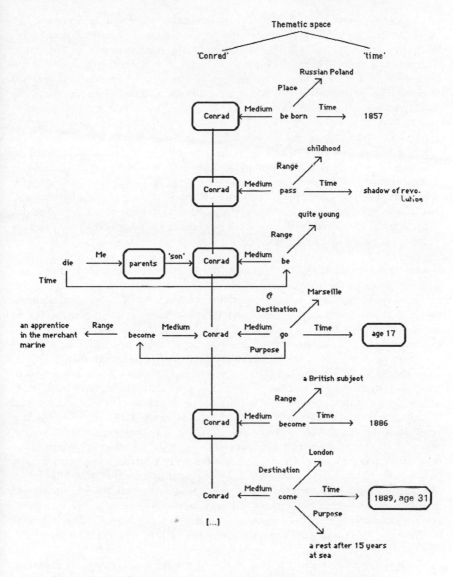

Figure 3.19 Semantic network partitioned into textual spaces

degree, and we need to think of a textual space not as a clearly bounded region but rather as a central region, the peak of prominence, from which one can move to more peripheral regions, the troughs of non-prominence. Such gradience is necessary not only to deal with degrees of thematicity and newsworthiness but also to handle identifiability by 'BRIDGING' (cf. Clark 1975; for example, bridging from a centrally identifiable whole to more peripherally identifiable parts).[17]

The use of textual spaces defined on an ideational semantic network can be illustrated by adding thematic spaces to Figure 3.18; see Figure 3.19. With the exception of Conrad's parents, the thematic spaces are either Conrad or a time. Thematic spaces in an ideational semantic network can be seen as a model of the systemic understanding of Theme and method of development articulated in Martin (in press), where field corresponds to what has been discussed in terms of ideational semantic networks here:

> Method of development . . . establishes an angle on the field. This angle will be sensitive to a text's generic structure where this is realised in stages. Method of development is the lens through which a field is constructed; of all the experiential meanings available in a given field, it will pick on just a few, and weave them through Theme time and again to ground the text: to give interlocutors something to hang on to, something to come back to, an orientation, a perspective, a point of view, a perch, a purchase.

The speaker thus selects 'THEMATIC SPACES' as points of entry into larger regions of the ideational semantic network. From the listener's point of view, these thematic spaces constitute indications of where to integrate the new information being presented in the text – cf. Reinhart (1982). If we think of the listener's processing of a text as being partly a matter of expanding his or her current semantic network with new information, the thematic spaces guide him/her to appropriate expansion points.

In the Conrad biography there are essentially two competing types of node to partition as a thematic space: Conrad and some significant time, although his works come in as another type of Theme in the second half of the text not diagrammed in Figures 3.18 and 3.19. The writer has resolved the conflict by alternating between the two candidates; in the segment shown in Figure 3.19, temporal Themes are selected when there is a transition in Conrad's life associated with Conrad's move to a new destination (Marseilles, London).[18] Here Conrad remains the Subject of the clause. But, even when Conrad is thematic, the discoursal movement through the semantic network is still essentially a chronological one (with certain elaborating excursions realized in dependent clauses). This takes us to the point where we can raise the question of how to model textual transitions.

So far I have hinted at the possibility of taking a 'snapshot' of a textual wave by partitioning a semantic network into textual spaces representing wave peaks (crudely, since the spaces are discretely bounded regions at this stage). This still leaves us with the task of modelling the dynamic character of the textual metafunction – the wave in motion or the TRANSITIONS between different textual states. To do this, to deal with what Grosz (1978: 233) called the dynamic requirement on focus representation, we can use one of the mechanisms developed in computational linguistics for dealing with 'DISCOURSE HISTORY'. Grosz used the computational notion of a STACK to model transitions or shifts from one focus space to another; see

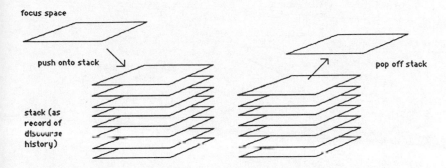

focus space

push onto stack

pop off stack

stack (as record of discourse history)

Figure 3.20 The stack as a model of successive textual states

Figure 3.20.[19] As a discourse develops, focus spaces are stacked one on top of another so that the most recent is always on top of the stack. The stack itself can thus be used as a record of progression through discourse time. Now the stack is always manipulated from the top: if a new focus space is to be added to the stack, it is pushed on to the top of the stack; and if an old one is to be removed, it is popped off the top of the stack.

For instance, the succession of thematic spaces might include from bottom to top: *'at the age of seventeen', 'in 1889, at the age of thirty-one', 'on this short London holiday'*. While the account based on the stack mechanism is a very explicit model of how textual states of prominence might get manipulated in the development of discourse, it is very clear from a functional-linguistic point of view that the stack is too simple a record of discourse history. In particular, it represents a discourse as a flat structure; it does not represent the kind of hierarchic constituency organization or internal interdependency nesting that various approaches to discourse have revealed (cf. section 3.3 above): see, for example, Fox (1987) on reference and rhetorical organization (modelled in terms of Rhetorical Structure Theory). A typical guidebook text would illustrate the issue with respect to Theme: while the global principle of development is a spatial one (say, that of the walking tour) and is constructed in spatial Themes, this type of text often changes locally to other principles, such as the temporal one reflected in <u>As the battle ended,</u> <u>the last six cadets</u> are said to have wrapped themselves in the Mexican flag **and** . . . *jumped from the hill to their deaths* **rather than** *surrender to the U.S. forces*, which occurs on a walking tour of a park in Mexico City. After this temporal detour the text returns to the spatial development, where it left off: see Figure 3.21. This is quite typical of Theme selection in discourse (cf. suspended exchanges in conversations). There is no problem with returning to the earlier principle for moving from one Theme to another although it has been interrupted; it may be necessary to use a strategy for marking the return Theme, such as *as for, as to, regarding* + NOMINAL GROUP.

To model the kind of situation that I have just illustrated, McCoy and Cheng (1991) propose hierarchic trees as a mechanism for controlling focus

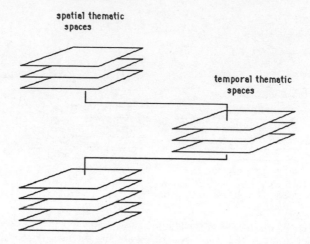

Figure 3.21 Detour through temporal stack, with return to spatial one

shifts and Hovy (1989) relates this work to Rhetorical Structure Theory. Bateman and Matthiessen (1989) suggest that Rhetorical Structure Theory can be used to model transitions in a text from one textual state to another. As already noted in section 3.6, these rhetorical transitions constitute the method of development of a text. The Conrad biography illustrates this principle but in a slightly complex way: the main type of transition is temporal sequence, which means that thematic spaces including times are likely and that shifts from one space to another will occur along with the sequence in time; but sequence often also involves a constant participant (Conrad in this text), which is then also a likely thematic candidate.

By way of conclusion, it is important to note what the modelling of the textual wave as sketched here involves: when we model it, we map the wave metaphor on to another ideational metaphor – that of textual spaces within an ideational space. The point of this translation is that this second metaphor corresponds to an explicit, implementable computational model; in other words, we have a way of grounding the metaphor. I have suggested one approach which involves the three wave characteristics identified in section 3.3:

(i) second-order → space on top of ideational semantic network,
(ii) peak of prominence as textual state → textual space (in ideational network),
(iii) dynamic → mechanism for moving from one textual space to another, e.g. a stack of textual spaces or rhetorical transitions as in Rhetorical Structure Theory.

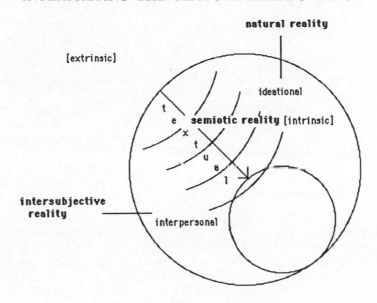

Figure 3.22 The textual metafunction

3.8 CONCLUSION: MISINTERPRETATIONS AND INTERPRETATIONS

In this paper I have discussed the interpretation of the textual metafunction. I identified the three properties of the textual metafunction just listed above in section 3.3, elaborated them further in sections 3.4–6, and used them as the basis for modelling in section 3.7. Let me try to summarize the discussion here: see Figure 3.22. The ideational and interpersonal metafunctions are oriented towards realities that are extrinsic to language and they semanticize these realities as ideational and interpersonal meanings by CONSTRUING natural reality (ideational) and ENACTING intersubjective reality (interpersonal). This creates the condition for a higher-order kind of reality – semiotic reality: a world of meanings intrinsic to language. This is the domain of the textual metafunction; it is oriented towards semiotic reality and semanticizes it as information that can be shared by PRESENTING ideational and interpersonal meaning as text in context. The textual metafunction is thus second-order: semantically, it is oriented towards semiotic reality; and it draws ideational and interpersonal modes of expression into textual service, as carriers of textual waves. At the same time, this means that it acts as an important principle in the organization of semiotic reality: semiotic reality has to be such that it can be shared as text in context. One way of achieving an appropriate textual organization is to reconstrue semiotic reality by means of grammatical metaphor.

The textual metafunction is a dynamic resource; and it is realized as a textual movement. It does not treat a text as a synoptic whole but as a

Table 3.4 Misinterpretations and interpretations of textual properties

property	misinterpretation	interpretation
dynamic	aspect of parole/utterance rather than langue/clause	textual systems are systemic; both static and dynamic
wave	structurally external, peripheral	this reflects an experiential vantage point; peaks are prominent and the experiential nucleus is often merely transitional
second order	temporally/logically later than 'core' grammar: post-production unit as stylistic adjustment or packaging	ordering in abstraction and circumstantially; simultaneous or (dynamically) even prior

constant process of unfolding: the textual resources are specifically concerned with the management of this unfolding as a structured movement, and the structure is wave-like; it embodies peaks of prominence and troughs of non-prominence.

In Figure 3.22 I have shown the textual metafunction as a snapshot of a wave motion carried by the other two metafunctions. The three textual properties of wave shape, dynamicity and second-order orientation discussed here are, I believe, important steps towards interpreting the textual metafunction. But we have to be careful in drawing conclusions about the nature of the textual metafunction based on them: they have clearly been the source of misinterpretations of the textual metafunction (for further discussion and illustration see also Matthiessen and Martin 1989; Martin n.d.). Table 3.4 lists misinterpretations of the textual metafunction that have arisen, together with the interpretations that I believe are appropriate.

I will just review the issues briefly; some I have already touched on. (i) Because of its second-order character (section 3.5), the textual metafunction has often been assumed to be ordered later temporally than the 'core' grammar, as a kind of post-production unit for 'stylistic adjustments' or 'packaging'. This view mistakes an ordering in abstraction for a temporal one. As I have tried to show, there is good reason for assuming that the textual metafunction motivates ideational decisions: transitivity selections may be made in such a way that an appropriate textual organization of a clause is achieved (see the discussion of ideational grammatical metaphor in section 3.5). On balance, it seems there is good reason to treat the textual metafunction as simultaneous with the other two; no metafunction is ordered temporally before the others.

(ii) Because the textual metafunction employs a wave-like mode of expression, with peaks of prominence at the beginning and, typically, the end of the clause, the peaks of textual prominence have often been described as external or peripheral to the nucleus of the clause. This view mistakes the experiential organization of the clause for the textual one: experientially, the Process of a clause's transitivity structure is typically nuclear, and textual peaks of prominence may very well be peripheral in relation to this experiential nucleus, being circumstances associated with the Process rather than directly involved in it or elements without any role at all in the transitivity structure of the clause. But this is only the experiential perspective; from a textual point of view, the textual peaks are exactly that – they are what is textually central to the clause. The experiential nucleus, the Process, will in fact often fall within a textual trough – it is textually non-central to the clause.

(iii) Because the textual metafunction is dynamic rather than static, it has sometimes been said to be part of *parole*, or the utterance, rather than *langue*, or the clause. That is, it is treated as something that arises in the process of instantiating language. This view mistakes instantiation for dynamic potential: there can be no instantiation without potential, no *parole* without *langue*; this becomes quite clear when we try to model language explicitly. The textual metafunction is just as systemic, just as much part of the linguistic potential, as the other two metafunctions. The difference has to do with the nature of the potential: it is dynamic rather than simply static.

These interpretive differences rest on the three textual properties of second-order nature, wave-like organization, and dynamicity. In addition, there are at least two other kinds of common misinterpretations of the thematic contribution to the textual metafunction deriving from important properties. These are listed in Table 3.5 together with the interpretations I believe to be the appropriate ones.

Table 3.5 Misinterpretations and interpretations of Theme in particular

property	misinterpretation	interpretation
iconic realization (THEME)	initial position has no unified meaning; only marked cases (ideational) are topical	iconicity is a feature, not a bug; it is common but not necessary
non-representational, so particularly ineffable	ideational bias: focus on topical themes, interpreted by lexical semantics on glosses	all themes are created equal

(iv) Thematic prominence is realized by initial position; this is an iconic realization of the 'point of departure' of textual movement forward in a clause. Because initial position (realization) is iconic with point of departure (textual function), it is sometimes thought to be meaningless: linguists may think that 'POINT OF DEPARTURE' simply means 'initial position'. But this is to confuse the function being realized with its realization, and if we can establish a model of textual movement through semantic space (cf. section 3.7 above) it is possible to see that point of departure is grounded in a model that is quite distinct from realizational categories such as linear sequence. It is also important to note that the category of Theme, glossed as 'point of departure', is not necessarily realized by initial position in the clause. On the one hand, other positions may be thematically significant, as in English with THEME SUBSTITUTION, where the thematic wave is a compound one, with two peaks of prominence (e.g. *they're not university calibre obviously*, the students on the whole; see Halliday 1967/8). On the other hand, languages may use special thematic markers to pick out the peak of a thematic wave, as in Japanese (*wa*) and Tagalog (*ang*).

(v) The textual metafunction is non-representational; it is not a resource for construing reality. Consequently it is hard to represent the textual metafunction (see section 3.2 above). It is, for instance, hard to gloss the category of Theme; and it is particularly hard to gloss Themes with a non-representational function alongside the thematic function itself, that is, to gloss interpersonal and textual Themes. As a result, Theme is often misinterpreted as being only 'topic' (as pointed out by Halliday 1985: 39) – that is, as the ideational type of Theme that is the easiest to gloss as 'what the clause is about'. The interpretation of Theme as 'topic' fails to show that all Themes are created equal: textual and interpersonal Themes make the same contribution to the development of the discourse as topical (ideational) ones do.

The misinterpretations are all clearly related to properties of the textual metafunction. One common thread is that they are based on PARTIAL views of the textual metafunction; and the vista point is often the ideational metafunction rather than the textual one. I have suggested that in an important sense interpretation is an ideational act. That is, the act of interpretation introduces an ideational bias. To avoid accounts of the textual metafunction that are partial and ideationally biased, we have to operate with global models of language in context and we have to try to understand and model the metaphorical expansion of the semantic system needed to deal with the textual metafunction.

NOTES

1 The technical account may be based on the theory built into ideational lexicogrammar rather than on an independent study of the phenomenon to be interpreted. This has arguably happened in speech act theory, where theoreticians have drawn on verbal transitivity within the ideational metafunction rather than interaction within the interpersonal metafunction; Edmonson (1981: 22) notes that 'what Searle characterises and classifies are not units of conversational behaviour, but concepts evoked by a set of lexical items in English – illocutionary verbs. The criterion for the existence of an illocutionary act of a specific kind is essentially the existence in English of a term which may be used in an explicit performative formula in the alleged performance of that act.'

2 Compare also language itself, construing discourse development in terms of abstract space: *in the first place, here, leaving that aside, to resume, to get back to the point, elsewhere; point, place, ground, field.*

3 Another source of interpretation of textual categories is the conduit metaphor (cf. Reddy 1979): the textual metafunction is seen as a way of packaging meaning. This type of metaphor is, I believe, quite misleading and has none of the interesting features of the metaphors concerned with (motion through) abstract space.

4 That is: 'CONTENT' wave (metaphorical construal) redounds with 'EXPRESSION' wave (congruent construal). Thus the English system suggests one way in which the wave metaphor we use to construe the textual metafunction may be grounded in a model.

5 The thematic grammatical wave in English is like the rhythmic wave: peak declining into trough. In contrast, the information wave typically starts with a trough and builds up to a peak: see section 3.1.

6 This also happens within the systemic part of the textual metafunction: the English voice system conflates the interpersonal Subject with one of the experiential participants.

7 The gradual transition between the two peaks can be 'MEASURED' in terms of degrees of topicality and newsworthiness in the discourse: see, for example, Thompson (1987) on the relative topicality of Medium and Beneficiary in the sequences MEDIUM ^ BENEFICIARY and BENEFICIARY ^ MEDIUM (the so-called 'dative' shift) – the topicality is higher for the participant to the left and thus closer to the thematic peak of the clause.

8 Even here constituency does play a role. The intonational prominence achieved through the major pitch movement takes place within one syllable, the tonic syllable, but as we move up one stratum from phonology to lexicogrammar this translates into a grammatical constituent: in the unmarked case, the New includes at least that grammatical constituent within which the tonic syllable falls.

9 Daneš (1974) introduces the concept of 'HYPER-THEMES' to show how particular themes may anticipate the thematic progression in a text; but these hyper-themes are still clausal themes rather than discoursal themes (see Martin n.d. for this point).

10 To take an example from R. Quirk and J. Svartvik, *A Corpus of English Conversation* (1980), p. 438: //4 we haven't got a **man** //1 we've got a whole **department** //. Here there is lexical repetition rather than ellipsis or substitution within the Given; but the example is very close to the following variant with ellipsis: //4 we haven't got a **man** //1 but a whole **department**//.

11 Once some piece of information has become given or identifiable it is likely to retain this status in the discourse; thematic status is also often maintained, but not necessarily.

12 Referential strategies are also sensitive to the rhetorical development of a text: see Fox (1987), and cf. Hinds (1977) on paragraphing and reference. On the relationship between rhetorical development and the selection of New see Fries (forthcoming, b).

13 However, over extended discourse REFERENCE in particular still contributes to a kind of wave-like periodicity: long stretches of pronominal reference (the unmarked strategy) interrupted occasionally by full nominal reference (the marked strategy). This periodic pattern is an important feature of text; and it shows clearly that what we have to explain is the use of full nominal reference and not, as is typically assumed, the use of pronominal reference.

14 Semantic networks were first developed in computational linguistics by Ross Quillian (e.g. 1968) in the 1960s and have undergone considerable development

since then, to a significant extent as a response to Woods (1975); there are obvious parallels with the networks used in Stratificational linguistics, with system networks and with Jay Lemke's thematic formations.

15 The text presents instantial meanings concerning Conrad; I have not represented the semantic systemic potential that these meanings instantiate. This potential would include, among other things, a hyponymic taxonomy.

16 Alternatively, we can define processes in terms of the semantic network – processing for moving through it and 'LINEARIZING' it as text; textual states such as Theme could then be modelled by making the process visit nodes in the network in a certain sequence (cf. Sowa 1983b).

17 Grosz (1978: 273) operates with both explicit focus and implicit focus. When a physical object in the semantic is in explicit focus, its sub-parts are in implicit focus.

18 One could, of course, write the text in such a way that times consistently fall within the thematic spaces: compare the different thematic versions of texts provided in Fries (1981) and Martin (n.d.).

19 As an ordering principle the stack, where the principle is 'first in, last out', differs from the queue, where the principle is 'first in, first out'. For a discussion of the stack in the modelling of exchange see O'Donnell (1990).

REFERENCES

Bateman, J. (1989), 'Dynamic systemic–functional grammar: a new frontier', *Word* 40, 1–2.

Bateman, J., and Matthiessen, C. (forthcoming), 'The Text Base in Generation', paper presented at conference on Language and Text Research, Xi'an Jiaotong University, Xi'an, to appear in selected papers from the conference, H. Bluhme (ed.), Amsterdam, Benjamins.

———— (1991), *Systemic Linguistics and Text Generation: Experiences from Japanese and English,* London, Pinter.

Brachman, R., and Levesque, H. (eds) (1985), *Readings in Knowledge Representation,* Los Altos, Morgan Kaufman.

Bundy, A. (ed.) (1986), *Catalogue of Artificial Intelligence Tools,* second, revised edition, Berlin and New York, Springer Verlag.

Catford, I. (1977), *Fundamental Problems in Phonetics,* Bloomington, Indiana University Press.

Chafe, W. (1979), 'The flow of thought and the flow of language', in T. Givón (ed.), *Syntax and Semantics* 12, *Discourse and Syntax,* New York, Academic Press.

Clark, H. (1975), *Bridging,* in *TINLAP-1,* reprinted in P. Johnson-Laird and P. Wason (eds) (1977), *Thinking: Readings in Cognitive Science,* Cambridge, Cambridge University Press.

D'Andrade, R. (1987), 'A folk model of the mind', in D. Holland and N. Quinn (eds), *Cultural Models in Language and Thought,* Cambridge, Cambridge University Press.

Daneš, F. (1974), 'Functional sentence perspective and the organisation of the text', in F. Daneš (ed.), *Papers on Functional Sentence Perspective,* The Hague, Mouton, pp. 106–28.

Edmonson, W. (1981), *Spoken Discourse. A Model for Analysis,* London, Longman.

Enkvist, N.E. (1987), 'Text strategies: single, dual, multiple', in R. Steele and T.

Threadgold (eds), *Language Topics: Essays in Honour of Michael Halliday* II, Amsterdam, Benjamins.

Firbas, J. (1987), 'On two starting points of communication', in R. Steele and T. Threadgold (eds), *Language Topics: Essays in Honour of Michael Halliday* I, Amsterdam, Benjamins.

Fox, B. (1987), *Discourse Structure and Anaphora: Written and Conversational English*, Cambridge, Cambridge University Press.

Fries, P.H. (1981), 'On the status of theme in English: arguments from discourse', *Forum Linguisticum*, reprinted in Janos S. Petöfi and Emel Sözer (eds) (1983), *Micro and Macro Connexity of Discourse*, Papers in Text Linguistics 45, Hamburg, Buske.

—— (forthcoming a), 'Patterns of information in initial position in English', in P. Fries and M. Gregory (eds), *Discourse in Society: Functional Perspectives*, Norwood, Ablex.

—— (forthcoming b), 'Towards a discussion of the flow of information in a written English text'.

Grosz, B. (1978), 'Discourse knowledge', in D. Walker (ed.), *Understanding Spoken Language*, New York, North Holland.

Grosz, B., and Sidner, C. (1986), 'Attention, intentions and the structure of discourse', *Journal of Computational Linguistics* 12.3, 175–205.

Halliday, M.A.K. (1967), *Intonation and Grammar in British English*, The Hague, Mouton.

—— (1967/8), 'Notes on transitivity and theme in English', *Journal of Linguistics* 3.1, 3.2, 4.2.

—— (1975), *Learning How to Mean*, London, Edward Arnold.

—— (1977), *Aims and Perspectives in Linguistics*, Occasional Papers 1, Sydney Applied Linguistics Association of Australia.

—— (1978), *Language as Social Semiotic: the Social Interpretation of Language and Meaning*, London, Edward Arnold.

—— (1979), 'Modes of meaning and modes of saying', in D.J. Allerton, E. Carney and D. Holdcroft (eds), *Function and Context in Linguistic Analysis: Essays offered to William Haas*, Cambridge, Cambridge University Press.

—— (1982a), 'It's a fixed word order language is English', *I.T.L. Review of Applied Linguistics*, 67–8, 91–116.

—— (1982b), 'How is a text like a clause?' in S. Allén (ed.), *Text Processing: Text Analysis and Generation, Text Typology and Attribution*, Stockholm, Almqvist & Wiksell, pp. 209–47.

—— (1984), 'On the ineffability of grammatical categories', in A. Manning, P. Martin and K. McCalla (eds), *The Tenth LACUS Forum 1983*, Columbia, S.C., Hornbeam Press.

—— (1985), *An Introduction to Functional Grammar*, London, Edward Arnold.

—— (1988), 'On the language of physical science', in Mohsen Ghadessy (ed.), *Registers of Written English: Situational Factors and Linguistic Features*, Open Linguistic series, London and New York, Pinter.

—— (1990), 'New ways of meaning: a challenge to applied linguistics', *AILA*, April.

—— (1992), 'How do you mean?', this volume.

Halliday, M.A.K., and Hasan, R. (1976), *Cohesion in English*, London, Longman.

Halliday, M.A.K., and Matthiessen, C. (in preparation), *Turning the Tables: a Linguistic Interpretation of Cognition*, Berlin, de Gruyter.

Hasan, R. (1985), 'The texture of a text', in M.A.K. Halliday and R. Hasan, *Language, Context, and Text: Aspects of Language in a Social-semiotic Perspective*, Geelong, Vic., Deakin University Press.

Hendrix, G. (1978), 'Semantic knowledge', in D. Walker (ed.), *Understanding Natural Language*, New York, North Holland.

—— (1979), 'Encoding knowledge in partitioned networks', in N.V. Finder (ed.), *Associative Networks*, New York, Academic Press.

Hinds, J. (1977), 'Paragraph structure and pronominalization', *Papers in Linguistics* 10, 77–99.

Hovy, E., with K. McCoy (1989), 'Focusing your RST', eleventh Conference of Cognitive Science Society.

Kies, D. (1988), 'Marked Themes with and without pronominal reinforcement: their meaning and distribution in discourse', in E. Steiner and R. Veltman (eds), *Pragmatics, Discourse and Text: Some Systemically-inspired Approaches*, London, Pinter.

Lemke, J. (1984), *Semiotics and Education*, Toronto Semiotic Circle Monographs, Working Papers and Prepublications, Toronto, Victoria University.

Longacre, R. E. (1986), 'Adverbial clauses beyond the sentence', in R. Longacre and S. Thompson, 'Adverbial clauses', in T. Shopen (ed.), *Language Typology and Description*, II, *Complex Constructions*, Cambridge, Cambridge University Press.

McCoy, C., and Cheng, J. (1991), 'Focus of attention: constraining what can be said', in C. Paris, W. Swartout and W. Mann (eds), *Natural Language Generation in Artificial Intelligence and Computational Linguistics*, Dordrecht, Kluwer.

Mann, W., and Thompson, S. (1987), *Rhetorical Structure Theory: a Framework for the Analysis of Texts*, ISI/RS-87-185, to appear in *IPRA Papers in Pragmatics*.

Mann, W., Matthiessen, C., and Thompson, S. (1989), *Rhetorical Structure Theory and Text Analysis*, USC/ISI Report; also to appear in W. Mann and S. Thompson (eds), [*Diverse Descriptions of a Text*], Amsterdam, Benjamins.

Martin, J.R. (in press), 'Life as a noun', in M.A.K. Halliday and J.R. Martin (eds), *Writing Science: Literacy as Discursive Power*, London, Falmer.

—— (in press), 'Theme, Method of Development and Existentiality: the Price of Reply', Department of Linguistics, Sydney University.

Mathesius, V. (1975), *Functional Analysis of Present Day English on a General Linguistic Basis*, The Hague, Mouton.

Matthiessen, C. (1988), 'Representational issues in systemic functional grammar', in J.D. Benson and W.S. Greaves (eds), *Systemic Functional Approaches to Discourse: Selected Papers from the Twelfth International Systemic Workshop*, Norwood, Ablex; also as ISI/RS-87-179.

—— (1990a), 'Language on language: the grammar of semiosis', to appear in *Social Semiotics* 1.2.

—— (1990b), 'Metafunctional complementarity and resonance', Department of Linguistics, Sydney University.

—— (1990c), 'Lexicogrammatical Cartography: English Systems', Ms, Department of Linguistics, Sydney University.

—— (1991), 'Lexico(grammatical) choice in text-generation', in C. Paris, W. Swartout and W. Mann (eds), *Natural Language Generation in Artificial Intelligence and Computational Linguistics*, Dordrecht, Kluwer.

—— (in preparation), *Systemic Functional Grammar in Natural Language Processing*.

Matthiessen, C., and Halliday, M.A.K. (1990), 'Systemic functional grammar', in F. Peng and J. Ney (eds), *Foundations of Syntax: an Advanced Study of Current Theories of Syntax*, Amsterdam and London, Whurr & Benjamins.

Matthiessen, C., and Martin, J.R. (1989), 'A response to Huddleston's review of Halliday's *Introduction to Functional Grammar*', Department of Linguistics, Sydney University.

Matthiessen, C., and Thompson, S. (1989), 'The structure of discourse and

"Subordination"', in J. Haiman and S. Thompson (eds), *Clause Combining in Grammar and Discourse*, Amsterdam, Benjamins.

O'Donnell, M. (1990), 'A dynamic model of exchange', *Word* 41.3.

Ochs-Keenan, E., and Schieffelin, B. (1976), 'Foregrounding referents: a reconsideration of left-dislocation in discourse', in *Proceedings of the Second Anuual Meeting of the Berkeley Linguistic Society*, Berkeley.

Painter, C. (1984), *Into the Mother Tongue*, London, Pinter.

Quillian, M.R. (1968), 'Semantic memory', in M. Minsky (ed.), *Semantic Information Processing*, Cambridge, Mass., MIT Press.

Reddy, M. (1979), 'The conduit metaphor: a case of frame conflict in our language about language', in A. Ortony (ed.), *Metaphor and Thought*, Cambridge, Cambridge University Press.

Reinhart, T. (1982), *Pragmatics and Linguistics: an Analysis of Sentence Topics*, Bloomington, Indiana University Linguistics Club.

Scragg, G. (1976), 'Semantic nets as memory models', in E. Charniak and Y. Wilks (eds), *Computational Semantics*, Amsterdam, North Holland.

Sowa, J. (1983a), *Conceptual Structures*, Menlo Park, Addison-Wesley.

―――― (1983b), 'Generating language from conceptual graphs', *Computers and Mathematics with Applications* 9.1, 29–43.

Thompson, S. (1984), 'Grammar and written discourse: initial *v.* final purpose clauses in English', *Nottingham Linguistic Circular* 13; also in *Text* 5.1/2, 55–84.

―――― (1987), 'Information flow and "dative shift" in English discourse', to appear in a forthcoming *Festschrift*.

Whorf, B.L. (1956), *Language Thought and Reality: Selected Writings of Benjamin Lee Whorf*, ed. by J. Carroll, Cambridge, Mass., MIT Press.

Woods, W. (1975), 'What's in a link: foundations for semantic networks', in D.G. Bobrow and A. Collins (eds), *Representation and Understanding: Studies in Cognitive Science*, New York, Academic Press.

ACKNOWLEDGEMENTS

In this paper I draw gratefully on discussions of textual issues over a long period of time with John Bateman, Peter Fries and M.A.K. Halliday. I would also like to thank Martin Davies and Louise Ravelli for their valuable comments on a draft version and participants at the Systemic Congress in Stirling for their comments on the material I presented orally there. I remain responsible for all errors.

4 Interpersonal meaning in discourse: value orientations

J.L. Lemke

4.1 SEMIOTIC FUNCTIONS AND SEMANTIC RESOURCES

Language is a resource for the construction of social reality. I want to pose some questions regarding the kinds of resources which language makes available to us for that construction. In sketching a programme for answering these questions I will be guided by a particular view of the nature of social reality as multiple and heterogeneous. My first objective will be to broaden and deepen our sense of the 'interpersonal' dimension of meaning, i.e. the kinds of meanings which the linguistic systems Halliday (e.g. 1978) has assigned to an INTERPERSONAL METAFUNCTION have evolved to help us make. I want to push our conception of this kind of meaning, made in every group, every clause, utterance and text, beyond a simple social interactionist model to one consistent with a more complex view of social reality. I then want to focus on one or two specific aspects of this kind of meaning and consider what sorts of social 'work' we do with the linguistic resources available, in texts and in discourse.

Language is one of many SEMIOTIC RESOURCE SYSTEMS, each of which provides us with the means to perform certain generalized SEMIOTIC FUNCTIONS: Presentational, Orientational and Organizational (cf. Lemke 1989a: 37–9, 1990: 194–8). Every act of semiosis, every utterance or other act of social meaning-making, relies for the sense that can be made of it in a community on systems of meaning-making practices that deploy the resources of semiotic systems in specific ways which are simultaneously PRESENTATIONAL, ORIENTATIONAL, and ORGANIZATIONAL.

Language as a resource for making meaning has evolved to enable communities to construct elaborate social realities in this way. Its specific semantic resources are co-deployed in ways which reflect the generalized semiotic functions of its social use, and this in turn produces important interdependencies among these semantic resources. These interdependencies are most evident when language is deployed in the semantic unit we call TEXT and the corresponding social practice we call DISCOURSE. A TEXT SEMANTICS or DISCOURSE SEMANTICS builds on the foundations of lexicogrammatical semantics, taking its analyses of the meaning options of a language at word, word-complex, group, phrase, clause and clause-complex ranks, and considering how local and global text meanings depend on the co-patterning and interdependencies of lexicogrammatical choices through a text.

What, specifically, should we expect to find linguistic resources FOR? What are the general social semiotic functions that shape the semantics of natural language? In the largest sense, we use language, in conjunction with other semiotic resource systems and their associated social practices (drawing, gesturing, etc.) to construct multiple social realities. We both ENACT these realities, in the sense that we perform the social practices that constitute them according to changing but identifiable patterns of redundancies (SEMIOTIC FORMATIONS, cf. Lemke 1984a, 1989b, 1990), and we also CONSTRUE them, in the sense that we make sense of them, or parts of them, implicitly through these same semiotic practices, and explicitly by metasemiotic practices (such as naming and describing, as in linguistics and sociology).

There are MULTIPLE social semiotic realities because all social communities are heterogeneous: there are multiple practices and systems of interrelated practices that do not agree. According to different semiotic codes of construal, there are always alternative ways to intepret what the 'present context' is, and there are different patterns of redundancies between contexts and the actions deemed appropriate or meaningful in those contexts (generalized HETEROPRAXIA). These diverse, sometimes compatible, sometimes conflicting or simply incommensurable codes coexist, usually not peacefully, in the same community and even within the same sub-community, social individual, or discrete text or event. In so far as the meanings are made linguistically, this phenomenon is generally known as HETEROGLOSSIA (Bakhtin 1935, Lemke 1988a).

The construction of a social reality is accomplished semiotically through the three simultaneous semiotic functions already named. The Presentational function of semiosis constructs describable things, including events, processes, relations and sequences, and variously interconnected systems of these. The semantic resources of language most directly subserving this function are those Halliday (1985) has characterized as the IDEATIONAL or EXPERIENTIAL systems of meaning choices in the lexicogrammar. In text semantics and discourse analysis these are the resources that are deployed in the identifiable patterns I have called THEMATIC FORMATIONS (Lemke 1983, 1985, 1988b, 1990, in press a) and which are essentially intertextual in nature and are woven together to create the complex Presentational texture of a text.

But, whatever Presentational reality we may construct, we do not construct it in isolation from a social context. All meaning is made in some immediate CONTEXT OF SITUATION (itself a variable social construction) and some wider CONTEXT OF CULTURE (the more slowly changing macrosocial envelope of innumerable microsocial events). Every semiotic act partially sustains or alters (or both) social relations: both microsocial relations among the participants in a social event and, in a constitutive sense, macrosocial relations among social categories and sub-communities. Social relations are negotiated and contested in social events, and the very codes of heteropraxic diversity in a community are juggled in their ongoing and changing relations to one another through these same events. The universe of social heteropraxia is multidimensional to a very high order. Every act, every utterance, can be construed from many social viewpoints and potentially belongs to many orders of social relations. When we make meaning, we must establish or construe an ORIENTATION in this complex social space.

The lexicogrammatical systems Halliday refers to as INTERPERSONAL ones are clearly associated with the Orientational semiotic function in language. They provide semantic resources for establishing the 'give and take' of language in action: mood systems and more delicate characterizations of speech act functions. They also provide the resources of MODALIZATION and MODULATION, which enable us to establish a stance or orientation towards the probability of a Presentational proposition or towards the degree of inclination or obligation attaching to a proposal (cf. Halliday 1985: 334–40). At the level of text-semantic analysis we are just beginning to understand the language system's Orientational resources, and we will explore some of them in more detail below.

Finally, there is the Organizational function of semiosis: the creation of larger semiotic 'wholes' which articulate 'parts' in characteristic kinds of relations to one another to produce a sense of the whole being structured or organized, rather than being simply a collection of parts which have only arbitrary relations to one another. In language the structure and texture of TEXTS which distinguish them from mere collections of words, or even of clause-complexes, is an instance of the Organizational function at work.

The Organizational semantic resources of language at the lexicogrammatical level of analysis are referred to by Halliday as TEXTUAL systems. At the text-semantic level of analysis there are the textual and intertextual resources of GENRE STRUCTURES, RHETORICAL FORMATIONS, thematic (multi- and co-variate) structuring (Lemke 1985, 1988b, in press a), and some sort of global patternings of Orientational resources (cf. Thibault in press a; Martin in press). In the larger Discourse Analysis perspective, which connects language use to the wider social practices to which it contributes, there are also the very poorly understood resources which enable us to make language BECOME situationally relevant, to create wholes in which text is articulated with other modes of action and features of situational context (cf. Lemke 1984a and Silverstein 1976 on creative and presupposing indexicals).

4.2 HETEROPRAXIA AND ORIENTATIONAL TEXT SEMANTICS

What is there in a text that enables us to determine how it orients itself in the universe of social diversity? If there are multiple social realities being constructed in a community, how does this multiplicity evidence itself in any given text? If the text deploys a consistent code, if it speaks with a single, pure (idealized) social 'voice' (which is rare because of the pervasive contradictions and disjunctions of social ideologies), that very 'voice' is definable only by its *valeur*-relations to other such voices. Pure codes of heteropraxia, like pure voices of heteroglossia, are idealizations constructed by the analyst as reference points for characterizing real, mixed texts and performances.

A useful assumption was first made by Bakhtin (Voloshinov 1929, Bakhtin 1935): that all texts are at least 'dialogical' if not multivocal. Every text-meaning is made in a social universe where alternative or contrary meanings have been or readily could be made. A text is dialogical in the sense that the intertextual contextualization of its meaning includes or is likely to include intertexts from divergent social viewpoints. Lexical choices are always made against the background of their history of use in the community, they carry the 'freight' of their associations with them, and a text must often struggle to appropriate another's WORD to make it its own. So also with choices of register and genre, and even choices of dialect and language.

All linguistic choices are meaningful, not just syntagmatically (in relation to other choices in their functional units at various ranks on various levels), or paradigmatically (in relation to other possible choices within the same local code), but also INDEXICALLY and INTERTEXTUALLY in relation to the various collocations, typically applicable intertexts, and situational and cultural redundancies of any choice or pattern of choices in a heteroglossic community. The entire social universe frames every utterance, every text. Each community and sub-community construes meaning by associating to any text (according to many, mutually divergent sets of rules) other texts, text-types, situation-types and cultural stereotypes which serve to assign it a position in the meaningful social universe. Its position, as Bakhtin saw, is not determined merely by its Presentational reality, by its propositions and proposals, but by its Orientational stance in a social universe of differing viewpoints, by its explicit and implicit VALUES AND SOCIAL INTERESTS, by its social self-positioning and its social positioning by and in relation to those who construe it.

4.3 INTERPERSONAL MEANING: TOWARDS A BROADER SEMIOTIC INTERPRETATION

The sophisticated theoretical framework I have been sketching here is needed to move us beyond simpler perspectives that are no longer sufficient when we have to analyse Orientational text semantics. The naive view is that texts are simply the products of authors or speakers, who address themselves in an immediate context of situation (face-to-face dialogue or the contexts of production and interpretation of written texts) to other participants, all within the context of a shared context of culture. Linguistic resources are then seen as having a primarily communicative function, in the sense of the exchange of messages or meanings. In this picture the interpersonal resources of language are primarily interactional in nature: they help us to establish the social relations between participants in the dialogue. Mood and more delicate characterizations of speech acts tell us who is doing what to whom, and some allowance is made for the tenor of intimacy or social distance, and the negotiation of power relation- ships between interlocutors. In this highly atomized, individual-centred view, individual speakers and their relations to one another are central, and social relations are built up through the linguistic interactions of speakers (cf. Martin's discussion of TENOR, 1990: 30–3).

Modality and Modulation would seem to be less central interactional resources in such a model; they are just the speaker's private opinion intruding into the ideational communication. Most peripheral of all would be such phenomena as 'attitudinal epithets' and the general 'purr v. snarl' features of lexical choices (cf. Martin 1990: 26–7, which finds the connec- tion of Attitude to the definitive interpersonal system of Mood by far the most problematic). What unifies these various semantic resources? Is it simply the 'attitude' of a speaker? And what, epistemologically, is an 'attitude' in a speaker? Is it not just another of the mentalistic notions of individualist folk psychology, as objectionable in a semiotically based linguistics as the notion of speaker 'intentions' or of 'ideas' psychologically anterior to semiosis, theoretically prior to social practices, and metaphysically 'existent' in some ultimately theological notion of 'mind'?

The semiotic case against mentalism is well known (Lemke 1989c, 1990; Thibault 1986), but it is harder to free our discourse from the associated habits of centralizing the speaking individual, of giving context of situation (communicative context) and the communicative function priority over context of culture (intertextual context) and the constitutive function. Moreover, we tend very much still to give precedence to the ideational aspect of language before its social aspect.

In the more complex theoretical picture I think we need, the primary function of language, and of all semiosis, is to create, sustain and change social reality. I do not want to privilege the Orientational semiotic function in this view, but I do want to lean against the prevailing discourse which seems to me (try as it may to do otherwise) to privilege Presentational meanings. The Orientational function could as easily be called the Social- constitutive function. Its essence is not simply the expression of the speaker attitudes but the construction, through the text, of the world of social diversity. What matters, then, is not so much that this speaker 'has' this attitude, but that the text has meaning in a community where there is a system of specific, divergent possible attitudes, and that the text is constructed within that universe of attitudes even as it helps in turn to construct it. This 'universe', moreover, is not simply an agnation of possi- ble 'attitudes' but a structured system of relations among possible attitudes, with redundancy relations linking them to speaker social roles, positions and presentational discourses (SOCIOTYPES rather than 'individuals' as such, cf. Lemke 1988c) and to situational circumstances. There is also a second-order system of redundancy relations (metasystem), the system of heteropraxia (the full sense of 'context of culture' here) in which the first-order systems of redundancy relations (specific, divergent local codes of social reality) coexist and conflict within the total social semiotic system of the community. In very simple terms, the codes by which we construe social relations from actions themselves form a larger system in which the total 'social reality' of a community looks different to those differently positioned within it.

The semantic resources of language, then, enable texts to construct relations which help to constitute the social universe, both in the local sense of multiple social realities, differently seen from different social viewpoints within a community, and in the global sense of the relations among those viewpoints (as seen from *each* viewpoint!). The SYSTEM OF SYSTEMS, or system of heteropraxia, thus potentially depends on an infinite regress, and is not a well defined theoretical 'object', but it is useful nonetheless as a name for the theorist's praxis (cf. Lemke 1984a: 99–104).

In this more elaborate picture, what is central to the social semiotics of language use are the semantic resources for using presentational realities (i.e. ideational meanings) as tools for the construction of this diverse, structured heteroglot social universe of 'ways of being in the world' (i.e. of systems of social practices). The ideational *can* thus be seen as SECONDARY (for the moment), a mere tool or pretext for sustaining or altering, buttressing or contesting, a structure of social interests, values and points of view. Individual speakers or writers are themselves socially constructed (as individuals, as social persons, as sociotypes; cf. Lemke 1988c) through their own and others' texts in this (and in other semiotic) ways. The text can now be analysed as a site of struggle, or at least of 'juggle', among the various voices of social heteroglossia, and each element and feature of the text (lexical item, clause, thematic formation, genre structure, lect, etc.) taken as indexical of the text's own voice(s) *and* as indicating the social stance, viewpoint or orientation of the text toward the rest of the social universe it is, at least in part, co-constructing.

It was also Bakhtin (1935) who first observed that texts position or orient themselves in the world of social heteroglossia through how they DESCRIBE (the ideational, Presentational aspect of the text; his 'ideological') and through how they VALUE (his 'axiological'). This is a fundamental sociosemiotic insight. We describe, present, construct, construe and 'see' different realities, depending on our position in the social system. We also ascribe different and often diverging or contradictory values to the elements we describe, and we favour or oppose various alternatives in varying degrees (cf. Mansfield 1987 on Northern Ireland; Lemke 1988a on gay rights). Thus, apart from the ways in which Presentational thematic formations are indexical of social viewpoints and are metadiscursively related to one another by a text's 'heteroglossing practices' (cf. Lemke 1988a), it is the ways in which texts construct VALUE ORIENTATIONS that can be regarded as central to the Social-constitutive function of language.

Attitudinal epithets and 'purr *v*. snarl' features can now be seen as much more central to the Orientational semiotic function in language, realizing semantically at a fairly delicate level of lexical choice the fundamental VALUE of Goodness (including Desirability, Morality, Appropriateness, Efficiency, etc.). Modulation, expressing inclination and obligation in respect of proposals (offers and commands), clearly conveys a value orientation in this general sense, and specific systems of more delicate choice in Mood (e.g. within Offers, between Promises and Threats) also essentially distinguish what is deemed good *v*. bad.

Modality can be seen in part (Probability systems) as orientation to another possible VALUE: Certitude (in some epistemologies, 'truth'; in others, 'warranted assertability') in all its various subjective and objective, explicit and implicit guises (Halliday 1985).

There are, of course, many other VALUES for which language provides Orientational resources. Predictability is an interesting one, of particular importance as a value in the culturally relatively recent technocratic ideologies (Lemke in press b), though we may regard it as a special case of a much more general Orientational resource: Expectability. This is realized in part through the other systems of modality (Usuality) but is also found in expressions such as *just two, only one, even Jim, done already?, nevertheless* . . ., and other signals of contrary-to-expectations. In fact there seem to be an amazing variety of resources for indicating whether a presentation is or is not in CONFORMITY with expectations. It is perhaps precisely this conformity which is the underlying social value, rather than the apparently more neutral notion of expected *v*. surprising. This is an area of the lexicogrammar and the semantics where considerably more work in systemic linguistics is needed and could be very helpful to discourse analysts.

In this deliberately counterweighted perspective it is perhaps not so surprising that the basic distinctions of Mood are no longer so central to the social function we originally connected with interpersonal systems in the grammar. The Mood system essentially helps to establish the exchange relations between interlocutors. From the Social-constitutive perspective this is merely the most microsocial extension of the resources of language for establishing relations among social positions and viewpoints. But the Mood system, fundamental as it is in the grammar, seems quite subordinate to a social semiotic formation like Genre (at the text-semantic level of analysis) as a resource for constituting these relations, even at the microsocial level.

One cannot say, for example, that those who ask for information or for goods-and-services are necessarily in the process of constituting themselves (and their kind, their social position) as having less power or control in relation to the possessors of the information or goods-and-services. Teachers ask questions as part of a speech genre that constitutes quite the reverse relation between the social positions of Teachers and of Students. Even the unmarked, congruent demand for goods-and-services, the imperative command, seems to imply, against logic, the ability of the one who lacks to compel the one who has, for it is only in such genres that it is used, being replaced by mood metaphors otherwise. The Mood system provides the resources for the realization of complementary moves in these exchange Genres, but it is the genre as a social formation that provides the linguistic resource for construction of (micro- and macro-) social relations.

4.4 GENRE AND THE SOCIAL-CONSTITUTIVE FUNCTION IN TEXT

Let me try to formulate a notion of Genre as a category of semiotic formation, and then consider in particular its role in describing textual patternings of Orientational meaning. An ACTION GENRE is an activity-type, i.e. a socially identifiable, recognizably reproducible constellation of actions that has social meaning *as a whole* in some community. We may choose to further describe the actions, each of which has meaning, or at least meaning potential (rather like lexical items in language) according to the semiotic interpretive and enactive practices of the community, in terms of paradigmatic meaning features (as in a system network) or not, as we like. In any case the social meaning is definable by the 'VALENCES' or 'reactances' of the activity-type, i.e. by its place in the overall system of metaredundancy relations among social practices that constitute the social semiotic system of the community.

Generally the constellation is at least partly one involving syntagmatic relations among acts, particularly the minimal relation of succession (equivalent to temporal sequentiality for most purposes). A Genre, then, is a constellation of meaningful acts, with relations of simultaneity and succession, which has a social meaning as a whole, i.e. as itself, beyond that of its constituent acts.

When people habitually, or at least recognizably and reproducibly, combine actions in ways that make sense socially, they are usually doing social work, and most of the time they are reproducing patterns of social action that are reproduced a lot under similar circumstances in their community. They are doing the important work of maintaining the metaredundancy relations of their social semiotic, and usually also maintaining the material fabric of their community as well. Genres are part of the evidence for social metastability. They are useful to the analyst because they do recur in the same form, more or less, again and again. They are also useful to the community for the same reason. Action genres are the heart of a community as a dynamic open material-semiotic system. Genres are, in sociological terms, 'institutions'.

Since they are doing primary social work, genres embody primary social relations: usually they construct PARTICIPANT ROLES (p-roles) which redound with p-roles in other action genres to constitute social person-types and social categories (including gender, class, etc.). A person who enacts a particular role in one genre does not have, in any real social system, equal probability of enacting all other roles in all other genres. Socially, you are what you do, and you are made to be that by doing so (cf. Bernstein 1981; Bourdieu 1972). In constructing p-roles, genres construct the relations among the p-roles and between the p-roles and the processes (actions) of doing – which is much the same thing, obviously. Translated to the macrosocial level of description, this is macrosocial structure. Genres are simply 'intermediate formations' in the dialectic between micro-(individual transactions, performances, co-actions) and macro-analysis. (Note that, as in the grammar, 'participants' include things and ideas as well as persons.)

A genre, then, in this more specific sense, is an activity-type (as social semiotic formation) in which successions (including branching successions as in a flow chart with contingencies and conditioned probabilities of branch selection) of action chords (the simultaneous acts, in the terminology of music) construct participant roles with specific social relations to one another and to the action processes in which they participate, including power and affinity relations, and specific actional relations among the action processes themselves, structuring the activity flow (i.e. actional text) in multivariate, univariate and covariate ways. (See Lemke 1985, 1988a, b, 1990, in press a) on semiotic modes of structuring.)

Many action genres are enacted at least in part through language. From the viewpoint of language, or at least of linguists, any genre that employs the semiotic resources of the linguistic system to any extent at all becomes a language genre (or just 'genre'), such as a speech genre or written genre, and all the rest becomes 'context'. It is an important question how satisfactory an account of genre can be that assumes that the distinctive features of a genre and its principles of structuration are entirely linguistic principles.

Because language is well adapted to DESCRIBE action genres, it is easy to borrow the semantics of its descriptive resources to claim a linguistic basis for its Organizational principles. For example, imagine a surgical operating theatre in which the surgeon successively calls for 'scalpel' 'clamp', etc., in the course of a standard operation. The operation itself is certainly an instance of an action genre, an institutionalized semiotic-material (i.e. actional) formation. Does the verbal component of this action constitute a TEXT? Is there a language genre to which this text belongs (i.e. which is realized ultimately by this text)? On the surface, without knowledge of context, the text is just a List of words, which *is* a language genre, but not a useful one for analysing the social meaning of the language used on this occasion.

We could imagine adding to our transcript information on the phonology of these utterances, from which conceivably we could infer that each is a minor clause (or severe ellipsis) realizing the discourse semantic features of a demand for goods. We now have a 'text' consisting of a sequence of demands with a certain consistency of semantic field ('surgery : implements'), speech function (demand for goods) and conceivably a few mode-like elements as well. But if we go on either to define a register-like relation of lexicogrammatical choices to situational context, or to define a language genre of the surgery operation, I think that we would in fact mainly be employing our cultural knowledge of the action genre rather than any linguistic features that all texts of this situation-type have in common. It is the non-linguistic action sequence of the operation that makes sense of the order in which implements are demanded, which implements are demanded when, and why they are demanded at all. If we try to characterize the genre from which this text is derivable, it does not seem plausible that the social meaning relations among its schematic structure elements are in any fundamental sense linguistic relations. The essence of this argument is easily extended to well recognized language genres like sets of instructions, recipes and even descriptions of events and narratives.

What is happening here? We know that as we move from the uses of language we call language-in-action to those we call language-as-reflection the 'autonomy' of the text appears to increase and the notion of language genres makes more sense. But we need to recognize that we can argue both ways along this cline. Just as it is possible to begin with the most nearly autonomous uses of language (written genres of exposition, reflection, fictional narrative), define language genres for them in abstract terms, and then construct analogous language genres for the least autonomous uses, so also we can begin with action genres, where they most clearly reflect the actional relations structuring events, and extrapolate this approach to all uses of language.

Any written genre can be described in terms of the action genre of writing that produces its texts (or, in the context of interpretation, rather than production, of the action genre of active-reading of such texts). The process is even more obvious in the case of speech genres. The theoretical problem in all this is that every description of actions and actional relations is necessarily a description in language (or in some specialized abstract symbolic extension of language, which would be equivalent to another linguistic register, and whose employment is potentially another language genre). Where language has evolved to give us (adequate?) descriptions, there is not much to choose between the results of the two approaches. Where it has not, our efforts merely have the effect of extending it.

One important difference, however, is in the relation of text and context in the construction or interpretation of Genre. A linguistic text may be essentially incomplete from the actional point of view. There are many elements in the schematic structure of the action genre of the surgical operation which are not linguistically realized and are therefore not represented in the linguistic text and cannot, by the usual procedures of genre analysis, be represented in the language genre constructed for this speech event. Thus the connections between elements in the language genre, the types of relations among them which propose the basis of their social meaning-relations to one another, and from which are derived our accounts of participant roles and their relations (and so the whole edifice of social analysis; cf. Ideology in Martin 1985), are clearly defective. There are missing elements, missing intermediaries and mediating actions, which potentially can (and generally do) significantly alter the nature of the meaning relations among the elements that do have linguistic realizations.

This defect is not necessarily critical in models (like Hasan's 1985 GSP) where the schematic structure specifies only ordering relations among elements, not meaning relations, but obviously such descriptions are themselves only 'schematic' in the broadest sense, and incomplete. Certainly they are incomplete for the purposes of social analysis. In models like Ventola's (1987) it is possible to specify non-linguistic actions, in which case one is ultimately moving towards an action genre perspective.

No number of texts of the surgery type would be sufficient grounds for inferring a genre description adequate in respect of social meaning. An adequate model will have to be supported by other kinds of evidence as well. That evidence might in practice be intertexts such as folk-model narratives of a stereotypical action text ('First the surgeon asks for a scalpel, then he makes an incision . . .'). Obviously we must establish a methodology and criteria of quality for evidence of this kind, as well as of other sorts (videotapes of actual operations, medical illustrations, written surgical procedure instructions and records, lay v. technical folk narratives, actual recorded narratives v. the analyst's personal narrative schema, etc.) And as we move to social analysis of meaning relations, p-roles, etc., still more sorts of evidence and other criteria must come into play: evidence about surgeon–assistant relations (from both points of view), technical accounts of the reasons for procedures and sequences, etc.

Once more, then, the usefulness of Genre as a theoretical construct is its depiction in a unitary way of a relatively stable, self-contained mode of social action, a Doing-X. The characterization of a Genre should include: (i) the actions that constitute (optionally and obligatorily, under various circumstances, including those generated by previous actions within the dynamic realization of the genre) in simultaneous and successive combinations a complete Doing-X; (ii) the participant roles of socially constituted persons and other entities constructed at least in part by Doing-X; (iii) the social meaning relations of the action chords to each other, of the action chords to their participant-roles, and of the p-roles to each other (including at least the thereby constituted relations of power and affinity as defined above); (iv) the normative and (indexically indicative) exceptional realizations of the actions through the resources of language and other semiotic systems to the degree of delicacy warranted by the commonality of action texts of the genre (down to differences that do not make a difference in Doing-X) and any social meanings attaching to alternative realizations (differences that make a socially meaningful difference in How-X-Was-Done or various recognized sub-type genres of Doing-X).

It should be clear that Genre affects Orientational meaning primarily by the selection of a genre itself, and within that by socially meaningful variants of realization (sub-types and non-type defining but still socially meaningful 'manners' of realization). So far as textual patternings of Orientational meaning are concerned, there are the multivariate structures of action sequences, which also contribute to Presentational and Organizational patternings, of course (reflecting the unitary quality of Genre), but which are specifically Orientational in so far as they establish implicit (e.g. Writer–Reader in written monologue genres) or explicit (as in dialogue genres) social relations among social-person (or more generally sociotype or social category) p-roles and also in so far as they necessarily construct some relations between the p-roles and Presentational meanings (cf. between social voices and thematic formations).

My principal concern from here on will be with textual patternings of Orientational meaning, with how the operation of the Social-constitutive function of language leads to patternings across a text of these meanings and therefore (and therefrom) global co-patternings in selections from many lexicogrammatical systems, especially those associated with the interpersonal metafunction in Halliday's grammatics.

4.5 GLOBAL VALUE-ORIENTATIONAL PATTERNS IN TEXT

It is often noted that the textual realization of interpersonal meaning choices in the lexicogrammar pattern in ways other than segmental, constituency, multivariate, 'particle-like' modes. This is a special case of what happens for Orientational meanings generally in text. In text-semantic analysis, of course, even Presentational meanings have global patternings across a text (cf. cohesion chains, cohesive harmonies, Hasan 1984, in Halliday and Hasan 1989; thematic-formation textures and patterns such as the Nexus pattern, Lemke 1990, in press a). All the primary semiotic functions are realized in both multivariate and covariate structurings globally across a text. We have already discussed Genre, whose schematic structure provides a multivariate scaffolding across a text for Orientational (e.g. p-roles), Presentational (e.g. genre constituents with thematic formation-specific features), and Organizational (e.g. the primary logical meaning relations among constituent elements of a schematic structure that make it a 'whole') meaning. I believe that Genre is the only basis of global, text-spanning MULTIVARIATE structure for all the semiotic functions. All other global structural patternings are covariate.

These covariate structural patterns may be characterized at the formal level as of several sorts. There are the general PROSODIC (field-like) type, which are like 'chains' or 'strands' appearing and reappearing, or rising and falling in prominence, through a text, in a non-connected fashion. Further structuration arises through the simultaneously interplay of these strands (cf. theme-weaving, the Nexus pattern, cohesive harmony, all studied with respect to Presentational meaning so far: Lemke 1988a, b, in press a; Hasan 1984), rather as in musical composition theory.

The commonly used term 'prosodic' patterning, usually very little specified, seems to be essentially a synonym for covariate structuring. The nature of covariate structures can be rather precisely defined, in contrast to multivariate ones (Lemke 1985). More specific, single-strand, patterns include the Culminative pattern, in which the degree of some feature

intensifies monotonically to some maximum, or Climax, which may then
optionally be followed by a significantly weaker reappearance, or by a
monotonic decrease. All the patterns of Tone systems can in principle be
accommodated in such a scheme (rising, rise–fall, etc.), though some (like
monotonic falling) do not seem favoured for global rhetoric (unless
complemented by other patterns on other strands).

Finally, there is the further special case of PERIODIC (wave-like)
patterns, on one strand, or in the relations among multiple strands. In
these there is repetition of three or more parallel cases, with a stronger
sense of true Periodicity as the number of parallels increases. An
interesting issue here is the 'timing' of periodicity, which requires a
'clock'. Since all such timing is relative, only another periodic phenomenon
can provide such a clock, and perhaps intuitively we use Organizational
periodicities as the base clock for judging others. There does not seem to
be any need to privilege this function in this respect, though it does seem
to be true that, at the lexicogrammatical level, textual systems more
regularly have periodic realizations than do ideational or interpersonal
ones. It is quite possible that univariate patternings lie on the border
between multivariate and periodic covariate types (e.g. the regular
'periodic' taxis and conjunctive options at the end of each clause, the turn-
taking options in dialogue structure, etc.).

In order to have a look at the kinds of covariate patternings of Orientational, social-constitutive meaning in text, I want to present brief
summaries of some patterns I have found in the analysis of two specific
texts. In each case I have focused attention on the least studied aspects of
Orientational, social-constitutive meaning: the deployment of lexicogrammatical resources to construct value orientations towards the Presentational
content of the text and to construct macrosocial relations between social
viewpoints or interest groups (especially in the first text). I have also
considered at some points various other microsocial, interactional relations.
These analyses are part of more general investigations of global semantic
patternings in these texts, including action genre analysis, not reported
here.

Text A (see appendix) consists of approximately three paragraphs from
near the opening of *The Hippies* (Wolfe 1968), a book that purports to be
a contemporary, personal journalistic account of the Hippie community of
San Francisco in 1967. The Author (i.e. my reconstruction of an authorial
text-voice) seems to have extremely ambivalent feelings about his subject.
His discourse mixes, constructs and reconstructs a number of (idealized)
social discourse types (social 'voices' in the world of discourse heteroglossia), each with its characteristic value orientations. The text makes
sense to us in large part against the background of our own models of the
heteroglossic relations of various known social viewpoints towards its
Presentational themes. Those themes include HIPPIES, DRUG USE,
SEX, RELIGION, HYGIENE, URBAN INDUSTRIALISM and
NUCLEAR WAR, among others.

Discourse analysis of Value-orientational prosodies and Social-constitutive textwork (only two among many Orientational and Presentational dimensions of the text semantics which I have analysed) reveals an interesting semantic patterning in this text. The details of the text analysis cannot be presented here, but I will summarize the results and provide one or two examples of the patterning I have identified. The methods of analysis are still tentative. Value-orientational prosodies are outlined mainly from assessments of the degree (High, Median, Low) and polarity (Positive, Negative) of valuational lexis over suitable grammatical units (groups, clauses, clause complexes). Orientational patterns of the VALUING type are not bound by such constituency units, however, and extend their prosodic-like reach over stretches of text as long as, say, lines 27–40 in text A. A preliminary account of this type of text analysis is available in Lemke (in press b), under the heading of 'axiological analysis'.

The patterning through the text of the social-constitutive work of constructing 'the Hippies' in a mainly oppositional relation to 'the old society' is closely bound up, not surprisingly, with the value-orientational prosody patterns. The two support and reinforce each other in this text. The analysis of heteroglossic relations of ALLIANCE and OPPOSITION has already been described in Lemke (1988a).

Text A fairly clearly exhibits smaller to larger scale repeated instances of specific textual patternings of value-construing Orientational meanings. The general pattern is one of, first, ascriptions of negatively valued epithets and (more often) processes or thematic discourses, followed by an ascription (or projection) of opposition to something which is itself strongly negative in a more widely shared value system. In Social-constitutive terms, this pattern first constructs a heteroglossic social opposition over value issues which is then partly deconstructed by emphasis on important shared values. Within these larger Negative–Oppositional and Positive–Allying movements, there are smaller-scale repeated patternings of value prosodies as well. (Table 4.1.) Note that, in the two more extended instances, the Positive–Allying movement begins immediately after the Climax of the Negative–Oppositional (Negative Climax: 21, 31–3). Cf. patternings in text B, described below.

To illustrate the realization of the pattern and the sorts of surface features of the text on which its identification relies, here is a brief account of one shorter and one longer instance, excerpted from a more detailed account.

Line 25 begins with Hippie characteristics that are negatively valued from the mainstream viewpoint (and positive from within the Hippie community), but pivots on *aliens*, which, read dynamically at this point, is negative, but retroactively is much more ambivalent, if not positive. What follows it is what the Hippies are ALIENATED from (lines 25–6), an instantiation of the thematic formation of Industrial Urbanism with its widespread negative valuation, shared by Hippies and many mainstream discourse traditions. The negatives are activated here both by *alien* (one is alienated usually from something negatively valued) and by the negative tradition on 'Machine Age' (Machines, Bad; People, Good) and the

Table 4.1 Instances of the pattern in text A

	Negative–Oppositional	Positive–allying
Line	[end 2] & 7–8	9
Lines	10–14; 15–21	22–23
Lines	24–25	25–26
Lines	27–33	33–40

sinister reading that is then possible of 'living in the shadow'. This phrase has two readings, one in the discourse of <INDUSTRIAL URBANISM – NEG> has a resonance with 'the valley of the shadow of death', and the other is simply a commonplace idiom for NEAR BY. The first meaning does the valuational and Social-constitutive work, the second the Presentational, though both can be construed in either way.

Once again, as in lines 7–9, the Hippies are characterized as Alien but sharing a mainstream antipathy to something strongly negative. This pattern is repeated again in lines 27–40, again with the univariate rhetorical structure of *amplificatio*, within a more unusual structure discussed above, which is essentially the Projection that, as via the paraphrasal report in lines 7–9, puts into the mouth of Hippie discourse a whole cultural catalogue of mainstream-value based negative valuations of the Old Society as a whole.

Within the first *amplificatio* we get the now overused parallelism of 'they knew' (lines 27–9) introducing a sequence of negatively valued characterizations of the Hippie life style (cf. lines 17–23). The last time we had this, it ended with what was either ambivalence or contemptuous irony (lines 22–3). Here it progresses in a Culminative prosody, not perhaps monotonic, but close enough for a prosody: *hair and dress* is mildly negative by stereotype of the long-haired, unkempt, crazily and probably dirtily dressed hippie (cf. line 25); *got their highs* is an instance of DRUG–NEG (cf. lines 19, 22); line 29 is less clear, but would probably be interpreted as either crazed or drug-crazed; *smelling*, line 30, would be read in the thematics of <body odour, dirty>, though it could also go to <incense, marijuana>; line 31 is another extremal point (analogous to line 21 more than to line 22) of DRUG–NEG with resonances to <drug psychosis>. At this point we once again have almost a diatribe against the Hippie life style, and again very solid Social-constitutive work of building the OPPOSITION of <HIPPIE> and <MAINSTREAM> communities.

But now we get a very important move in the text's Orientational meaning. Line 32 uses *and* as a closure signal for the univariate sequence, is valuationally more neutral (*chanting* is value-ambivalent between 'Gregorian chant' and *pagan chanting*) and serves mainly as a projector (*chanting* as verbal process). Line 33 now reaches yet another peak of negative mainstream valuation with 'Fuck you' repeated twice. This dynamically retrocontextualizes *chanting* into the negative 'mindless chant of the mob' and the 'screaming obscenities' view of, for example, the counter-cultural

Berkeley Free Speech Movement. Apart from its sexual lexis, it is indexical of non-middle-class threats and the 'mindless violence' which Anglo-American (and generally north European) middle-class culture fears as much or more lurking beneath its own tight control of emotions as from 'the lower orders'.

Line 33 continues, *fuck you and your nuclear bombs*, which marks a sudden pivot in structure (the beginning of the next *amplificatio*, lines 33–40) and a reversal in value orientation of the text voice between <HIPPIE> and <MAINSTREAM>. *Nuclear bombs* is the first of a new catalogue of items negatively valued by Hippie discourse and also by major segments of Mainstream discourse, even dominant segments (though dominant in value-discourse genres, not in action genres). The projection makes the Hippies be against what is BAD, which makes them good, or more specifically makes their discourse in alignment, even in heteroglossic ALLIANCE with mainstream discourse. It is difficult here to hear the text voice, the value orientation of the author, as other than in sympathy with the Hippies, and we now go back to lines 9, 25–6 and even 22–3, rereading them for possible Hippie sympathies.

The value prosody in lines 33–40 stays at a consistently high negative level, with a microrhythm born of the univariate periodic parallel structure, marked by the repeated *your . . . .* It is not noticeably culminative, and it again uses the pleonastic out-of-breath (cf. lines 22–3) technique (and the Presentational summary-category *your whole way of . . . life*) to bring the structure to a sense of closure.

More detailed analysis of this text suggests that there may well be textual patterning of Orientational meaning at many levels of scale across the text. Prosodic patternings do not need to respect scales and can be scale-invariant. We perhaps err in using the clock of multivariate structural scales as a yardstick for looking at the structural effects of prosodic patterning. On the other hand, our notion of structure is very much conditioned by multivariate patterns in many semiotic domains, constructed with many semiotic resource systems. We should consider closer analysis using models in which there are multi-stranded co-patternings (general co-variate 'chains' or more 'periodic' waves of intensity of different scales) that, in so far as their relations of simultaneity with respect to one another are somehow foregrounded in the text, lead to patternings that appear to have definite scales (as with theme-weaving and localized patterns made by the superposition of different periodic 'waves').

Let us turn now, though even more briefly, to text B, which is a transcription from a radio broadcast in Australia (see Thibault 1989). The radio programme followed a format in which the Host (a broadcaster) invites listeners to telephone him and speak on the air about various topics of current interest. In text B one such Caller responds to the Host's previous introduction of the topic of 'women working'. There is here again a repeated value-prosody patterning across the text. In this general pattern the Caller's discourse grows progressively more strongly negative in the valuation it constructs towards working mothers until an extreme negative

Table 4.2 Repetitions of the pattern

Caller	Negative	Culmination	Host positive
Lines	13–23	22–23	24–25
Lines	26–32	[Pre-empted]	33–36
Lines	37–54	54	55–58
Lines	60–68	68	[Bid to terminate]
Lines	70–73	73	[Call-Termination]

(the Culmination) is reached, at which point Caller is interrupted (or at least there is a turn exchange) and the Host proceeds to construct a more positive discourse on the topic. The details of the pattern are somewhat more complicated, with some internal variations and smaller-scale patterns.

The entire text of the Call between the Opening/Greeting and the Closing/Goodbye, except at most for bits of adjunct metadiscourse, is covered by repetitions (with variation) of the global value-prosody pattern described in these examples. This pattern is repeated, in effect, five times (once with the Caller Negative climax pre-empted, twice with the Host Positive element replaced by termination moves). These are shown in Table 4.2. These elements take on a quasi-structural appearance only because the turn-exchange structure is part of the realization of the pattern. In fact there is sometimes a continuation of a value-prosody across a turn exchange boundary (e.g. at 25–6, 32–3, 36–7). Note also that there are many back-channels from Host-as-listener to Caller-as-speaker, but that full turn-exchange ALWAYS and ONLY takes place immediately following a distinct culmination ('NEGATIVE CLIMAX') in the negative value-prosody.

Within the thereby distinguishable Caller–Negative and Host–Positive parts of the pattern we can identify smaller-scale prosodic patterns in the value-orientational meaning, and specific strategies (e.g. the very common Concessive and Replacive rhetorical formations with weak negative or positive first elements allowing for contrastive strong negative second elements). Here is a brief excerpted account of one instantiation of the pattern.

A clear example of this pattern can be seen over lines 37–54 (Caller's rising negative, culminating in line 54) and lines 55–8 (Host's strong and sustained positive), again with a turn-exchange. This is a long and complex section. It begins in lines 37–8 with a mild negative (*lacking*) framing a long series of strongly lexical positives (*nicety, reassure, cuddle, love*) that create a weakly positive tone locally, despite the overall negative valuation. The shift to a more clearly negative tone begins in line 39 with *mum bawls them out*, which builds up through line 41 and gets an emotional reinforcement in lines 43–4. Lines 45–9 tell a little story and end on a strong negative (*not getting proper sleep*), again reinforced emotionally in 51–3, which is much more negative even than the similar construction in lines 43–4, and finally the true negative climax is reached in line 54, *they're not really caring for their children*, which is a direct intensification of the previous climax in lines 22–3. This new version is not very far from the extreme *they don't really care for their children*, especially in the context of the previous clause.

Again the Host takes a hand and introduces the explicitly positive *good, good* (line 55) and speaks about a *good solution* and then emphasizes *care about kids* and altruistic behaviour *opening up your home*. The lexis is all positive, and so is the thematics. The only global linkage to Caller's negatives comes through the term *solution*, which acknowledges the existence of a Problem (rhetorical formation). But all the emphasis here is on the (positive) Solution.

Globally, there is an almost PERIODIC patterning to the negative-positive alternation of the value-prosody. Caller–Negative portions tend to be longer; Host–Positives briefer. The periodic quality is based in the continual, unintermitted repetition of the pattern rather than in any strict regularity of recurrence in time. (It is possible that in a larger sample of texts of this genre we might find some maximum time, for example, that Host will allow Caller to speak without Host taking a full turn-at-talk. This would tend to create some sort of true chronological periodicity.)

We have seen something similar in the 'Hippies' text (text A), where there was a recurring pattern of negative ascription toward the hippies, ending (with some variations again) in a more positive valuation based on common rejection of yet another negatively valued phenomenon. We saw there too an internal patterning on smaller scales, and we would no doubt see a larger patterning on longer scales if we were to analyse more the full text from which this short segment was excerpted.

There is much more yet to be done in the enormous area of study of resources for Orientational meaning in text and textual patternings of Orientational meanings on different scales. We have touched only briefly here on the role of Expectation-constructing resources, on heteroglossing practices (cf. Lemke 1988a), on the general Social-constitutive work of Orientational meaning in texts, and on patternings with respect to other kinds of values than those in the Goodness system. I believe that future developments of a precise and sophisticated model of how Orientational meanings are made will be of great use in the analysis of ideology, social value systems, social heteroglossia and heteropraxia, and the general study of processes of social and cultural change (see Lemke forthcoming).

APPENDIX

Text A

AN ANNOUNCEMENT	1
Gathering of the Tribes	2
Saturday, January 14, 1967, 1–5 P.M.	3
Polo Field, Golden Gate Park	4
Powwow and Peace Dance to be celebrated	5
with leaders, guides, and heroes of our generation	6

[Two paragraphs omitted describing the setting and the organizers; third paragraph begins, 'Ron had a vision.' Then:]

The be-in would serve as a gathering of reincarnated Indians	7
who would form small tribal settlements one day,	8
away from the noise and turmoil of America's over-populated urban centers.	9
Hence, the call to San Francisco was issued as a 'Gathering of the Tribes'.	10
Thousands of tribesmen read it . . . in the *Oracle* . . .	11
in the New York *East Village Other* . . . in the *Los Angeles Free Press*	12
. . . in the *Berkeley Barb* . . . in the Detroit *Fifth Estate* . . .	13
in publications that mom, dad, church, school, and the old society hardly imagined were in existence.	14
But *they* knew, the tribesmen, the members of the New Community –	15
the beatniks, hippies, flower childen, love generation.	16
They knew because they had their own thing going,	17
gathering together in communal apartments,	18
smoking marijuana cigarettes,	19
listening to rock and roll records,	20
stroking each others' genitals,	21
taking trips into other realities through their new magic elixir of love: LSD,	22
the modern American version of the gateway to paradise.	23
They knew who they were,	24
these bearded, long-haired, barefoot, unscrubbed aliens from the Machine Age	25
living in the shadow of its factories and office buildings.	26
They knew by the way they wore their hair and dressed;	27
they knew by the way they got their highs;	28
they knew by staring each other in the eyes,	29
by smelling each other,	30
by taking off the tops of their heads together with new drugs,	31
and by chanting their theme to the world:	32
Fuck you, fuck you and your nuclear bombs,	33
your eternal fighting,	34
your eight-to-five jobs,	35
your all-white suburbs with boxes all in a row coming out the same,	36
your racial ghettoes,	37
your memorized prayers to God in houses of golden idols,	38
your politics,	39
your whole way of neat-ordered-regulated-uniformed-stifling way of life.	40
They got the message of the New Community's First Human Be-in,	41
and then they did their own thing with it. . . .	42

Text B

[Prefatory remarks by Ollie (host) based on published survey:]

Ollie. . . . two-thirds of women in Britain now work	1

but only 14 per cent of people believed their families benefited from it. 2
About 30 per cent of the sample thought being a police officer or a bank 3
manager was a man's job 4
and that secretaries should be women. 5
A third felt that way about nurses. 6
But the results in the periodical *British Social Attitudes* showed 7
most people still viewed women primarily as homemakers. 8
Just 12 per cent of married couples surveyed shared the housework. 9
You might have a few thoughts on that. 339–1000. 10
And as I've said, feel free, if you wish, to discuss something else as well. 11

[A range of other topics were discussed; then the following call-in phone conversation begins:]

Ollie. 'Kerry good morning 12
Kerry. 'good morning ah. my point of ah. was on women working. 13
'not that I want to buy into the argument that women are less 14
'capable than men 15
'I think they are capable 16
'but from the point of view of **children** they leave with babysitters 17
I wanted to sort of point out. that. do they is what they earn. 18
the career. or what they can buy with their money 19
worth what they're doing to their children. 20
because even though they may be good babysitters very caring **women**. 21
I still feel that they're neglecting their duty 22
to bringing up their own children 23
Ollie. umm so you still think their place is in the home 24
not because they're incompetent but because they're more needed there 25
Kerry. well. the needs of their children is what I'm looking at. 26
Ah. I've been associated with children that are being minded 27
and I feel distressed at the way the childen are brought in very 28
early in the morning 29
sometimes maybe they've been up at half past five. 30
they're very sleepy. they're very lethargic. 31
even though they get good care where they are. they're well dressed 32
Ollie. surely that's the crucial thing isn't it? 33
the quality of their care. 34
I mean there will be some parents who are probably better out 35
working in the sense that their children might do better 36
Kerry. could be too because children at home are still lacking the 37
nice [niceties] of being cuddled and being reassured and being loved. 38
a lot of children are just. you know. mum bawls them out all day 39
don't do this don't do that 40
Ollie. mmm 41
Kerry. and that's not building. ah. very secure individuals 42
and eh I just felt sorry for these children that are left 43
and that there's a substitutes always give them the cuddles. like. 44
um. one little girl was up even though she gets up at half past six 45
she's very often out till late at night. and do you know what? 46
when she says I'd rather have McDonald's or we ate Chinese last night 47
and she's out late at night at restaurants with her parents and not 48

getting proper sleep	49
Ollie. mmm	50
Kerry. and I just see the distress in these little these real littlies	51
they they want to be with their mums but their mums have got other	52
things on their minds.	53
they're not really caring for their children	54
Ollie. a good. good solution might be for people like you	55
who really do care about kids and don't like to see that	56
to perhaps provide the sort of care by opening up your home	57
to take in other kids	58
I don't know	59
Kerry. it's distressing	60
Ollie. mm	61
Kerry. because you get them back	62
and you know that their parents are just bundling them off with a	63
dummy and a bottle where they should be being trained.	64
and they should be you know at two years old off the dummy and off	65
the bottle and out of nappies	66
Ollie. yeah	67
Kerry. that's a lazy parent	68
Ollie. all right Kerry well	69
Kerry. there are statistics about um breaking breaking up homes hmm	70
broken homes. apparently they said that quality time a parent to a	71
child is only about thirteen minutes a day.	72
yet with working parents it must be a lot less	73
Ollie. yes sometimes it is that's true ok thanks very much for that	74
Kerry. thank you	75
Ollie. bye Kerry	76

REFERENCES

Bakhtin, M.M. (1935), 'Discourse in the novel', in M. Holquist (ed.) *The Dialogic Imagination* (1981), Austin, University of Texas Press.

Bernstein, B. (1981),'Codes, modalities, and the process of cultural reproduction', *Language in Society* 10.3, 327–64.

Bourdieu, P. (1972), *Outline of a Theory of Practice*, Cambridge, Cambridge University Press.

Halliday, M.A.K. (1978), *Language as Social Semiotic*, London, Edward Arnold.

——— (1985), *An Introduction to Functional Grammar*, London, Edward Arnold.

Halliday, M.A.K., and Hasan, R. (1989), *Language, Context, and Text*, London, Oxford University Press.

Hasan, R. (1984), 'Coherence and cohesive harmony', in J. Flood, (ed.), *Understanding Reading Comprehension*, Newark, Del., International Reading Association.

Lemke, J.L. (1983), 'Thematic analysis, systems, structures, and strategies', *Semiotic Inquiry* 3.2, 159–87.

——— (1984a), *Semiotics and Education*, Toronto Semiotic Circle Monographs series, Victoria University, Toronto.

——— (1984b), 'Textual Politics, Heteroglossia and Discourse Analysis', paper presented at the International Summer Institute of Structural and Semiotic Studies, University of Toronto, June.

——— (1985), 'Ideology, intertextuality, and the notion of register', in J.D. Benson and W.S. Greaves (eds), *Systemic Perspectives on Discourse*, pp. 275–94, Norwood, N.J., Ablex.

——— (1987), 'The Topology of Genre, Text Structures and Text Types', City University of New York, mimeo.

——— (1988a), 'Discourses in conflict: heteroglossia and text semantics', in J.D. Benson and W.S. Greaves (eds), *Systemic Functional Approaches to Discourse*, pp. 29–50, Norwood, N.J., Ablex.

——— (1988b), 'Text structure and text semantics', in R. Veltman and E. Steiner (eds), *Pragmatics, Discourse, and Text*, pp. 158–70, London, Pinter.

——— (1988c), 'Towards a social semiotics of the material subject', in T. Threadgold (ed.), *Working Papers*, 2, *Sociosemiotics*, pp. 1–17, Sydney, Sydney Association for Studies in Society and Culture.

——— (1988d), 'Literacy, Language Conflict, and Social Change', paper presented at Boston University Language Conference.

——— (1989a), 'Semantics and social values', *Word* 40.1–2, 37–50.

——— (1989b), 'Text Production and Dynamic Text Semantics', paper presented at the sixteenth International Systemic Linguistics Congress, Helsinki; to be published.

——— (1989c), 'Social semiotics, a new model for literacy education', in D. Bloome (ed.), *Classrooms and Literacy*, pp. 289–309, Norwood, N.J., Ablex.

——— (1989d), 'Literacy and Diversity', paper presented at Murdoch University (Australia) *Language in Education* conference. to be published in proceedings.

——— (1990), *Talking Science, Language, Learning, and Values*, Norwood, N.J., Ablex.

——— (in press a), 'Intertextuality and text semantics', in M. Gregory and P. Fries, (eds), *Discourse in Society, Functional Perspectives*, Norwood, N.J., Ablex.

——— (in press b), 'Technical discourse and technocratic ideology', in M.A.K. Halliday, John Gibbons and Howard Nicholas (eds), *Learning, Keeping, and Using Language: Selected Papers from the 8th AILA World Congress of Applied Linguistics, Sydney 1987* II, pp. 435–60, Amsterdam, Benjamins.

——— (in press c), 'Language diversity and literacy education', *Australian Journal of Reading*, special issue for the International Year of Literacy.

——— (in press d), 'Heteroglossia and social theory', in New York Bakhtin Circle (eds), *M.M. Bakhtin, Radical Perspectives*, Minneapolis, University of Minnesota Press.

——— (forthcoming), 'Discourse, system dynamics, and social change', in M.A.K. Halliday (ed.), *Language as Cultural Dynamic*, special issue of *Cultural Dynamics*.

Mann, W.C., and Thompson, S. (1987), 'Rhetorical structure theory: a theory of text organization', in Livia Polanyi (ed.), *The Structure of Discourse*, Norwood, N.J., Ablex.

Mann, W., and Matthiessen, C. (1987), *Rhetorical Structure Theory and Systemic Approaches to Text Organization*, Marina del Rey, USC/Information Sciences Institute.

Mansfield, A. (1987), 'A Cartography of Resistance: the British State and Derry Republicanism', doctoral dissertation, University College of North Wales.

Martin, J.R. (1985), 'Process and text', in J.D. Benson and W.S. Greaves (eds), *Systemic Perspectives on Discourse*, pp. 248–74, Norwood, N.J., Ablex.

——— (1990), 'Intrinsic Functionality', University of Sydney Linguistics Department, mimeo.

——— (in press), 'Macroproposals: meaning by degree', in W.C. Mann and S.A.

Thompson, (eds), *Discourse Description*, Amsterdam, Benjamins.

Poynton, C. (1984), 'Names as vocatives', *Nottingham Linguistics Circular* 13, 1–70.

Silverstein, M. (1976), 'Shifters, linguistic categories, and cultural description', in K. Basso and H. Selby (eds), *Meaning in Anthropology*, Albuquerque, University of New Mexico Press.

Thibault, P.J. (1986), *Text, Discourse, and Context: a Social Semiotic Perspective*, Toronto Semiotic Circle Monographs, Toronto, Victoria University.

——— (1989), 'Semantic variation, social heteroglossia, and intertextuality', *Critical Studies* 1.2, 181–209.

——— (in press a), 'Interpersonal meaning and the discursive construction of actions, attitudes, and values', in M. Gregory (ed.), *Relations and Functions within and around Language*, Norwood, N.J., Ablex.

Ventola, E. (1987), *The Structure of Social Interaction: a Systemic Approach to the Semiotics of Service Encounters*, London, Pinter.

Voloshinov, V.N. (M.M. Bakhtin) (1929), *Marxism and the Philosophy of Language*, Cambridge, Mass., Harvard University Press (1986 edition).

Wolfe, Burton H. (1968), *The Hippies*, New York, New American Library (Signet Books edition).

Part III. Lexicogrammar

5 Transitivity/ergativity: the Janus-headed grammar of actions and events
Kristin Davidse

5.1 INTRODUCTION: THEORY AND DESCRIPTION

The theoretical stance most fundamental to an appreciation of Michael Halliday's descriptive work is his belief in the non-arbitrary relation between semantics and lexicogrammar (cf. Halliday 1985: xiii–xxxv). In positing that the relation between semantics and lexicogrammar is 'natural' and non-arbitrary (with the lexicogrammar realizing or 'encoding' the semantics), two things are being asserted: firstly, the lexicogrammar is not independent of the semantics; secondly, the semantics is not independent of the lexicogrammar. Formal theories such as Transformational Grammar are, of course, founded on exactly the opposite premises, viz. that syntax IS autonomous and that semantics is concerned with establishing objective truth conditions within the frame of a universal logical model. Both these premises have come under attack from the growing opposition to formalist thinking on the contemporary linguistic scene.

Linguists rejecting the dogma of 'autonomous syntax' used to be very much in a non-mainstream position, but they are becoming less and less so. Bolinger's bold theoretical credo has always been that a difference in syntactic form signals a difference in meaning (Bolinger 1968). In her tellingly titled and equally bold book *The Semantics of Grammmar* (1988) Anna Wierzbicka time and again shows that the purely syntactic rules of a-semantic generative grammar simply do not work. She then comments (p. 55):

> Fictions of this kind not only fail to explain the facts, but, moreover, they distort those facts. They fail to reveal the beautifully functioning, sensitive, subtle mechanism that the syntactic system of a language really is, and present instead a bizarre, chaotic, 'mindless' collection of arbitrary rules and equally arbitrary exceptions to the rules.

At the same time that 'autonomous syntax' was being increasingly questioned and challenged, Lakoff (1987; and Lakoff and Johnson 1980), with his well-known attacks on the 'Myth of Objectivism', began to wake the linguistic community up to the fact that there might also be something wrong with the model-theoretical approaches that were being used to account for semantics and pragmatics. Nishimura (1989) develops Lakoff's line of thinking into a particularly penetrating critique of 'objectivist semantics'. 'Objectivist semantics' operates on the tacit assumption that each extralinguistic situation has a specific (universal) organization which is independent of the alternative language-specific representations of that situation and which we have intuitive access to. Most of the 'case grammars' and descriptions of 'states of affairs' are based on such naive realism. For instance, Fillmore's case roles in the semantic 'deep structure' are basically intuitively reasonable *pre*-linguistic notions. In its – praiseworthy – attempt to take meaning seriously, generative semantics also operated with a form of 'objectivist semantics': it tried to account for all kinds of fictional 'synonymy' and 'identical semantic relations' which were defined in referential rather than in linguistic terms. As noted by Martin (1990: 24), 'in its twilight years generative semantics obliterated the boundary between language and the world'. Unfortunately, it has left many people with the mental reflex that 'deep' semantic relations are somehow totally divorced from lexicogrammatical regularities. On the contrary, as Halliday has always stressed, any good semantic generalization should be based on the best possible elucidation of lexicogrammatical patterning: semantic categories should have 'linguistic reality'.

This retreat from two of the central features of TG is, in fact, nothing but a rediscovery of Whorf's programme for the 'exact science' of linguistics: 'Linguistics is essentially the quest for MEANING' (1956: 73) as engendered by lexation and grammatical patternment (p. 261).

It is important to evoke this wider linguistic context to stress, within the systemic debate, that the question of the non-arbitrary relation between semantics and grammar stands as a central theoretical issue to be discussed in linguistics. Yet Butler (1985: 171), taking (degrees of) autonomous syntax and objectivist semantics as his unquestioned norm, rejects the postulate of a semantically motivated grammar without any reflection or argumentation, as if it were a totally unreasonable position to hold. And in his review of *An Introduction to Functional Grammar* Hudson (1986: 799) makes the wonderfully ambivalent comment: 'Halliday aims much higher than most of us and really believes in the idea that a language is a system where everything hangs together.'

Indeed, for someone who believes that the grammar of a language is driven by its semantic principles, those deep semantic 'persuasions' (Whorf 1956: 81) could be compared to strong currents in the ocean, which are manifested by very many interconnected waves and ripples. Similarly, the categories and models of grammatical semantics are realized by the more obvious phenotypical patterns as well as by a whole array of cryptotypical reactances. On the other hand, if the semantic motivation of syntax is not recognized, the 'form' of language will be perceived as an ocean of separate waves and ripples, unrelated to the deeper semantic currents. The waves that are then selected for description will have to be very 'visible', clear-cut patterns that can stand on their own as scientific facts.

One area of research that may have been held back by the latter kind of approach is that of the transitive versus the ergative characteristics of languages. For instance, in his standard article 'Ergativity', Dixon (1979) recognizes a language as ergative only if it displays some very clear-cut patterns – or phenotypes – of ergative grammar such as ergative case morphology or ergative co-ordination. By these standards English is not an ergative language: it is said to have only lexical ergativity. The implication seems to be that the ergative principle is of little importance in English clause grammar. However, to 'semantic grammarians' the strict separation of grammar and lexis, particularly in the area of experiential grammar, is artificial and counterproductive. Moreover, ergative lexation is the most overt, but by no means the only, realization of ergativity in English.

Halliday has always held that all languages are a mixture of ergative and transitive, and that English is no exception. He has been joined in this belief by Langacker, who notes:

Because these groupings are most frequent and visible in the realm of case marking, it is common to speak of NOMINATIVE/ACCUSATIVE v. ERGATIVE/ABSOLUTIVE ORGANIZATION – or more simply, of ACCUSATIVITY v. ERGATIVITY. Nevertheless, these patterns have numerous other linguistic manifestations. In fact, every language probably uses both patterns in one fashion or another, though the mixture varies and a particular pattern is often predominant.

[1989: chapter 9, p. 3]

In this paper I will show that it is essential to account for both the transitive and the ergative systems in order to even begin to describe with any accuracy the grammar of actions and events, i.e. of material processes, in English. As a rule, linguists have not done this, but have simply generalized in terms of one system, either the 'causative' model associated with the ergative principle or the 'action chain' model embodied by the transitive principle. The specific mixture of transitive and ergative in English material processes is perhaps rather elusive because it offers an uncanny double-imposure of similarity and distinctness. There is very real semantic neutralization and grammatical generalization across the two types. But if one digs a little deeper the very distinct cryptogrammars of transitivity and ergativity can be revealed; these allow one to give a sharper elucidation of and a more precise paradigmatic location to many constructions that have been long-standing problem cases in the grammar of actions and events.

The main claim I want to put forward is that the grammar of material processes is 'Janus-headed', that it is governed by the two distinct systems of transitivity and ergativity. To a certain extent, this claim squares with work within other schools of linguistic thought, although it has never been made so strongly. Within the typological tradition, Dixon (1979: 116 ff.)

recognizes a certain distinction between transitives, on the one hand, and 'causative' transitives or 'lexical ergatives', on the other, but he regards intransitives as a uniform group. Within Government and Binding, in contrast, intransitives are divided into 'pure' intransitives and ergatives (Keyser and Roeper 1984: 382) but transitives are regarded as a fully homogeneous group. In this paper, however, it will be argued that both the EFFECTIVE and the MIDDLE voice have distinct transitive and ergative categories and structures (sections 5.3–4). Moreover the transitive and ergative systems each create their own kind of 'metaphorical' PSEUDO-EFFECTIVE structure (section 5.5). The manifold grammatical and semantic differences between these structures can ultimately all be referred back to the 'natural', non-arbitrary relation of these structures to the transitive and ergative semantic models (section 5.2).[1]

5.2 PRESENTATION OF THE TRANSITIVE AND ERGATIVE SYSTEMS

Throughout his work on experiential grammar Halliday (1967a, b, c, 1968, 1985) has developed what are, in my opinion, the sharpest characterizations in the literature of the transitive and ergative semantic models. The essence of this characterization will be outlined briefly here.

5.2.1 The transitive system

The transitive system, says Halliday (1985: 145), realizes a PROCESS AND EXTENSION model. Its point of departure is that of an Actor performing an action. Now, it can be left at that: the action ends, as it were, with the Actor. We then have an INTRANSITIVE clause, e.g. *The lion is running*, which is characterized by an Actor·Process structure. But the action does not have to stop at the Actor·Process complex; it can also be extended or 'go through' (*trans-ire*): it can direct itself on to a Goal, e.g. *The lion is chasing the tourist*. Such a clause has a *transitive* constellation with a 'doer' (Actor)·Process·'done to' (Goal).

In contemporary English the intransitive and semantically related transitive structures tend to be realized by different lexemes:

The lion is running	The lion is chasing the tourist
The water is flowing	The water is flooding the river banks
She is cycling	She is pedalling her bike
The baby is playing	The baby is manipulating her toys

Of course, we do get clauses such as *The Light Brigade is charging, God saves, She is eating*, but I regard these as inherently goal-directed, i.e. with an 'unexpressed' Goal that is not overtly realized (cf. Kress 1976: 159; Hasan 1987: 49). Even though the Goal is not explicitly stated, the experiential constellation of these clauses clearly implies that there IS a Goal on to which the actions of charging, saving and eating are directed. No doubt this is a fluid transition area: the implication of a Goal might seem more compelling in, for instance, *God saves* than in *She is eating*. But, generally, the contrast 'not goal-directed' versus 'inherently goal-directed' tends to go hand in hand with realization by different lexical verbs.

5.2.2 The ergative system

With the ergative system the picture is completely different: it realizes an INSTIGATION OF PROCESS model. We have a process in which one participant, the Medium, is crucially involved. If only the process and its central participant are expressed, we have a Medium·Process structure, e.g. *The glass broke*. The central variable here is not extension but instigation: is the process 'self-instigated' or 'externally instigated'? If it is represented as 'externally instigated', it will be expressed by an Instigator[2]·Process·Medium structure, as in *The cat broke the glass*.

Within the ergative paradigm, the middle *The glass broke* has a very specific value: its experiential structure neutralizes the features 'self-instigated' and 'externally instigated'. *The glass broke* is synonymous neither with *The glass broke itself* nor with *The glass was broken*, but 'syncretizes' (cf. Greenberg 1966: 27) these voice distinctions. Consequently the ergative middle is characterized by an essential vagueness: it leaves open whether or not the process is self-instigated or instigated by an external agent. This vagueness can be resolved by either the co-text or the context. For instance, in a piece of dialogue like *Look! The door is opening! – Yes, Lizzy's opening it!* the self-instigated interpretation is excluded by the next move in the discourse. The vagueness of the ergative middle can also be resolved by the extralinguistic context. For instance, in the context of having a circuit breaker installed, one could say *The electricity will switch off immediately in the event of a short circuit*. This sentence will be understood as 'it will turn itself off', not 'it will be turned off by an Instigator external to it'. But the very fact that either of these two features can be excluded shows that both 'self-instigated' and 'externally instigated' are inherently associated with the ergative middle.

How does English, which does not have ergative case marking, actually manage to realize the ergative semantic model of events and happenings? With languages that do have ergative case marking the ergative structures are realized as in Figure 5.1. But contemporary English, to realize the ergative representation of events and happenings, exploits the characteristic FLEXIBILITY of its ergative process lexemes to pattern with the Medium only as well as in Instigator–Medium constellations. It is precisely because the lexeme remains the same that a clause such as *The glass broke* is perceived as a Medium·Process constellation proportionate with an Instigator·Process·Medium structure such as *The cat broke the glass*, rather than as an Actor·(intransitive) Process constellation.

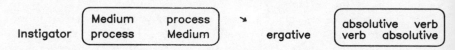

Figure 5.1 Realization of ergativity through ergative case marking

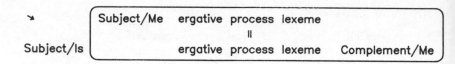

Figure 5.2 Realization of ergativity through ergative lexation

What I will concentrate on in my discussion is that the transitive and ergative models have different grammatical centres and different 'directionalities'. The transitive system is Actor-centred: its most central participant is the Actor, and the Actor–Process complex is grammatically more nuclear and relatively more independent. The basic Actor–Process frame can be extended only to the RIGHT to include a Goal. The ergative system, in contrast, is Medium-centred, with the Medium as most nuclear participant and with a more nuclear, independent Medium–Process complex. Here the basic Medium–Process constellation is opened up to the LEFT to incorporate the Instigator. Schematically this can be represented as in Figure 5.3. This ties in completely with the 'logic' of transitive and ergative case marking: in a nominative language the nominative – or the case which expresses the transitive and the intransitive Actor – is the most basic case, which is mostly indicated by its zero morphology; in ergative languages the absolutive, or the case which expresses the ergative 'Object' and the non-ergative 'Subject', is the most basic one, usually marked by zero morphology.

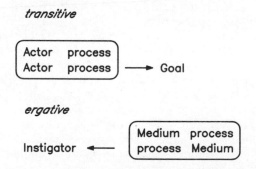

Figure 5.3 The different nuclei and the different directionalities of the transitive and ergative constellations

5.3 TRANSITIVE/ERGATIVE EFFECTIVE STRUCTURES

5.3.1.1 Internal prototypical structure of the category 'transitive: effective'

Linguists have generally found it intuitively acceptable that the Actor of 'goal-directed' clauses – or some vaguer notion, since the transitive and ergative models are never distinguished – is typically conscious, and mostly human and volitional. In this section I will argue that clauses expressing intentional transitive action have some unique grammatical and semantic characteristics which enable them optimally to realize the notion of 'goal-directed action'. Transitive constellations with unintentional or inanimate Actor can be shown to be partial instantiations of this central constellation. In other words, the category 'transitive:effective' has internal prototypical structure: its most characteristic features cluster in 'intentional goal-directed action'.

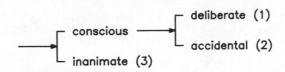

Figure 5.4 Intentionality of the Actor's action: a system network

With transitive:effective clauses, the dimension of 'intentionality' applies to the RELATION between the Actor and the process–Goal complex. Intentionality of an action presupposes an Actor endowed with the (higher) gifts of consciousness. But 'not intentional' has two meanings, viz. 'lack of control' (with a conscious Actor) and 'absence of intentionality' (with an inanimate Actor). The system network shown in Figure 5.4 captures the various values of 'intentionality' that can be associated with the Actor–action relation. This gives us the following structure types:

(1) The teacher hit the child.
(2) John accidentally hit Mary in the face.
(3) The arrow hit the target.

One of the most distinctive 'reactances' of intentional goal-directed action to the Actor-centred transitive prototype pertains to the AMBIGUITY of its nominalizations with *of*-periphrasis. The ambiguity of nominalizations such as *the shooting of the hunters* or *the eating of the children* has often been remarked on: *the hunters* and *the children* can be interpreted either as Actor or as Goal of the 'shooting' and 'eating' respectively. What has not been observed, as far as I am aware, is that this ambiguity is typically associated with deliberate goal-directed action, cf. also *the kissing of Mary, the charging of the enemy, the driving of Joan, the painting of David.* All other 'effective' constellations, i.e. those instantiating the general Agent·Process·Affected

schema,[3] generally allow only the Affected to appear as *of*-Complement.
The only other structure type where a nominalized process + *of* +
Agent might occasionally occur is inanimate transitive action:

The tile hit the old lady.

The hitting of the tile was a tragic coincidence.

Inanimate transitive action is the closest instantiation of the intentional
transitive prototype and arguably involves a hint of personification of the
inanimate Actor.[4] Accidental transitive clauses generally do not allow the
Actor to appear as *of*-Complement:

Mary grazed her hand.
≠ The grazing of Mary
The grazing of her hand

With ergative structures, including intentionally instigated ones, it is
absolutely impossible for the Agent to appear as *of*-Complement:

John opened the door.
≠ The opening of John
The opening of the door

Mary spread the news
≠ The spreading of Mary
The spreading of the news

The nominalizations with *of*-periphrasis of the Agent represent different
experiential contents from the original clauses, precisely because *of John*
and *of Mary* are automatically understood as 'of the Affected'.

Nominalization is the result of a process of grammatical metaphorization
in which the constituents of a clause are recoded with the functional
resources offered by the nominal group: the process is reified into an a-
temporal Thing and the direct participants in the process have to be coded
as Modifiers. Langacker (1989: chapter 1, p. 13 f.) notes that the structural marker *of* expresses an *intrinsic* relation such as part–whole, kinship
or possession; because a process's inherent participants have this kind of
intrinsic relation to the process they can appear as Complement of *of*. My
point, then, is that, for all the effective clause types of English, the Affected
is the most inherent participant, since it is only the Affected that can be
coded as Complement of *of*, except for intentional goal-directed action
where the nominal *of*-periphrasis shows BOTH Actor and Goal to be fully
inherent participants. This points to the unique nuclearity of the Actor–
Process complex in intentional goal-directed action.

A second 'reactance' pointing to the nuclearity and relative
independence of the Actor–Process complex, particularly when the action
is intentional, is formed by what has traditionally been called the 'absolute

construction'. Within the material process paradigm, intentional transitive clauses quite freely allow a natural absolute construction:

The teacher hit.
The Light Brigade charged.

Accidental transitive action generally cannot be expressed without explicitating the Goal:

Mary grazed her hand.
≠ Mary grazed.

However, non-intentional transitive events with inanimate Actor can occasionally be represented by absolute constructions: *Unfortunately, the tile struck/hit* (describing the event of the tile falling on the old lady). With ergative processes it is totally impossible to isolate the Agent–Process complex in an absolute construction: *John broke the glass* does not lead to a corresponding absolute *John broke. John broke* is immediately interpreted with *John* as Affected rather than as Agent of *broke*, i.e. as an ergative middle. The ergative paradigm is Affected-centred, in contrast with the transitive paradigm, which is Agent-centred (cf. Fawcett 1980: 140).

There is a subtle but interesting semantic correlate to this nuclearity of the Actor–Process complex. Most intentional transitive clauses allow of two interpretations as regards the 'success' of the goal-directed action. Take *He's hitting me! The dog's biting me!* Normally, when such clauses are used, we take it that the action ended in successful contact with the Goal. However, you could also say *Help! The dog's biting me!* when its fangs are not yet actually in your leg but when the dog has the very clear intention of sinking its teeth into you. All other types of material effective clauses allow *only* of the reading in which the Affected is successfully affected:

*John accidentally hit Mary, but Mary was not hit.
*The arrow is hitting the target, but the target is not hit.
*Mary is burning the meat, but the meat is not burnt.

As observed by Nishimura (1989: 15) the meaning of 'goal-directed action' can usually be decomposed into an action component and a goal-achieving component. Intentional transitive clauses most strongly activate the action component, the notion that an Actor consciously targets an action on to a Goal, and this to the extent that 'goal achievement' is not even necessarily implied. Once again, this is a feature unique to intentional goal-directed action, attributable to its strong Actor-centredness. In transitive clauses with inanimate or unintentional animate Actor the semantic focus of the action process shifts from the action component to the goal-achieving component. Hence these two structure types can be referred to as 'goal-achieving' transitive clauses, as opposed to the intentional 'goal-directed' prototype.

5.3.1.2 A note on the facility-oriented passive

A clause type whose characterization has often been marred by imprecise location with regard to the transitive and ergative paradigms is the 'process-oriented' (Halliday 1967b: 47 ff.) or 'facility-oriented' (Fawcett 1980: 148) passive, e.g.:

(1) These tomatoes peel well.
(2) Those muffins eat easily.
(3) My bicycle rides easily.

These clauses are not ergative middles. In principle, they do not allow of an ergative middle agnate:

*(1) These tomatoes are peeling now.
*(2) Those muffins are eating now.
*(3) My bicycle is riding now.

Rather, these examples illustrate a construction type characteristic of the transitive system. They instantiate a Subject/Goal·Process·(implied) Actor structure, whose participants stand in a passive inherent voice to the process; example (2), for instance, can be paraphrased as 'Those muffins can easily be eaten by the (implied) Actor(s).'

The Subjects *these tomatoes, those muffins, my bicycle* are Goals, not Mediums: they do not actively co-participate in the process as Mediums do. *The tomatoes* in example (1), for instance, do not 'do' the peeling the way *the glass* 'does' the breaking in *The glass broke*:

What the glass did was break.
* What the tomatoes did was peel.

Moreover, unlike ergative middle clauses, examples (1)–(3) realize a feature of (inherent) agency. Even though the syntax does not allow of the Actor's being expressed, the experiential structure DOES imply that the tomatoes are peeled by someone, or that the bicycle is being ridden by someone. The facility-oriented passive is used to make a judgement about the feasibility of the transitive process, WITH IMPLIED REFERENCE TO THE INHERENT ACTOR.[5] If an ergative middle is used to specify the quality or the feasibility of a process, e.g. *In the event of an accident the glass will break neatly*, then it does this WITHOUT NECESSARILY IMPLYING AN EXTERNAL AGENT. The ergative middle leaves it open whether the action was self-instigated or externally caused. The reading that 'in the event of an accident the glass will break ITSELF neatly' is a valid alternative here.

Once the difference between the transitive facility-oriented passive and the ergative middle is recognized, clauses that are blends of transitivity and ergativity can be tackled, e.g.:

(4) That car drives easily.
(5) Those books sell like hot cakes.
(6) Those clothes wash easily.

The exponential paradigms of these experiential constellations show that they are blends of transitivity and ergativity. Examples (4) and (6), for instance, allow both for the typically transitive absolute (*John is driving*, *Mother is washing*) and for the ergative middle (*That car was driving too fast*, *Those clothes are washing at the moment*). Hence, examples (4)–(6) can receive a Goal·Process·(implied) Actor reading, for instance as in (5), 'Those books can be sold like hot cakes (by the distributors)', AS WELL AS a Medium·Process reading 'those books sell (themselves) like hot cakes', which is supported by the possibility of an ergative reflexive agnate *Those books are selling themselves, as it were*. Unless one sees that precisely this complementarity – the transitive versus the ergative representation of a process – is at stake in examples (4)–(6), the real subtlety of the facts of English goes unnoticed.

5.3.2.1 Prototypical structure of the category ergative:effective

Within the ergative paradigm there is no linguistic support (of the kind just discussed for the intentional transitive Actor) for claiming prototype status for the intentional Instigator. The performance of a DEED is typically deliberate, but not the INSTIGATION of an event. It can also be noted in this context that *the fact that* . . . nominal groups with postmodifying 'fact' clauses fit naturally into the Instigator slot, whereas they are excluded from the typical Actor slot: *The fact that boiling water was poured into it broke the glass /* The fact that he aimed well hit the target*. Embedded processes cannot 'act', but they can 'instigate' an event. The prototypicality of the intentional, typically human, Actor hinges on the strong Agent-centredness of this structure. But the ergative paradigm is Medium-centred: the Medium–Process complex is its most nuclear unit. Not surprisingly, the shift towards 'less prototypical' structures is, within the ergative paradigm, associated with the Medium–Process complex.

For prototypical ergativity in English it is essential that for the effective there should be a corresponding, typically ergative, syncretistic middle with the same process lexeme: *The cat broke the glass/The glass broke*. This type of effective structure optimally realizes the meaning INSTIGATION-OF-A-PROCESS. On the border between the transitive and the ergative paradigms we find clauses with potentially 'ergative' process lexemes whose specific constellations do NOT allow of an ergative middle, e.g.:

Mary changed the baby.   ≠ The baby changed.
John opened a bank account.   * A bank account opened.

Because the most distinctive feature of the ergative system, the syncretistic middle, is lacking, these constellations shift towards the transitive paradigm. However, they are not prototypical Agent-centred Actor–Goal constellations: they do not allow for the absolute, or for *of*-periphrasis of the Agent in nominalizations:

Mary changed the baby.
≠ Mary changed.
≠ The changing of Mary

Therefore a case can be made that these structures are analysed better in terms of the more general schema Agent–Affected than in terms of the more specific functions Actor–Goal or Instigator–Medium, whose most typical characteristics they precisely lack. Because they are predominantly transitive, but with the 'instigative' meaning reminiscent of ergativity, these structures can be referred to as INSTIGATIVE ACTIONS.

5.3.2.2 Ergative instigation versus analytical causation

Few questions have intrigued linguists more than the difference between what are traditionally known as lexical causatives such as *John killed Bill* and *John opened the door* versus grammatical causatives such as *John caused the door to open*. However, because the transitive and ergative cryptotypes have not generally been distinguished within the category of 'lexical causatives', the debate so far has not come to grips with the complexity of the facts of language. In a first point (i) it will be shown that the 'Medium'–Process complex is increasingly 'independent' in transitive:effectives, ergative:effectives and analytical causatives (in that order). In a second point (ii) the difference between ergative 'instigation' and grammatical 'causation' will be discussed.

(i) Fodor (1970) attacked the view that lexical and grammatical causatives, more specifically *kill* versus *cause to die*, were synonymous. He argued that the former express one-event causative situations and the latter two-event causative situations. Take examples such as:

(1)   *John caused Bill to die on Sunday by stabbing him on Saturday.*
(2) * *John killed Bill on Sunday by stabbing him on Saturday.*

With *cause to die* we have two discrete events, 'cause to die' and 'die', hence these two events can be represented as distinct in time and space. But *kill* represents, as a cohesive unit, only one unanalysed event; therefore it is impossible to attribute different time/place specifications to it (as in example (2)). Similarly, we can have:

(3) *John caused Mary to die, and it surprised me that he did so.*
                                                  she did so.
(4) *John killed Mary, and it surprised me that he did so.*
                                          **she did so.*

Because *cause to die* expresses a two-event situation, it can provide two 'propositional antecedents' to DO SO: *John causes Mary to die* and *Mary dies*. But, because *kill* expresses an unanalysed event, it can provide only the antecedent *John kills Mary* and not something like *Mary dies*.

The problem with Fodor's characterization of the difference between lexical and grammatical causatives is that he looks only at a transitive process, *kill*, as representative of 'lexical causatives'. The picture becomes more complex if ergative processes are brought in. If we consider the 'reactances' of ergative structures to operations in the areas of circumstantial modification and cohesive presupposition, ergative constellations turn out to represent something in between 'two-event' grammatical causatives and 'one-event' transitive:effectives.

Thus, in ergative clauses, it is possible for circumstances to modify ONLY the MEDIUM–PROCESS complex. In transitive clauses, by contrast, circumstances necessarily modify all of the ACTOR–PROCESS–GOAL nucleus. Compare:

trans.:　(1) *The cook pounded the meat for ten minutes.*
erg.:　(2) *The cook boiled the meat for fifty minutes.*

Sentence (1) implies that the cook's pounding and the meat's getting pounded are fully co-extensive in time and space. Sentence (2) implies that *the meat boiled for fifty minutes*, but it does not entail that the cook engaged in a boiling activity for fifty minutes. The INSTIGATION-OF-THE-PROCESS and the INSTIGATED PROCESS are not necessarily co-extensive.

Secondly, the MEDIUM–PROCESS nucleus within the ergative:effective cannot be substituted, but it can be referred to (cf. Lakoff and Ross 1972):

(a) *Mary changed John, and it surprised me that she did so.*
            **he did so.*
(b) *Mary changed John, but it took her a whole lifetime to
    bring it about.*

As pointed out by Halliday and Hasan (1976), a reference item refers to a *meaning*, whereas with substitution a piece of WORDING which retains its grammatical function and class is carried over. The ergative *Mary changed John* does not provide a grammatically identical piece of wording *John changed* that can be substituted by *so*, but it does allow the independent meaning 'John changed' to be picked up by reference. In contrast, the GOAL–PROCESS complex within the transitive:effective can be neither substituted nor referred to.

(a)　*John killed Mary, and it surprised me that he did so.*
            **she did so.*
(b) * *John killed Mary, but it took him six months to bring it about*

Both these REACTANCES indicate that the MEDIUM–PROCESS complex has some degree of grammatical independence in ergative:effective structures, although this independence is less strong than that of the CAUSED PROCESS CONSTELLATION in grammatical causation. But the GOAL–PROCESS complex in transitive:effective structures has no independence at all.

Within the transitive paradigm, the Goal has no relation of its own – grammatical or semantic – to the process: the process is being done to it, but the Goal itself does not 'do' the process. It is, as it were, a totally 'inert' Affected. Within the ergative system, something is being done to the Medium AS WELL AS the Medium itself 'doing' the process. It is characteristic of the central ergative participant that it co-participates in the process; the ergative middle allows one to isolate the Medium in its 'doing' relation to the process. This difference between the transitive and ergative system can be illustrated with familiar examples such as (1) *John threw the ball* (transitive) and (2) *John opened the door* (ergative). In (1) the Actor *John* does the 'throwing', but *the ball* does not actively participate in the action of 'throwing'. Hence the *do*-probe applies to all of the clause, but not to the GOAL–PROCESS complex: we can say *What John did with the ball was throw it* but not **What the ball did was throw*. In (2) Instigator *John* 'affects' *the door* by instigating its opening, but *the door* co-participates in the process of 'opening'. Therefore we can say both *What John did to the door was open it* and *What the door did was open* (cf. Halliday 1968: 136 ff.).

In this context it should be remembered that Halliday (1985: 145) has characterized the transitive model as a LINEAR model and the ergative model as a NUCLEAR one. In the transitive model there is 'energy input' only at the level of the Actor, while in the ergative model there is 'energy input' at two levels: that of the Instigator within the outer ring and that of the Medium within the inner ring (cf. Langacker 1989: chapter 9, p. 3). Schematically this can be shown as in Figure 5.5. Structurally as well as semantically, a transitive effective structure has only one processual layer, whereas an ergative structure has two processual layers.

the transitive model   **the ergative model**

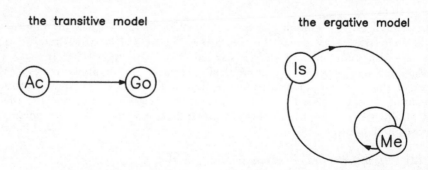

Figure 5.5 The transitive model (*left*) and the ergative model (*right*)

(ii) The attempt to characterize the difference between (ergative) lexical causatives and grammatical causatives has given rise to one of the most stubborn fictions in descriptive linguistics, namely that lexical causatives always imply 'direct action' by the causer on the causee (e.g. Lyons 1968: 365; Lakoff 1977: 244; Vendler 1984: 299). Shibatani (1976: 31 ff.) pushes this fiction to its extreme with his notion of 'manipulative causation'. He claims:

> In a situation where the causee is involved as a non-volitional entity, the causer must physically manipulate the causee in effecting the caused event. It is this situation involving MANIPULATIVE CAUSATION that the lexical causative form usually expresses.
>
> [p. 31]

Analytical causatives, where the Causer role is further removed from the Causee role in the grammatical structure, are then said – often with the invocation of distance iconicity – to express 'non-direct action' from the causer on to the causee. As, for instance, Vendler (1984: 299) puts it, 'By using *make, get* or *cause* we imply some indirectness, or a roundabout way of getting the thing done,' e.g. *making* or *causing the arm to rise* would imply that this happened 'by lifting the arm with the OTHER hand or by stimulating the subject's brain'. However commonly this explanation has been espoused by linguists, a host of counter-examples can immediately be given. *The boss works his secretaries from eight till six* does not refer to a situation in which the boss physically manipulates his secretaries, and if I were to ask someone to open the outside door of an apartment building by pressing a button on the twentieth floor I would say: *Could you open the door, please?* not *Could you cause it to open?*, even though no physical manipulation of the causee, *the door*, is involved. Similarly, if pupils wish to support the arm they raise with their *other* arm, I would still say *The pupils raised their hand* not *The pupils made their hand rise*.

In this section I will argue that the differences in meanings encoded by the ergative:effective and by the analytical causative are tied up with the distinction which the grammar makes between direct participants in the process, circumstantial elements attendant on it, and some transitional category like 'indirect participants' that lie between these categories. The iconicity principle obtains between the abstract grammatical frame of circumstantial setting versus process–participant(s) nucleus and its meaning, not between syntax and the referential situation. Also, attention has mostly been concentrated on the 'causer' and the nature of the causation. As indicated by Halliday (1968: 195 ff.), the crucial distinction between ergative:effectives and analytical causatives is related to the nature of the 'Medium'–Process complex in both types of structure. The principle is as follows: ergative structures ALTER the inherent voice of the Medium–Process complex; analytical causation does NOT alter the inherent voice of the process–participant(s) complex to which it adds a feature of 'causation' (Halliday 1968: 198).

In terms of the generalized model,[6] analytical causation adds a feature of 'agency' (structurally realized by causative Agent + causative process) to the basic structures of all process types. This implies that, if the feature 'causation' is added to an effective structure which already has an Agent in it, a secondary Agent is brought into the constellation (Halliday 1985: 53). Restricting ourselves to the material process paradigm (representing 'Medium' as Me and Agent as Ag) we get:

Transitive

    (1a). *John* ('Me') *fell into the pool.*
    (1b). *Peter* (Ag) *made John* ('Me') *fall into the pool.*

    (2a). *John* ('Mc') *ran away.*
    (2b). *Peter* (Ag) *made John* ('Me') *run away.*

    (3a). *John* (Ag) *threw the ball* ('Me').
    (3b). *Peter* (Ag_2) *made John* (Ag_1) *throw the ball* (Me).

Ergative

    (4a). *The ball* (Me) *rolls.*
    (4b). *Peter* (Ag) *made the ball* (Me) *roll.*
    (4c). *Peter* (Ag) *rolled the ball* (Me).

    (5a). *The soldiers* ('Me') *are marching.*
    (5b). *The general* (Ag) *is making the soldiers* ('Me') *march.*
    (5c). *The general* (Ag) *is marching the soldiers* (Me).

As pointed out by Halliday, the essential thing about analytical causation is that it leaves intact the inherent voice of the process–participant(s) constellation to which it is added. The relation of *John* to *fall* in (1a) is SUPERVENTIVE, i.e. the action is not engendered by the participant but supervenes (Halliday 1968: 198). And it remains a SUPERVENTIVE action in (1b). All that (1b) says is that Peter caused John not to control his falling into the pool; it may be that Peter pushed him, but Peter may also have done something indirect like put soap on the tiles or tied a string to make 'John fall' – the analytical causative does not specify the nature of the causative Agent's involvement. In (2a) the relation of *John* to *run away* is not superventive – John initiates and controls his running away – and as such it is retained in (2b). Once again, note that the *make*-causative does NOT specify the nature of the extra-linguistic causation: Peter may have positively chased John, he may have frightened or hurt John, thus indirectly causing John to run away, or Peter may have looked so terrible that he involuntarily made John run away. (It is certainly not the case that analytical causatives EXCLUDE the interpretation that manipulative causation was involved in the extralinguistic situation.) Example (2b) simply states that 'because of (some action or something associated with) Peter,

John decided to run away'. Example (3a) is a prototypical transitive clause with a relation of 'deliberateness' between the intentional Actor *John* and the goal-directed action *throw the ball*. Example (3b) leaves intact the control and intentionality of the action. Note in this context that – if intonation is disregarded – *Peter did not make John throw the ball* has two possible interpretations: (1) 'John decided to throw the ball but it was not because of Peter'; (2) 'Peter tried to function as "cause" of John's throwing the ball, but John decided not to throw the ball'.

With examples (4a)–(4c) we are at the heart of the problem of lexical ergative versus analytical causatives As we have seen above, the syncretistic middle neutralizes the voice distinction associated with the relation between Medium and process: in terms borrowed from Talmy's (1985) semantics of 'force dynamics', *the ball* in *The ball rolled* is represented as manifesting a tendency towards rolling, but whether this tendency is intrinsic or externally instigated is left open. The analytical causative retains this essential voice vagueness; the meaning of (4b) *Peter made the ball roll* can be paraphrased as 'the ball manifested its (intrinsic or externally instigated) tendency to rolling because of Peter'. This sentence could be used with reference to the most varied extralinguistic situations, including that of Peter kicking the ball, which could be alternatively referred to by (4c) *Peter rolled the ball*. Against all truth semantics, let it be said again that, even though (4b) and (4c) COULD be used to refer to the same extralinguistic situation, they mean different things. *Peter made the ball roll again* (but not *Peter rolled the ball again*) could also be used, for instance, if Peter had pumped up a flat ball and so restored the ball's capacity to manifest its tendency to roll. The essential thing about (4b) is that it retains the neutralized voice of (4a).

The central meaning of the ergative:effective lies in its resolving the voice vagueness of the middle: *Peter rolled the ball* makes it clear that the process of rolling was instigated by the external Instigator *Peter*. By removing the vagueness in the inherent voice of the middle, the effective CHANGES that inherent voice. Exactly the same principle applies to the special ergative sub-type of 'INSTIGATION-OF-ACTION' such as (5c) *The general is marching the soldiers*. Here the corresponding middle is a non-superventive intransitive clause: (5a) *The soldiers are marching*. But, unlike most intransitive clauses, this sub-class is 'instigatable': it is possible to bring an Initiator such as *the general* as direct participant into the constellation. This suppresses the features of 'control' and 'initiative force' associated with the *soldiers–march* complex in (5a) and turns *the soldiers* in (5c) into what Halliday (1967a) has called an 'ENFORCED Actor'. INSTIGATION-OF-ACTION ergative structures are used mostly in contexts of coercion (*John is galloping the horse*, *The boss is working his secretaries from eight till six*) or of essential aid (*Peter stood the drunk up*, *Mother sat the baby up*), where the features of 'control' and 'initiative force' usually associated with the Actor-process complex are cancelled. You would not say *Mother made the baby sit up* – rather than *Mother sat the baby up* – precisely because a young infant cannot 'self-instigate' the action of sitting up but has to be propped up, after which she can 'do' her own sitting. But, referring to older children, you would use *Mother always made us sit up straight at the table*, not normally *Mother always sat us up straight at the table*, because the latter suggests that mother had to pull each of the lazy creatures into the desired position rather than appeal to their free will to instigate a decent posture themselves.

A functional analysis of the different structures realizing 'instigation' versus 'analytical causation' will allow us to clarify these distinct notions further. To questions such as

Why did the ball roll?
Why are the soldiers marching?

the ergative:effective provides the answer:

Well, because it *was* roll*ed* (by Peter).
because they *were* march*ed* (by the general).

These answers say, in effect, something like: you are looking at it in the wrong way – the BALL was not the principal energy source of the 'rolling', PETER was. Or *the soldiers* are not the 'free' but the 'enforced Actors' of the 'marching', which is being instigated and controlled by *the general*. Instigators such as *Peter* and *the general* are the Agents or the 'prime movers' of the process. Inherently circumstantial elements can never be coded as Instigators, because they simply cannot be conceived of as Agents, e.g.:

*The slope rolled the ball.
*Hunger marched the soldiers.

Analytical causatives, in contrast, DO allow both 'circumstantial'-type and 'agentive'-type causes to be coded as the 'second degree' (Halliday 1968: 195) Causer, and neutralize the distinction between them.

Peter made the ball roll.
The slope made the ball roll.
The general made the soldiers march.
Hunger made the soldiers march.

Because the material process (*roll, march*) is expanded by a causative process (*make*), the Causer is not part of the nucleus of experiential clause structure. The Causer is NOT a direct participant and it is NOT an Agent in the strict sense of an 'effective' Agent like the Actor or the Instigator. It is more of a circumstantial element, coded as an indirect participant. In analytical causatives the Medium remains the primary energy source of the process. Note in this respect that Manner circumstances modify the Instigator–instigated process relation in ergative:effectives, but the 'Medium'–process relation (not the Causer–caused process relation) in analytical causative constructions. Compare:

The boss works his secretaries very efficiently.
The boss makes his secretaries work very efficiently.

In the second sentence *the secretaries* self-instigate the process of 'working very efficiently', whereas in the first it is the initiating of their 'working' which is being done 'very efficiently' by *the boss*.

5.4 TRANSITIVE/ERGATIVE MIDDLE STRUCTURES

In this section it will be argued that the grammar of MIDDLE material processes is also fundamentally Janus-headed between transitivity and ergativity. Within the transitive paradigm, MIDDLE structures are 'intransitive', i.e. they are ACTOR–PROCESS constellations which do not extend to a Goal. Within the ergative paradigm, MIDDLE structures are 'non-ergative', i.e. they are MEDIUM–PROCESS structures which do not incorporate the structural role of an external Instigator.

The most crucial distinction between the intransitive and the non-ergative is that with the intransitive no Agent can be added, whereas with the non-ergative the frame can always be expanded to include an Agent:Instigator. We can, in principle enquire into the potential instigation of a non-ergative, but intransitives are essentially 'non-instigatable'.[7]

Intransitive

The children are swimming.   *Who's swimming them?
John stumbled.   *Who stumbled him?
The sun's shining.   *What is shining it?

Non-ergative

The door is opening.   Who is opening it?
That branch moved.   Who/what moved it?
The news spread.   Who spread it?

As noted above, the non-ergative is, in contrast with the intransitive, characterized by voice syncretism. The distinct 'voices' of the intransitive and the non-ergative are picked up, among other things, by certain principles within the grammar of the word. For instance, derivation of deverbal adjectives in -*able* is ruled out with intransitives, but it is possible with non-ergatives (Keyser and Roeper 1984: 400):

Intransitive	*Non-ergative*
*runnable	changeable
*faintable	breakable
*marchable	variable

Derivations from transitive processes, e.g. *edible*, *lovable*, obviously have a passive meaning: 'able to be eaten', 'able to be loved'. But the derivations from the ergative middles retain the voice neutralization characteristic of that constellation: *variable parameters*, for instance, evokes both 'the parameters are able to vary' and 'the parameters are able to be varied'.

5.5 TRANSITIVE/ERGATIVE PSEUDO-EFFECTIVE STRUCTURES

In sections 5.3–4, it has been argued that the grammar of both EFFEC-TIVE and MIDDLE material processes is governed by the distinct systems of transitivity and ergativity. But in between canonically MIDDLE and EFFECTIVE clauses lie those grammatically rather intriguing two-participant clauses that 'look' effective but are not, such as *The thief jumped the wall* and *The cooling system burst a pipe*. The Janus-headed transitive/ergative grammar of actions and events is particularly relevant to these structures. Unless we disentangle them into a transitive and an ergative 'pseudo-effective' type, we cannot satisfactorily 'locate' and describe them. At the same time, the very existence of these two types of non-effective structure adds further weight to the 'reality' of the transitive and ergative models.

5.5.1 Transitive PSEUDO-EFFECTIVE structures

Within the transitive paradigm we find, contrasting with the effective ACTOR–GOAL structures, pseudo-effective structures exemplified by clauses such as *They danced an energetic jig*, *They drove the whole distance*, *They crossed the field*. As suggested by their problematic passive and the inappropriateness of the *do to* thematic equative, these clauses are non-effective.

(Marked) mediopassive

An energetic jig was danced (by them).
The whole distance was driven (by them).
The field was crossed (by them).

Do to *thematic equative*

*What they did to an energetic jig was dance it.
*What they did to the whole distance was drive it.
*What they did to the field was cross it.

If these clauses do not represent an Agent taking effective action on an Affected, it is because the postverbal participant is not a 'done to', i.e. a Goal/Affected. Rather, this participant, which Halliday has called the Range, restates the process or specifies its extent or scope. One grammatical symptom of the 'non-affected' nature of the Range is that it can never take a resultative Attribute (which expresses the nature of the 'affectedness'). You can say *They trampled the field* (Go/Af) *flat* but not *They crossed the field* (Ra) *flat* (Halliday 1985: 131).

Not only are Ranges not Goals, they are not 'true' participants, either. As observed in Halliday (1967b: 58 ff.), elements such as *an energetic jig*, *the whole distance*, *the field* in the above examples seem to occupy some functional area in between participant and circumstance. To the extent that Ranges can become Subject of a passive they have – obviously – more participant status than straight circumstances; compare *They ran five miles* (Range)/*Five miles were run by them* with *They stayed five hours* (Circumstance)/*Five hours were stayed by them*. By the same token, ranged passives are always marked mediopassives, indicative of the limited participant status of the Range. Some sub-classes of Ranges are also characterized by a fairly systematic contrast with circumstances, which suggests that they are inherently more like a circumstance. It is to this sub-type of Range, rather than the 'cognate object'-type Range, that, for reasons of space, I will limit my discussion. For instance:

1(a). She prowled the city.
1(b). She prowled around the city.

2(a). The children rowed the lake.
2(b). The children rowed on the lake.

3(a). McMurtry climbed the mountain.
3(b). McMurtry climbed on the mountain

4(a). The thief jumped the wall.
4(b). The thief jumped over the wall.

5(a). She rode a horse called Swinger.
5(b). She rode on a horse called Swinger.

6(a). He has read that book.
6(b). He has read in that book.

As noted above, Ranges contrast with Goals in that they are coded as essentially 'non-affected'. The reason why the functional slot Range implies 'unaffectable' has to be sought in its inherent relation to circumstances. Ranged structures make participants out of elements that can also be coded as a Circumstance: they bring an element which in its alternative coding is only indirectly related to the process into the nucleus of the clause, where it interacts directly with the process. They also confer a degree of effectiveness on what are basically intransitive processes. The limited participant status of the Range is, as it were, the result of a 'promotion' from circumstance to pseudo-participant. Now, the ranged version always has a different meaning from the circumstantial one, and this difference can always be related to its having brought a circumstantial element into DIRECT INTERACTION with the Actor–Process complex. For instance, *rowing a lake* and *reading a book* imply, in contrast with *rowing on a lake* and *reading in a book*, that 'all' the lake is rowed and 'all' the book read: coding *a lake* and *a book* as a direct participant implies interaction with the totality of that participant. Much the same can be said about *climb the mountain*, which stresses the achievement of climbing 'all' the mountain. Langacker (1989: chapter 7, p. 12) notes that coding *the mountain* as participant rather than as circumstance represents *the mountain* more as the 'adversary' to be conquered in the process and stresses the difficulty of the task (cf. also *jump the wall*). Similarly, *prowling the city* suggests direct interaction with it (as in *doing the city*). *Riding a horse* highlights the aspect of 'controlling' the horse, in contrast with *riding on a horse*, which simply represents an intransitive process of motion with a circumstance specifying the vehicle of motion. We can conclude that this type of ranged structure imposes, as it were, a seemingly effective model of 'direct interaction between participants' on what can – mostly more congruently – also be coded as an intransitive process plus circumstance.

But ranged structures are never truly effective. Their processes are basically intransitive and their Ranges are inherently more like circumstances and cannot really be affected or acted on in the way a Goal from a prototypical transitive clause is. When *the teacher hits the child* the child is 'affected' by the action. Therefore the event can also be represented by an unmarked passive clause, with the participant 'being acted upon' or 'suffering the effects of the action' (Lyons 1968: 377) coded as Subject: *The child was hit by the teacher*. But when *Mary is prowling the city*, *rowing the lake* or *climbing the mountain* she is not really doing anything to the city, the lake or the mountain. Rather, she is involved in an activity IN the city, ON the lake and ON the mountain. Hence the oddity of, for instance, *The city is being prowled by Mary*. The 'natural' intransitivity of the congruent coding prevents the incongruent coding from becoming truly goal-directed.

This is why, in the generalized model, ranged structures are analysed as 'Medium'·Process·Range constellations, in contrast with Actor–Goal structures, which are an instantiation of the Agent·Process·Affected structure. Ranged clauses do not code an 'effective' Agent who initiates an action which 'affects' or is 'targeted at' the Affected. Ranged structures basically represent a middle process; the Range is not a real participant in that process but specifies its scope. It should immediately be added that this is a generalization over very many different instances which may range from almost fully middle clauses without passive (e.g. *They took a walk/*A walk was taken by them*) to almost fully effective clauses with only a slightly marked passive (e.g. *I'm reading a book/A book is being read by me*).

Ranged clauses fall strictly within the transitive paradigm as regards both their descriptive elucidation and their distribution. It is not possible to range ergative structures: we do not find clauses like *The wind broke a breakage*, *The door opened an opening*. Ranging is a logical possibility of the transitive system ONLY. Within the transitive paradigm the Actor is the most nuclear participant; this participant cannot possibly be 'reduced' or 'metaphorized'. The central transitive variable is: will the action extend or not to a Goal? (Hence the RIGHTward directionality of the transitive model.) The grammatical metaphor of 'ranging' operates on this area of variability within the model by creating a 'pseudo-extension' of the process. Cognate Ranges such as *sing a song, die a horrible death* restate the process: they represent 'an extension inherent in the process' (Halliday, 1967b: 59). Circumstantial Ranges draw an inherently circumstantial element into the clause nucleus, thus imposing a pseudo-effective model on what is congruently an intransitive process.

5.5.2 Ergative PSEUDO-EFFECTIVE structures

The ergative paradigm has its own type of pseudo-effective structure, exemplified by the following clauses:

(1) He fractured an arm in the accident.
(2) He burnt his eyelashes in the fire.
(3) The cooling system burst a pipe.
(4) The house blew a fuse.
(5) The car broke an axle.

The common tests of passivizability and *do to* thematic equative show that these two-participant clauses are not effective.

(1) *An arm was fractured by him in the accident.
    *What he did to his arm was fracture it in the accident.
(2) *His eyelashes were burnt by him in the fire.
    *What he did to his eyelashes was burn them in the fire.
(3) *A pipe was burst by the cooling system.
    *What the cooling system did to a pipe was burst it.
(4) *A fuse was blown by the house.
    *What the house did to a fuse was blow it.
(5) *An axle was broken by the car.
    *What the car did to an axle was break it.

So these clauses do not represent an Agent taking effective action on an Affected either, but here the reason they do not lies with the Subject, which is reduced in participant status to the point of no longer being an Agent. Notions essential to the 'Agent' of material processes are 'initiative' and 'responsible': the Agent is the participant who performs or instigates the effective action, and by virtue of this he is also held responsible for it (cf. Nishimura 1989). Take an ergative effective clause like *Lizzy burst the balloon*. Even if she did it accidentally, by coding *Lizzy* as Instigator, or

Agent, of the balloon's bursting, she is represented as 'responsible' for it. And, as shown by the passive *The balloon was burst by Lizzy*, this is an effective clause. It is precisely when any notion of 'responsibility' is absent that we no longer have an Agent relation, as in *The cooling system burst a pipe*. *The cooling system* did not initiate the bursting of the pipe and thus cannot be held responsible for it. This is a clause without the feature 'agency' and, hence, it is non-effective: **A pipe was burst by the cooling system*. All the Subjects of examples (1)–(5) are such non-agents.

Langacker (1989: chapter 8, p. 8 ff.) analyses these Subjects as Setting/Subjects:[8] like Ranges they are pseudo-participants with a functional affinity to circumstances. In order to appreciate the inherently 'circumstantial' nature of the Setting/Subject, it should be noted that it is a necessary condition for this construction that a relation of 'inalienable possession' should exist between the Subject and the Complement (Nishimura 1989): the Subject coincides with the Possessor, the Complement with the Possessed. Now, as noted by Halliday (1985: 122), possession also, in its broad sense of 'containment' and 'involvement', is a circumstantial notion. This provides a clue to the more congruent 'circumstantial' codings of examples (1)–(5), which are along the lines of:

(1b). His arm fractured on him in a car accident.
(2b). His eyelashes burnt on him in the fire.
(3b). A pipe burst in the cooling system.
(4b). A fuse blew in the house.
(5b). An axle broke in the car.

These are clearly middle ergative clauses with spatial circumstances that invariably imply a notion of inalienable possession, containment or a part–whole relation. Mostly, these clauses can be related to (truly) effective:ergative constructions with an Agent:Instigator/Subject such as:

(1c). The shock fractured his arm (on him) in a car accident.
(2c). The flames burnt the eyelashes (on him) in the fire.
(3c). Pressure burst a pipe in the cooling system.
(4c). A short circuit blew a fuse in the house.
(5c). The crash broke an axle in the car.

The ergative pseudo-effective construction is, just like a ranged clause, basically a middle constellation, semantically as well as grammatically. Its nucleus consists of an ergative process with its one real participant, the Medium, while its Subject is mapped on to the pseudo-participant Setting.

John	broke	his neck.
The cooling system	burst	a pipe.
Peter	grew	a wart.
pseudo-participant	process	true participant
Setting		Medium

It should be stressed that Setting-constructions (as defined here) are a logical possibility of the ergative system only. Within the ergative paradigm, the Medium is the most nuclear as well as an obligatory participant. Therefore the possibility is excluded of the Medium becoming involved in a metaphorical transfer and being reduced in participant status. The central ergative variable is: is the frame opened up to the LEFT to include an external Instigator, or not? It is these properties of the ergative system which make it possible to bring the circumstantial element 'Setting:Possessor' as a pseudo-participant and non-Instigator within the clause configuration.

Setting-constructions achieve a different semantic effect from the more congruent 'circumstantial' codings where the 'Setting:Possessor' appears as Circumstance. It is instructive to note that ergative pseudo-effective constructions can be used to represent the disastrous events that have befallen a person, for instance, *Just think of all the disasters that have happened to John lately: he's lost his wife, he's crashed his car and he's burnt his house.* These Setting-constructions do not mean that, in a certain sense, *John* caused these disasters or enabled them to happen – they mean precisely that *John* was not responsible for them at all. (One cannot use transitive constellations in this way. If we say, *John's killed his wife, he's destroyed his car and he's set fire to his house*, the Agent *John*, regardless of whether his actions were deliberate or accidental, is definitely held responsible.) The pseudo-effective *John's crashed his car* has as its non-metaphorical variant *John's car crashed on him*. By drawing the 'possessive:circumstantial' element *John* into the clause nucleus, the relevance of the middle process, *the car crashed*, to the Setting/Subject is foregrounded (cf. Langacker 1989: chapter 8, p. 8), and the fact that this process affected John is stressed. The congruent 'something happened on a setting' meaning is, in accordance with the leftward, 'inverted' directionality of the ergative model, dynamized into the meaning of 'a happening *affecting* its setting'.

5.6 CONCLUSION

The resources offered by material processes in English can now be represented by a system network. (Figure 5.6). This system network can be related 'downwards' to the grammar: each of its structure types is characterized by a distinct array of paradigmatically 'linked constructions'. For the distinct transitive and ergative categories and structures, the most obvious 'linked constructions' are the different voice paradigms of each structure type. However, the transitive and ergative semantic models are also realized by a far-reaching and deep-seated array of cryptotypical reactances: the different directionality and the differential ideational dependency grammar of transitivity and ergativity are picked up 'congruently' by specific patterns of clause grammar such as circumstantial

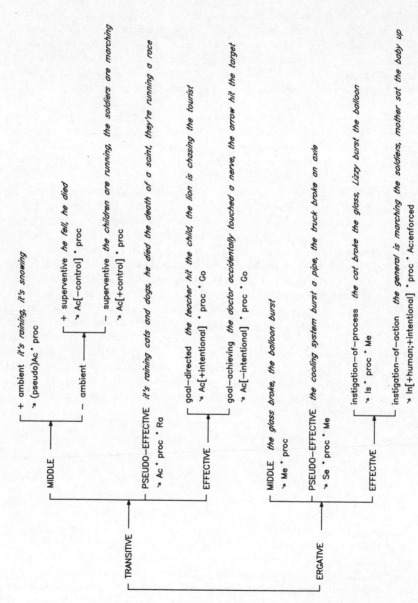

Figure 5.6 Material processes: primary experiential systems

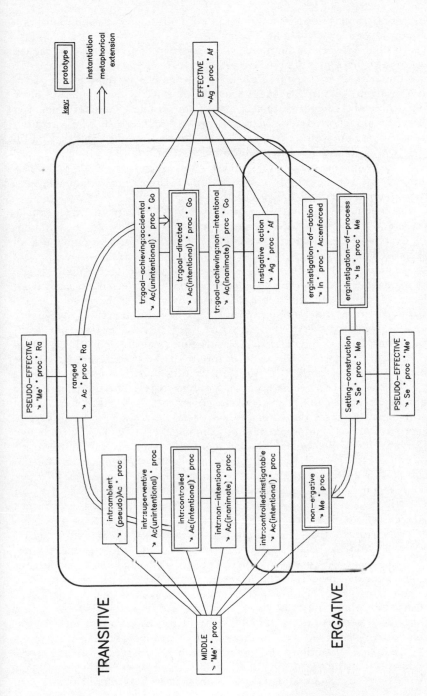

Figure 5.7 Material processes: schematic network

modification, and 'incongruently' by certain principles of nominalization and morphological derivation.

The system network of the material process paradigm can also be related 'upwards' to the semantics: these systems represent meaning primarily as choice rather than as structure. Therefore justice can be done to the essentially 'gradient' nature of language. (With strictly syntagmatic, more 'compartmental', categories this is almost impossible.) General categories such as Agent, Affected and 'Medium', as well as more specific categories such as Actor and Range, cover extended ground on the map of English experiential grammmar. Internally these categories are 'gradient'; they encode shifting meanings and these semantically shifting continua 'interlock' in a meaningful way with other clines. For language IS a system where everything hangs together functionally.

In the schematic network appearing as Figure 5.7 an attempt is made to represent the relations of intrastratal instantiation between the different structure types of the material process paradigm. The non-ergative and all sub-types of the intransitive can be seen as more specific instantiations of the 'Medium'-Process schema. The 'Medium' is the generalized single participant which has neither true agency nor real affectedness associated with it. Similarly, all the sub-types of transitive and ergative effective clauses constitute differentially fleshed out instantiations of the highly general Agent–Process–Affected structure. But there is no way the transitive and ergative pseudo-effective constructions can be generalized into a single schema. It would be counter-intuitive to attribute the transitive 'Medium'–Process–Range structure to a Setting-construction like *The house blew a fuse*, or to attribute the ergative Setting–Process–'Medium' structure to a ranged construction like *The thief jumped the wall*. Here the distinct transitive and ergative directionalities have to be taken into account.

There are also instantiation relations among the more specific transitive and ergative structure types. The prototypical structures within the transitive and ergative paradigms link up via a relation of (more or less) partial instantiation with the more peripheral structure types. The pseudo-effective structures constitute metaphorical extensions from one central structure type to another: from intransitive towards transitive for ranged clauses and from ergative towards non-ergative for Setting-constructions.

Recognition of the transitive/ergative cryptogrammar of material processes is indispensable to anything approaching an adequate, fine-grained description. Throughout this paper it has been shown that forcing a purely transitive model on to the resources of material processes leads to false generalizations, fictions and simplification of the real subtleties of English. One has only to think of the undifferentiated mainstream approaches to such issues as the ambiguity of process nominalizations, the 'absolute' construction, the facility-oriented passive, lexical instigation versus analytical causation, and pseudo-effective structures. But once one recognizes the distinct transitive and ergative cryptotypes, the whole system becomes more transparent and is seen to make sense. Because they are plausibly realized by the lexicogrammar, the transitive and ergative systems also offer plausible models for constructively – and creatively – interpreting our experience of actions and events.

NOTES

1 For reasons of space the discussion of many issues in this paper has of necessity been kept very brief. For a more detailed discussion of the questions touched on the reader is referred to Davidse (1991).

2 The 'agentive' participant of the generalized ergative constellation was labelled 'Cause' in Halliday (1968) and 'Agent' in Halliday (1985). For the ergative cryptotype within the material process paradigm I have chosen the more specific term 'Instigator'; one of the main points to be made in the following discussion is that the ergative:effective realizes the more specific notion of 'instigation' rather than simply 'causation'.

3 The view taken here is that there is no such thing as one generalized model in experiential clause grammar. Rather, different grammatical resources bring different general models to the fore. The general resource of causation foregrounds the generalized 'ergative' Agent·Process·Medium model. However, issues of EFFECTIVE voice and passivizability are discussed here, unlike in Halliday (1985: 150 ff.), in terms of a general Agent·Process·Affected schema. As pointed out by Hopper and Thompson (1980) and Rice (1987), the feature 'affectedness' is just as crucial to an understanding of effectiveness and passivizability as the feature 'agency'.

4 The relative 'closeness' of transitive clauses with inanimate Actor to the intentional transitive prototype is discussed in greater detail in Davidse (1991).

5 Langacker (1989: chapter 8, p. 3) makes exactly the same point concerning examples such as *This ice cream scoops out easily*: 'Certainly an agent is implied – we do not, for example, envisage the ice cream wielding a scoop and lifting itself out of the container. And while the ease or difficulty of carrying out the action is attributed to inherent properties of the subject, it can only be assessed as easy or hard in relation to the capability of an actual or potential agent.' He does not, however, point out that such constructions are restricted to transitive action processes.

6 The resource of causation foregrounds the generalized 'ergative' Agent·Process·Medium model. 'Medium' is put between inverted commas when it does not denote the prototypical Medium role found in the ergative cryptotype but a more schematic generalization of it.

7 The one exception to this principle is constituted by those controlled intransitives that can lead to coercive 'instigation-of-action' structures, such as *The boss works his secretaries*, *The general is marching the soldiers*.

8 I adopt Langacker's 'Setting' in preference to, for instance, Inoue's 'Experiencer' (1974), because it is evocative of the ambiguous participant/circumstance status of this specific role. I am, however, using 'Setting' in a more restricted sense than Langacker, i.e. not to cover all elements that are congruently coded by circumstances but only to refer to the pseudo-participant contrasting with the Agent:Instigator – the ergative counterpart of the Range.

134   KRISTIN DAVIDSE

REFERENCES

Bolinger, D. (1968), *Aspects of Language*, New York, Harcourt Brace & World.
Butler, C.S. (1985), *Systemic Linguistics: Theory and Application*, London, Batsford.
Davidse, K. (1991), 'Categories of Experiential Grammar', Ph.D. thesis, University of Leuven.
Dixon, R.M.W. (1979), 'Ergativity', *Language* 55, 59–138.
Fawcett, R.P. (1980), *Cognitive Linguistics and Social Interaction. Towards an Integrated Model of a Systemic Functional Grammar and Other Components of a Communicating Mind*, Exeter and Heidelberg, Julius Groos Verlag & Exeter University Press.
Fodor, T.A. (1970), 'Three reasons for not deriving "kill" from "cause to die"', *Linguistic Inquiry* 1, 429–38.
Greenberg, J.H. (1966), *Language Universals with Special Reference to Feature Hierarchies*, The Hague: Mouton.
Halliday, M.A.K. (1967a), *Grammar, Society and the Noun: an Inaugural Lecture delivered at University College London, 24 November 1966*, London, Lewis.
―――― (1967b), 'Notes on transitivity and theme in English' 1, *Journal of Linguistics* 3, 37–81.
―――― (1967c), 'Notes on transitivity and theme in English' 2, *Journal of Linguistics* 3, 199–244.
―――― (1968), 'Notes on transitivity and theme in English' 3, *Journal of Linguistics* 4, 179–215.
―――― (1985), *An Introduction to Functional Grammar*, London, Edward Arnold.
Halliday, M.A.K., and R. Hasan (1976), *Cohesion in English*, London, Longman.
Hasan, R. (1987), 'The grammarian's dream: lexis as most delicate grammar', in M.A.K. Halliday and R. Fawcett (eds), *New Developments in Systemic Linguistics* 1; *Theory and Description*, pp. 184–211, London, Pinter.
Hopper, P., and Thompson, S. (1980), 'Transitivity in grammar and discourse', *Language* 56, 251–99.
Hudson, R. (1986), 'Systemic grammar' (review article), *Linguistics* 24, 791–815.
Inoue, K. (1974), 'Experiencer', *Studies in Descriptive and Applied Linguistics* 7, 139–62.
Keyser, S.J., and Roeper, T. (1984), 'On the middle and ergative constructions in English', *Linguistic Inquiry* 15, 381–416.
Kress, G. (ed.) (1976), *Halliday: System and Function in Language*, London, Oxford University Press
Lakoff, G. (1977), 'Linguistic Gestalts', in *Papers from the Thirteenth Regional Meeting*, pp. 236–87, Chicago, Chicago Linguistic Society.
―――― (1987), *Women, Fire and Dangerous Things*, Chicago and London, University of Chicago Press.
Lakoff, G., and Ross, J.R. (1972), 'A note on anaphoric islands and causatives', *Linguistic Inquiry* 3, 121–5.
Lakoff, G., and Johnson, M. (1980), *Metaphors we Live by*, Chicago, University of Chicago Press.
Langacker, R. (1989), *Foundations of Cognitive Grammar. II, Descriptive Application* (preliminary draft), University of San Diego.
Lyons, J. (1968), *Introduction to Theoretical Linguistics*, Cambridge, Cambridge University Press.
Martin, James R. (1990), Review of Geoffrey Sampson, *Schools of Linguistics*, *Network* 13/14, 20–8.
Nishimura, Yoshiki (1989), 'Agentivity in Cognitive Grammar', Tokyo, Jissen

Women's University, mimeo. To appear in Geiger, A. and Rudzka-Ostyn (eds) (in press) *Conceptualizations and Mental Processing in Language*, Berlin, Mouton de Gruyter.

Rice, S.A. (1987), 'Towards a Cognitive Model of Transitivity', Ph.D. thesis, University of San Diego.

Shibatani, Masayoshi (1976), 'The grammar of causative constructions: a conspectus', in M. Shibatani (ed.), *Syntax and Semantics: the Grammar of Causative Constructions* 6, pp. 1–40, New York, Academic Press.

Talmy, L. (1985), 'Force dynamics in language and thought', in W. Eilfort *et al.* (eds), *Papers from the Parasession on Causatives and Agentivity*, pp. 293–337, Chicago, Chicago Linguistic Society.

Vendler, Z. (1984), 'Adverbs of action', in D. Testen, M. Veena and J. Drogo (eds), *Papers from the Parasession on Lexical Semantics*, pp. 297–307, Chicago, Chicago Linguistic Society.

Whorf, B.L. (1956), *Language, Thought and Reality: Selected Writings of Benjamin Lee Whorf*, Cambridge, Mass., MIT Press.

Wierzbicka, Anna (1988), *The Semantics of Grammar*, Studies in Language Companion Series 18, Amsterdam, Benjamins.

6 The place of circumstantials in systemic-functional grammar

William McGregor

6.1 INTRODUCTION

I begin this paper by posing four puzzles for the model of functional grammar advanced in Halliday (1985) – henceforth the IFG model – which I will assume represents the current systemic paradigm.

(i) In many languages it seems that a certain class of words – including some sub-set of the class of adverbials – may occur as immediate constituents of clauses, without an intermediate phrasal node.[1] For instance, in English the adverbial *upwards* would appear to be an immediate constituent of the clause *he climbed upwards*: there seems to be no convincing evidence that there is an intervening phrase (or group) node (see further section 6.2 below). Similar remarks apply to the corresponding word *thaanoonggoo* 'upwards', in *thaanoonggoo barwindi*, the translation equivalent of this clause in Gooniyandi (McGregor 1990a: 141, 151). This is in contradiction to the rank hypothesis of systemic theory, according to which a unit of a given rank must be a constituent of a unit of the rank immediately above (morphemes must be constituents of words, which must be constituents of groups/phrases, which must be constituents of clauses) – see, for example, Halliday (1961), McGregor (forthcoming). How can we account for this class of exceptions?

(ii) In some languages – e.g. Ungarinyin, Kija, Gurindji, among others in Australia and elsewhere – corresponding to directional expressions like *towards here*, *away from here*, etc., are bound morphemes which are attached to the verb (usually) or sometimes to the first constituent of a clause. Thus, in Ungarinyin, we have the suffix *-nya*, indicating movement away from the speaker, and the suffix *-lu*, indicating movement towards the speaker, as exemplified in (1) and (2) (from Rumsey 1982: 110, 112 respectively):

(1) *ba-nya*
    go-away
    'Go away!'

(2) *ba-lu*
   go-here
   'Come here!'

Items such as these also pose problems for the rank hypothesis. For, as morphemes, they should be constituents of words, which should be constituents of phrases. However, there is no evidence that nodes of either rank may intervene between the morpheme and the clause.[2] Like the words discussed under (i), these morphemes would appear to be immediate constituents of clauses.

Indeed, morphemes such as these appear to alternate with – and be replaceable by – full phrases, as illustrated by example (3):

(3) *balala*   *umbani*   *wurlan*   *di*
   spread:out   it:fell   language   it

   ungarinyin   *gandinya-biyny*   *ganda-biyny*
   Ungarinyin   w-class-ALL   w-class-ALL

'The Ungarinyin language spread out, way over that way, and in this direction.'

[Rumsey 1982: 63]

Since the phrases realize clausal circumstantial roles, it would seem reasonable to presume that the relevant morphemes do also. Moreover, they must do so directly, and not via intermediate, non-branching nodes. For there is no evidence that these morphemes can enter into syntagmatic relationships with other morphemes, the resulting syntagms constituting units of word or phrase rank.

It would surely be advantageous to be able to account for adverbial morphemes, whether free or bound, in a unified way, rather than be forced to posit different treatments in different languages. Other ways of incorporating the items discussed under (i) and (ii) should thus be sought.

(iii) In many languages (including English, Gooniyandi and Nyulnyul) adverbials may enter into syntagmatic relationships with phrases (usually prepositional or postpositional), forming what would appear to be complexes with them (Butler 1985: 21–4). This is illustrated in (4), where the adverbial *upstream* forms a complex with the prepositional phrase *to the farmhouse*, and the Gooniyandi example (5), in which the adverbial *gindiwa*, 'upstream', forms a complex with the postpositional phrase *doowoo-ya*, 'in the cave':

(4) *He walked **upstream to the farmhouse**.*

(5) *niyajingga*   *manyi*   *dagooddwaddinga*
   this:erg   food   he:put:it:repeatedly

   gindiwa   *doowoo*   *-ya*
   upstream   cave-   LOC

'He kept putting food up into the cave.'

This fact could be taken as evidence that adverbials are units of phrasal status. However, the problem is that, if this were accepted, it would be necessary to postulate that there are two nodes between the adverbial and morpheme, as illustrated in (6):

(6) Adverbial – Phrase rank
|
Adverbial – Word rank
|
Adverbial – Morpheme rank

Contrary to this hypothesis, there is no evidence that the two higher non-terminal nodes are branchable – a necessary requirement for the identification of constituency nodes.

There are at least two ways in which this problem could be resolved in a way consistent with the IFG model, both equally implausible. Firstly, it might be suggested that the adverbial and preposition in (4) together constitute a preposition group or complex preposition (Halliday 1985: 188–9). This suggestion fails because *upstream* and *to* do not cohere together as tightly as do the elements of the complex prepositions listed in Halliday (1985: 189). Indeed, an intonation break may even occur following *upstream*, with the adverbial and following prepositional phrase uttered in different intonation units, which fact strongly supports my contention that the adverbial and the prepositional phrase do form a complex. Another difficulty is that, even if this could account for the English phenomenon, it is not at all clear that the facts of Gooniyandi can be accounted for in a similar way: indeed, it would be necessary to permit complexes consisting of adverbial words and bound postpositions, which are always discontinuous.

Secondly, it could be proposed that the adverbial has word rank, but is at the same time a constituent of an adverbial group. Attention could be drawn to the fact that in *The stew was simmering gently* the adverbial *gently* can be modified by, say, *very*. But this does not really solve the problem. For, as Huddleston (1988:143) has pointed out, it is difficult to accept the need of a rank of adverbial group, given that it has univariate structure only – and no multivariate structure –according to Halliday (1985: 187–8). Thus (iii) remains a problem for the IFG model.

(iv) Why is it that sentences (7) and (8) are accorded vastly different structures in systemic theory? According to Halliday (1985), (7) is a single clause in which the *before* phrase functions as a circumstance of time; (8) is a clause complex in which the *before* clause provides temporal enhancement on the first clause.

(7) Actor   Process   Circumstance
    He   *left*   *before the debate.*

(8)   Clause$_1$ ×   Clause$_2$
    _____   _____

    Actor   Process   Conjunctive Adjunct   Actor   Process
    He   *left*   *before*   *the vote* *was taken.*

As Huddleston (1988: 145) points out, there seems to be no difference between the two sentences except for the fact that it is a phrase in (7) and a clause in (8) that indicates the time of the event. As he goes on to say,

It is strange that, in a theory that attaches prime importance to function, (4) [our example (7)] and (5) [i.e. (8)] should be given such radically different analyses on account of the difference in internal structure of the final elements.

[Huddleston 1988: 145]

Indeed, the case for viewing the two *before* constituents as fulfilling the same function is strengthened by Huddleston's observation that they can be co-ordinated, as in (9):[3]

(9) *He left before the debate and before the vote was taken.*

As we will see, these four problems are interrelated, and I shall be suggesting a framework which provides an answer for each of them. What I shall be proposing is that circumstantials do not constitute a class of ideational functions within the clause as per Halliday (1985). Rather, the items which are usually referred to as circumstances are related either to the remainder of the clause or to the verb phrase by one of the dependency relationships ENHANCEMENT, ELABORATION or EXTENSION (Halliday 1985: 196). As I have argued elsewhere (McGregor 1990b), the logical and experiential metafunctions must be rigidly separated: they do impose different structures on the clause, and should not be confused together under the rubric 'ideational metafunction' (cf. Halliday 1985: 101, 158). The dependence relationships belong specifically to the logical metafunction, and do not involve the experiential metafunction in any way, as suggested by Halliday's term 'logico-semantic relationships' (1985: 196). This suggestion permits a reduction in the number of primitives required in a systemic grammar: we need only the logical relationships of enhancement, elaboration and extension, and not the ideational roles of circumstance as well.

6.2 ADVERBIALS AND RANK

In McGregor (forthcoming) I propose that the best way round the problems which adverbials pose for the rank hypothesis is to assume that they are non-ranking items. That is, adverbials may be immediate constituents of clauses, and there is no need to postulate intervening phrasal (or group) nodes between them and the clause node in a constituency diagram. They can be regarded as immediate constituents, and yet non-ranking because, although they may be regarded as parts of a whole, they cannot be regarded as grammatically significant parts of that whole. For a part to be grammatically significant – to be a ranking constituent – it is required that it be associated with, and defined by, some function within the encompassing whole; see Haas (1954), McGregor (1990b, forthcoming) and Halliday (1985: 24ff.).[4] It follows that, if adverbials are non-ranking, they must not have functions in the wholes they are parts of; they must be no more than 'bits' of the clause which can be segmented by analytical tools. Thus in (10) and (11) the adverbials would not fulfil functions within the clause, although they are clearly 'parts of' the clause.

(10) *He drove quickly.*

(11) *He drove upstream.*

I have argued elsewhere (McGregor 1990b, forthcoming) that the functions of ranking linguistic units in the wholes to which they belong must belong to the experiential metafunction. (In other words, the experiential metafunction is constituted by part-to-whole relationships.) Non-ranking units do not have associated functions in the wholes of which they are parts, and thus have no significance in terms of the experiential metafunction. Granted that all linguistic units have some function associated with them, adverbials must fulfil some non-experiential function in examples such as (1)–(3) and (10)–(11). What might this be? My suggestion is that they realise a LOGICAL function, and are related by dependence to the remainder of the clause, or a constituent thereof (McGregor 1990b: 24). Moreover, this logical relationship is one of ENHANCEMENT (Halliday 1985: 196ff.). What I am proposing, then, is an analysis for (11) such as the one illustrated in (12). This means that *upstream* does not function experientially in (11), and is not 'visible' when the clause is considered from the perspective of the experiential metafunction. This paper explores some of the consequences of this hypothesis, and demonstrates that it permits a better account of the range of 'circumstantial' phenomena than does the IFG model.

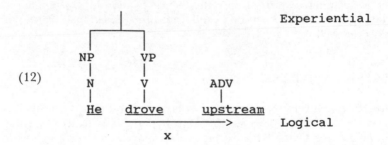

According to IFG, the adverbials in (10) and (11) share the same structural/functional relationship within the clause – they are both circumstances, although in (10) the adverbial functions as a circumstance of manner, whilst in (11) it functions as a circumstance of location (Halliday 1985: 137–40). However, it seems to me that there are some important differences between the two types of adverbial, differences which cannot be accounted for simply by different role labels. Firstly, only *quickly* can occur in a position immediately before the verb (*he quickly drove (along)*; *upstream* cannot occur in this position (*he upstream drove* is not acceptable). Secondly, although both adverbials may be modified, the type of modifier taken is different. Whereas *quickly* takes intensifiers which indicate a greater degree of the particular quality (e.g. *very quickly*), *upstream* takes exactives, which indicate that the orientation obtains precisely, and not just approximately (e.g. *straight/directly upstream*). Thirdly, and more weakly, it seems to me that *quickly* modifies the verb *drove*, indicating an inherent quality of the driving, whereas *upstream* seems to indicate a less inherent quality of the process, its direction, and instead modifies the whole situation referred to by the clause *he drove*.

The first and third of these differences can be accounted for in a revealing, and intuitively appealing, way within the framework I am proposing here, under the assumption that the difference lies in the fact that *quickly* is logically related to the verb *drove*, whereas *upstream* is logically related to the whole situation *he drove*. This would explain why *quickly* is consistently closer to the verb than is *upstream*. Further, it seems reasonable to suggest that *quickly* is in a relationship of elaboration – rather than enhancement – to *drove*, in as much as it indicates a quality of the motion, rather than embellishes around it.[5] That is, the adverbial *quickly* qualifies the verb *drove* in much the same way as *powerful* qualifies *locomotive* in *a powerful locomotive*. This might then explain why *quickly* and *upstream* select different sets of submodifiers. (This is the second difference commented on in the previous paragraph.) What we are suggesting, then, is that the structure of (10) is as shown in (13) below, which is quite different from (12), the analysis of the superficially similar (11). Here VP indicates Verb Phrase, which is defined as a construction consisting of a verb together with optional modifying or qualifying adverbials (possibly among other things).[6]

(13)   Experiential

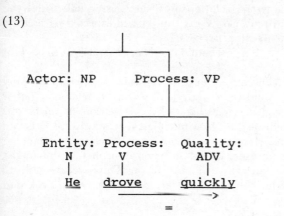

In proposing this way of distinguishing between manner and directional adverbials (exemplified by (10) and (11) respectively) it should be noted that I am concerned specifically with English. It is possible that in languages like Ungarinyin (some) spatial adverbials – possibly including -*nya*, 'away', and -*lu*, 'here', which are encliticized to verbs – actually do realize roles within the VP. Such a possibility would be perfectly consistent with the model outlined here, and merely reflect a cross-linguistic difference between English and Ungarinyin. There is no space to discuss this issue here, but it is one which will repay future investigation.

6.3 CIRCUMSTANCES AND ENHANCEMENT

I have proposed that adverbials do not realize experiential roles in clauses. This is just a special case of a more general proposal that there are no such 'things' as circumstances, conceived of as ideational roles (as per Halliday 1985) which embrace the functions of parts within dominating and encompassing wholes. Intuitively this can be interpreted as a suggestion that circumstances contextualize the core situation – the process together with the participants engaged in it (i.e. roughly the nuclear predication of Dik's (1989: 56) functional grammar – by relating it to something external to itself. They do not represent a part of the make-up of the situation, but rather are attendant to its core, or to one of the components of the core.[7] Thus, instead of ideational roles of circumstances we distinguish logical relationships of enhancement, elaboration and extension (Halliday 1985: 196ff.). There is no need for both circumstantial roles and logical relationships, and the latter can replace the former completely.

I am suggesting, then, that enhancement relationships be expanded considerably in scope from Halliday (1985), where they apply prototypically to clauses:

> As noted above, enhancing relationships are essentially between processes as a whole, and only rarely can they be interpreted as holding between particular elements of a process.
> [Halliday 1985: 253; cf. also p. 193]

This claim follows in part as a consequence of the mistaken view that only like objects – units of the same rank and class – can be related together logically, or form unit complexes together. There is reason to reject this restriction (McGregor 1990b: 36), and permit logical relationships between items of different ranks and classes. So, in addition to clauses enhancing other clauses, we can have phrases, words and even morphemes enhancing clauses (or constituents of clauses), and vice versa. Thus we are able to account for the following triplet in terms merely of differences in rank and class of the unit enhancing the clause *he left*:

(14) *He left early*

(15) *He left before the debate* (= (7))

(16) *He left before the vote was taken* (= (8))

Such triplets do not pose a problem for the rank hypothesis, if we regard the circumstance in each as not being a part of the ideational/experiential structure of the clause. Of course, Halliday (1985) considers only the 'circumstance' in (16) as standing outside the first clause, and the referent situation. And, as already mentioned, I agree with Huddleston that there seems to be no good reason for distinguishing the constructions. Huddleston (1988: 145ff.), however, takes this as evidence that the *before* clause in (16) is not in a dependency-type relationship with the previous clause, but rather is embedded in the first clause (and this occurs as part of an argument that rankshift and hypotaxis are not to be distinguished). In a reply to Huddleston (1988), Matthiessen has pointed out an important problem with this view: the *before* clause in (16) 'is immediately accessible to argumentation in discourse just as a paratactically related clause would be'. Accordingly, Mattheissen draws on agnation with another set of clause complexes, including examples such as (17) – an agnation which is inescapable, according to Halliday's arguments:

(17) *He left, and then the vote was taken.*

A more viable alternative is to interpret Huddleston's observation as evidence that the relationships in each of the three clauses are DEPENDENCY relations of ENHANCEMENT; indeed, the fourth type, exemplified by (17) can also be accounted for in precisely the same way. My proposal, that is, neatly captures the agnation between each of the four types under consideration, and for this reason is preferable to both Huddleston's and Halliday's proposals.

Matthiessen (1989) does indicate a way of accounting for the agnation noted by Huddleston, within a strictly IFG framework. He suggests that *before the debate* in (15) (= (7)) could be treated as an example of 'a metaphorically represented clause complex (*he left before they started to debate*, or the like) . . .'. It is not clear how seriously Matthiessen intends this suggestion to be taken, since he does not follow it up and admits that it does not account for other examples of prepositional phrases such as *He left before nine*. Furthermore, and more important, quadruplets resembling (14)–(17) are by no means restricted to English. In Gooniyandi, for instance, the following could be pointed to:

(18) *barngingi*   *gaddwaroo*   (Adverbial)
     I:started:back afternoon
     'I started back yesterday.'

(19) *barngingi*   *baddangga*   *-ya*   (Prepositional Phrase)
     I:started:back summer   -LOC
     'I started back in the summer.'

(20) *barngilangi*   *ngirndajinhingi*   *biliga*
    I:was:returning   from:here   middle

    barlanyi   *moordla*   (Hypotactic enhancement)
    snake   I:stepped:on:it
    'When I was going back, I stepped on a snake.'

(21) *barngingi*   *ngirndajinhingi*   *niyinhingi*
    I:started:back   from:here   then
    barlanyi   *moordla*   (Paratactic enhancement)

    snake   I:stepped:on:it
    'I started back from here, and then I stepped on a snake.'

It would seem rather unlikely that metaphor is involved if the same agnates
are identifiable in a number of languages, including languages as different
as English and Gooniyandi. As a general rule it seems to me preferable in
the first place to attempt to account for a given grammatical phenomenon
in terms of a grammatical system, rather than to resort to metaphor –
which is by no means to deny the existence and importance of metaphor
in grammar. Methodologically this means that we should attempt to incorporate as much as possible within the system of a language, and allude to
metaphor only as a last resort, not whenever problems arise. (Thus in
McGregor 1990b I point out that some other grammatical phenomena
which are treated as instances of grammatical metaphor in Halliday 1985
can in fact be analysed non-metaphorically.)

   In saying that 'circumstances' are not experientially identifiable parts of
clauses I am not, of course, suggesting that they may not themselves be
experiential entities, and thus amenable to constituency analysis into
experiential roles. This should be clear from my discussion of (14)–(16)
above. In order to make my position perfectly clear, I provide in (22)–(24)
analyses of (14)–(16) respectively. (Observe that in these diagrams *before* is
not treated as part of a prepositional phrase with the NP *the debate*. This
is because I regard it as a member of the class of RELATORS, which
indicate the relationship of some linguistic unit to another, and belong to

(22) **Experiential**

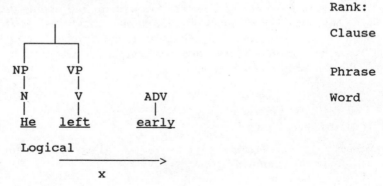

(23) **Experiential**

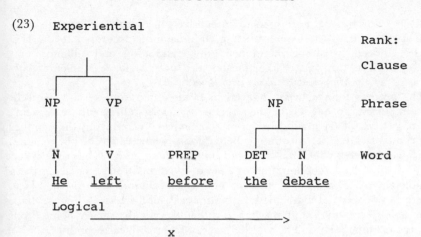

Logical

(24) **Experiential**

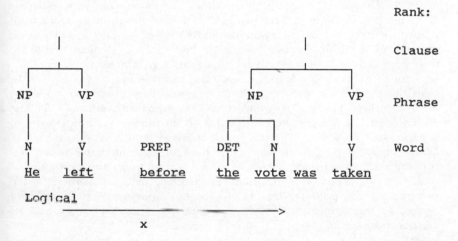

the 'textual' metafunction; McGregor 1990b: 18.)

6.4 CONCLUSION

What I have done in this paper is make a number of suggestions whereby
the four problematics identified in the introduction may be resolved. In the
process a revision of the IFG model has been proposed which departs from
it in a number of fundamental respects. The discussion has been largely
programmatic and exploratory, suggesting different (but certainly not new)
ways of doing things. I have not attempted to discuss the full range of relevant phenomena, presenting detailed arguments and justification for each

analysis. Nor have I attempted to categorize all logical relationships relevant to the class of items constituting circumstances according to the IFG model. Indeed, we have mentioned only elaboration and enhancement. However, it is possible that extension also occurs, for example in *with*-phrases, as in *Mary walked along with John*.

The process I have been engaged in is an important exercise in itself: it is important to engage in the process of theory refinement, embracing the objectives of (i) making it more economical by reducing the number of primitives; and (ii) accounting better for a wider range of phenomena. I believe that this paper has achieved both of these goals. Objective (i) has been satisfied by the elimination of a set of ideational roles, replacing them completely by a sub-set of the set of logical relations already in place. There is no need for both in the grammatical model. As to (ii), we have been able to provide some answers to difficulties for the theory pointed out by, for example, Huddleston (1988) and McGregor (forthcoming).

Both (i) and (ii) are theory internal. But we cannot leave matters at this point: we must consider also (i') is there any solid evidence for the proposals; and (ii') is it falsifiable – is there any observation that could be made which would contradict it? These are of course very different problems, rather more difficult to deal with than the problem of internal refinement and intermodel comparison. (ii') is, of course, a well known criterion of scientific theories (see, e.g., Popper 1968) – albeit not these days regarded as highly as it once was (see, e.g., Chalmers 1976: 57ff., who points to its theory-boundedness). But to my mind it is (i') which in practical terms is the most significant criterion: how would one go about justifying their position – what counts as evidence, and how is this evidence used in supporting the theory? (Note that in giving primacy to (i') I am not suggesting a return to the naive view of scientific endeavour as one of justifying hypotheses on the basis of, say, inductive reasoning. Rather, I am thinking of something which is admittedly theory-internal – much like the proof of a mathematical theorem. In other words it is the process, not the product, that is of greatest importance.) It is by these means, in my opinion, that one comes to understand a theory and its components.

One illustration of (i') is provided by examining a prediction of my model and arguing for its superiority over the corresponding prediction in the IFG model. This prediction relates to the interaction with Theme.[8] According to Halliday:

THE THEME OF ANY [English] CLAUSE, THEREFORE, EXTENDS UP TO (AND INCLUDES) THE TOPICAL THEME. The topical Theme is the first element in the clause that has some function in the ideational structure . . . .

[Halliday 1985: 56, his emphasis; cf. 1985: 54]

Thus, (25) would have a single Theme, the phrase *before very long*:

(25) *Before very long they heard Lily screaming as though somebody was dead.*

since this expression functions as a circumstance of time.

In line with my suggestion that the experiential and logical metafunctions must be distinguished in the structure of the clause, the characterization of topical Theme should be rephrased and restricted to elements which realize functions in the experiential structure of the clause (McGregor 1990c): the topical Theme of an English clause is the first element that has an experiential role in the clause. According to my analysis, *before very long* is in a logical relation of enhancement to the remainder of the clause. Thus there are two Themes, a logical Theme *before very long*, and an experiential Theme *they*. The first functions, as it were, to set the scene, relating it to the previous scene (compare Fries 1990; Downing 1990). The second functions to identify what the sentence is about: the *they* referred to, which is not a Theme according to the IFG model. In support of my contention that *they* is indeed a Theme, I would point first to the fact that, in this example, the Senser NP – likewise, an Actor NP in a material process clause – following a circumstantial element is typically in intuitive terms what the clause is 'about' (in its context of occurrence), and this is frequently identical with the paragraph theme: what the whole paragraph is about. Secondly, my approach permits us to capture the fact that exactly the same thematic relations are involved in examples such as (26), where according to IFG *they* would be Theme of the second clause.[9]

(26) *Before they had used up all their bullets, they heard Lily screaming as though somebody was dead.*

Owing to space considerations I cannot develop these ideas here but see McGregor (1990c).

Despite the advantages of the present approach to adverbial elements, I must conclude by acknowledging that I cannot yet answer one crucial question, pointed out to me by Erich Steiner: how is dependency to be characterized and defined in such a way as to make it operational – so that in a given instance we are able to determine whether two linguistic expressions are related in this way?[10]

NOTES

1 Of course, it would always be possible to postulate the existence of an intermediate node. However, it seems reasonable to demand that such nodes must always be supported by language internal evidence – the requirement of branchability – and should not be proposed merely for theoretical convenience.

2 This statement may seem to contradict the representations of (1) and (2), which show *-nya*, 'away', and *-lu*, 'here', as forming words with *ba*, 'go'. However, these are phonological, not grammatical (or ranked) words. The two morphemes

are strictly speaking enclitics, and are not constituents of a unit of the rank next above.

3 As Martin Davies (personal communication) has pointed out to me, Halliday is not entirely consistent in his analyses. Thus *as fast as he could caper* is treated as a circumstance in *and home he trot as fast as he could caper* (Halliday 1985: 106), but *as well as she could* is treated as a dependent, enhancing clause in *Alice crouched down among the trees as well as she could* (Halliday 1985: 270). Here also it is possible to co-ordinate the two, as in *and home he trot as fast as he could caper and as well as he could.*

4 Putting this in slightly different terms, I am suggesting that we need to distinguish between immediate constituents (any part of a whole which is not at the same time part of another part of that whole) and grammatical or ranked (Halliday 1985: 22) constituents (which are linguistic signs, i.e. correlations between linguistic forms and functions or roles of those forms in the thing of which the form is a part). It is only entities of the latter type, which involve form–function correlations, that are linguistically significant and fall on to the rank scale.

5 In support of this suggestion, observe that there exists what Halliday (1985: 113) refers to as an intensive attributive clause agnate with the clause with manner adverbial (*his driving was quick*), whereas, for the directional adverbial, the agnate attributive clause is circumstantial (*his driving was in an upstream direction*).

6 It will be observed that the VP defined in this way differs significantly from the verbal group of systemic functional grammar. Perhaps the major difference is that according to my analysis (McGregor 1990b: 30), auxiliary verbs do not belong to the verb phrase (or group) – experientially they are not a part of it. (This view is, of course, commonplace in transformational-generative theory.) Instead they relate interpersonally to the clause, which they hold in their scope.

7 It is necessary to add this proviso because sometimes locations constitute essential aspects of situations, as in *he lives in Prague* or *she put it in her pocket*. I would still argue that the locations do not constitute parts of the processes but rather serve to specify the (final) whereabouts of the Medium. It should be made quite clear that this is not a claim about the referent world, but rather a suggestion about the way in which language constructs it: an intuitive way of understanding the analyses proposed here.

8 Another area which would repay investigation is word order: whether the account of adverbial elements as dependents permits a ready explanation of the order of adverbial items (e.g. as per Hudson's 1987 adjacency principle).

9 Halliday seems to be aware of this problem, and appears to permit some thematic status to Subjects which are preceded by adverbial elements with the notion of displaced Theme: '. . . a topical element which would be unmarked Theme (in the ensuing clause) if the existing marked topical Theme [i.e. some adverbial or 'circumstantial' element] was reworded as a dependent clause' (Halliday 1985: 67 fn.). This seems an *ad hoc* addition to the theory; moreover, it does not help greatly in examples such as (25), where rewording by a dependent clause does not provide a congruent realization of the temporal duration.

10 The same problem arises for the constituency-based IFG model, and it would be not unreasonable to demand rigorous criteria for identifying constituency relations: in particular, to demand evidence that 'circumstantials' are indeed clausal constituents in the sense of being parts which fulfil some ideational role in the whole clause. Providing a label for a constituency node does not, of course, solve the problem.

REFERENCES

Butler, C. (1985), *Systemic Linguistics: Theory and Applications*, London, Batsford.
Chalmers, A.F. (1976), *What is this Thing called Science?* St Lucia, University of Queensland Press.
Dik, S.C. (1989), *The Theory of Functional Grammar* 1, *The Structure of the Clause*, Dordrecht, Foris.
Downing, A. (1990), 'On Topical Theme in English', paper presented to the seventeenth International Systemic Congress, Stirling.
Fries, P.H. (1990), 'Patterns of Information in Initial Position in English', unpublished manuscript.
Haas, W. (1954), 'On defining linguistic units', *Transactions of the Philological Society, 1954*, 54–84.
Halliday, M.A.K. (1961), 'Categories of the theory of grammar', *Word* 17, 241–292.
────── (1985), *Introduction to Functional Grammar*, London, Edward Arnold.
Huddleston, R. (1988), 'Constituency, multifunctionality and grammaticalization in Halliday's functional grammar', *Journal of Linguistics* 24, 137–74.
Hudson, R. (1987), 'Zwicky on heads', *Journal of Linguistics* 23, 109–32.
Matthiessen, C. (1989), 'A response to Huddleston's review of Halliday's *Introduction to Functional Grammar*', manuscript.
McGregor, W.B. (1990a), *A Functional Grammar of Gooniyandi*, Amsterdam, Benjamins.
────── (1990b), 'The metafunctional hypothesis and syntagmatic relations', *Occasional Papers in Systemic Linguistics* 4, 5–50.
────── (1990c), 'On the Notion of Theme in Semiotic Grammar', paper presented to the fourth International Conference on Functional Grammar, Copenhagen, June 1990.
────── (forthcoming), 'The concept of rank in systemic linguistics', to appear in E. Ventola (ed.), *Recent Systemic and other Functional Views on Language*, Berlin, Mouton de Gruyter.
Popper, K. (1968), *The Logic of Scientific Discovery*, London, Hutchinson.
Rumsey, A. (1982), *An Intra-Sentence Grammar of Ungarinyin, North-western Australia*, Canberra, Pacific Linguistics.

ACKNOWLEDGEMENTS

This is a revised version of a paper presented to the seventeenth International Systemic Congress, Stirling University August 1990. I am grateful to members of the audience for some challenging queries, and to Chris Butler, Martin Davies and Susanna Shore for useful comments on an earlier draft.

7 An initial approach to comparatives in a systemic functional grammar

Gordon Tucker

7.1 INTRODUCTION

This paper is of a methodological nature, in the sense that it describes and discusses the ongoing process of grammar development in a computational linguistic framework. Working within this framework, the linguist is constantly reminded that machines have the habit of 'generating' only what is explicitly specified by the grammar. Computational linguistics, therefore, can and does contribute substantially to the development and validation of an explicit model of language.

As the architects of a full-scale generative grammar construct their model they are ultimately called upon to solve those problems which have beset linguists and in particular generative linguists since descriptivism and generativism came of age. The problem of *wh* movement, for example, is not one which only linguists within the Chomskyan paradigm must solve. Any self-respecting generative theory, be it syntactically or semantically oriented, must ultimately produce a solution. Systemic functional approaches to language may be in many respects radically different from those within the Chomskyan and post-Chomskyan paradigms, but if we believe that meaning potential and a semantic system network approach can provide explanatorily adequate generative solutions then we must attempt to demonstrate it.

This is clearly not the first systemic discussion of comparison, despite what may seem to be implied by the title. It is discussed in some detail, for example, by Veltman (1982) and Halliday and Hasan (1976). What is addressed here specifically is the phenomenon of explicit comparative expansion, or more transparently, of what can follow *than* in comparative constructions. Moreover, the discussion is limited to a sub-set of comparative types. The range which any grammar must ultimately handle is illustrated and discussed by Huddleston (1967) and Quirk *et al.* (1985: 1134) and includes the following:

(1) Mary bought more records than Peter.

(2) Mary achieved more than Peter.
(3) Mary talks more than Peter.
(4) Mary is more talkative than Peter.
(5) Mary bought a more expensive car than Peter.
(6) Mary talks more quickly than Peter.
(7) Mary dictates more quickly than Peter writes.

Discussion here is restricted to the type represented by (4), that is, comparison in terms of the so-called predicative adjective. In systemic functional terms, and specifically within Fawcett's (1980) framework, we are concerned here with comparison centred around the realization of **quality of thing** as the Attribute in attributive relational processes. This is very much an Occam's razor approach, and in attempting to understand the problems involved with this one small sub-set it is hoped to throw light on the other types.

One of the problems for the generative grammarian is to account for the range of syntactic structures which can be found after the adjective in its comparative form, and I take the examples below to be representative of this range.

       It's taller . . .
  (8) . . . than five foot.
  (9) . . . than this one.
 (10) . . . than this one is.
 (11) . . . than I wanted.
 (12) . . . than (it was) yesterday.
 (13) . . . than I wanted it to be.
 (14) . . . than the shelves could hold.
 (15) . . . than would fit under the stairs.
 (16) . . . than anything that would fit under the stairs.
 (17) . . . than me.

7.2 THE STRUCTURE SET UP FOR QUALITY AND COMPARISON

For this and other related types of comparative meaning, the quantity–quality group or adjectival/adverbial group is the syntactic domain. Its structure provides three elements used by comparatives, namely: a(pex) for the quality itself, t(emperer) expounded by the item *more* (or conflated with the apex, as in the case of the morphological realization of the temperer +*er*), and the f(inisher), where we can make the standard of comparison explicit. Issues relating to the morphology of comparatives will not be discussed here.

Comparison is one form of modification or 'tempering' of a quality of thing expressed adjectivally. When a speaker chooses to temper a quality in comparative terms, he can then choose whether to make the comparison explicit or not. This, as can be seen in Figure 7.1, is realized at the finisher element of structure through structures following *than* (or *as* in

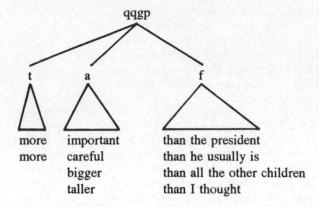

Figure 7.1 The partial structure of the quantity–quality group

'equality comparison'). We shall now examine possible structures, attempt to provide syntactic descriptions for them, propose a system network which explicates the meanings that are reflected in the various formal possibilities, and finally propose a set of realization rules.

7.3 THE SYNTACTIC STRUCTURE OF *THAN* CONSTRUCTIONS

7.3.1 General observations

Two observations at least can be made about *than* constructions in the case under examination here. First, *than* can be followed either by a nominal group or by a clause. Secondly, there appear to be various degrees of non-realization or ellipsis[1] in the structure following *than*. The construction *THAN* + NOMINAL GROUP is suggested by examples such as

(18) bigger than me
(19) taller than John

and we might represent this syntactically with *than* taken as the exponent of the **p**(reposition) in a prepositional group (pgp) and the nominal group (ngp) that follows as filling the **cv** (completive) (see Figure 7.2).

In the case of *THAN* + CLAUSE there is always some non-realization, in the sense that (20) below has one participant role missing. I take this to be a case of non-realization rather than ellipsis, since (21) is at best anomalous. We might assume, however, that there is an empty Attribute on the basis of rather uncommon clauses such as (22).

(20) than the boys are
(21) ?taller than the boys are tall
(22) John is taller than the bed is long.

An important issue here is whether it is desirable to generate a structure in which the Attribute is represented but not realized, or simply to leave this part of the structural tree totally unaccounted for. In the computational linguistics paradigm, with its concern for both generation and interpretation, we might adopt the principle that the more semantic information available in the syntax tree the easier becomes the task of deriving from it a semantic interpretation. In any case, we must provide a mechanism which generates a clause – in this case a relational clause in terms of transitivity – which has a participant role missing. In other words, when the system network for **situation** is re-entered, in order to generate the embedded *than* clause, the full range of options realized by different clause types is not available. We should remember that the justification for positing semantic options within the tempering system network, or indeed in any network, is that there is some reflex in form. The original choice of comparative and subsequent, more delicate choices determine the nature of the structure which carries them.

7.3.2 *THAN* + NOMINAL GROUP[2]

Nominal groups are essentially associated with filling participant roles in clause structure. Given that clauses are found after *than* in comparisons, we might be led to assume that the presence of a nominal group simply signals the omission of the rest of the clause, which is taken as recoverable in some way. What is there to say that *my brother* in (23) below is simply not the Subject of a clause, the rest of which is not realized? It would then be an alternative for (24) which, although still 'incomplete', at least contains a Predicator.

(23) bigger than my brother
(24) bigger than my brother is

If this were the case, everything that followed *than* could be accounted for as some more or less complete realization of a clause. A diachronic study of comparatives might well show that *than* structures started out as such, but at some stage in their development, perhaps even recently, the 'objective' form of pronouns in such structures appears, as in (25) below. This does not seem to me unrelated to the change in usage from (26) to (27).

(25) bigger than me
(26) It is I.
(27) It is me.

Quirk *et al.* (1985: 1132) discuss this point with reference to other types of comparative, giving examples such as:

(28) He loves his dog more than they.

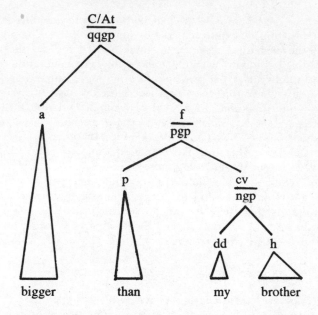

Figure 7.2 The syntax of *than* + nominal group

(29) He loves his dog more than them.

and suggest that in other styles (from the 'formal' one they are describing) (29) would replace (28), thus creating ambiguity of the kind more clearly seen in their example:

(30) He loves his dog more than his children.

They also note that in such cases *than* would be treated as a preposition in much the same way as the approach here. A significant point that they do raise is whether the use of the 'objective case' represents a meaning choice in the formal style they are describing. This point is central to systemic functional grammar, since we are attempting to capture the choices which speakers have available to them. What I wish to claim is that there is a choice between (31) and (32) below and that (33) belongs increasingly to an outdated form of language.

(31) he's taller than me.
(32) he's taller than I am.
(33) he's taller than I.

This is, of course, an arguable point, but one which takes into account the fact that usage is changing in this area. As I argue in section 7.3.1, there is a choice between simply wishing to make the comparison with a **thing** alone (the nominal group choice) or with a **thing** in a **situation** (the more explicit choice with a clause).

The presence of *than* structures with 'objective' pronouns, in the type of comparative under discussion here, is difficult to reconcile with the participant at Subject in clause structure, unless, of course, we adopt a transformational approach in which some form of 'subject to object raising' is proposed. However, such a proposal is inconsistent with the systemic linguistic principle which assumes that elements of structure are not generated and moved into their correct surface position but generated in their correct position from the start. Clearly, the underlying syntax of (34) cannot be proved to be one or the other.

(34) he's taller than John.

All that we can say is that there is a tendency to use the 'objective' pronoun in such cases or to opt for the clause with a Predicator, and, if this tendency is establishing itself, it may well be the case that, by analogy, the same underlying principle is at work when the **thing** is nominal rather than pronominal.

7.3.3 *THAN* + CLAUSE

In syntactic terms there seem to be three types of construction, all with some degree of ellipsis or non-realization. The first type, shown in the analysis in Figure 7.3, and which henceforth I shall refer to as Type I, contains a Subject which may or may not be co-referential with the Subject (or Complement) in the matrix clause (see examples (10) and (12) above). The Main Verb (M) tends to be of the same type as, and usually identical to, the Main Verb in the matrix clause.

The time reference may change as in example (12) and there may be a circumstantial role which reinforces the different time reference. The clause lacks a Complement, however. As I suggested above, we might take it that it is the participant role of Attribute which is not realized and that the Attribute would be realized by the same **quality** as the **quality** appearing at Attribute in the matrix clause. We can only speculate, however, since, unlike ellipsis, we cannot restore the clause to its 'complete' structure.

This second type of clause, henceforth Type II, is represented in Figure 7.4. This type is associated with verbs of cognition which may or may not have some form of complementation (see examples (11) and (13). When complementation is present it tends to be a clause with a Subject co-referential to the Subject in the matrix clause and an identical Main Verb. Once again the Complement is never realized and we might assume it to be the Attribute and a **quality** identical with the **quality** in the matrix clause. The range of cognitive processes which is found includes such verbs as *want, think, imagine, believe, intend, tell* and *say* Caution must be expressed at the claim that there is ellipsis after the Main Verb, since at times two types of complementation are possible, and it is therefore not always

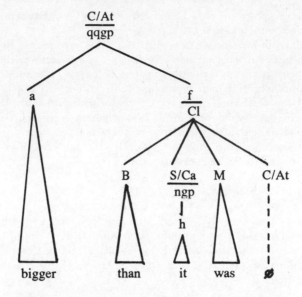

Figure 7.3 The syntax of *than* + clause (Type I)

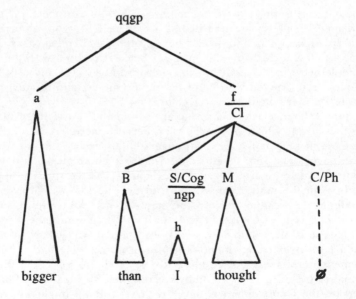

Figure 7.4 The syntax of *than* + clause (Type II)

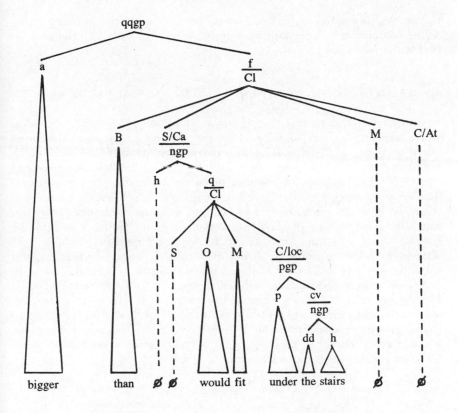

Figure 7.5 The syntax of *than* + clause (Type III)

possible to reconstruct the Complement with accuracy. The examples below illustrate this:

(35) than I believed it was
(36) than I believed it to be

The third type, henceforth Type III, although rarer than the first two, presents even greater syntactic complexity. It is illustrated by examples (14), (15) and (16) above. A possible solution to this syntactic puzzle is suggested by example (16) in which *anything* occurs after *than*. If we assume that something like *anything* is missing from the structure in (14) and (15), then we can treat whatever follows as a relative clause filling the qualifier of the head of a nominal group. The analysis in Figure 7.5 pushes this hypothesis even further by suggesting that the nominal group is in fact the Subject of an attributive clause which has a non-realized verb, identical to the verb in the matrix clause, and an unexpounded Complement/Attribute implicitly indicating an identical quality to that expressed in the matrix clause. An alternative hypothesis would be to analyse the nominal group as the completive in a prepositional group as was the case with the analysis in Figure 7.2.

7.4 SEMANTIC CONSIDERATIONS AND THE SYSTEM NETWORK

In section 7.3 I suggested that there are four major syntactic structures which appear after *than*, one based on the nominal group and three types based on the clause. We now need to examine the kinds of meaning which are conveyed by these structures, and by any more delicate variations which they may exhibit, in order to postulate a tentative system network. The syntactic categories that have been used are 'functional' in nature and therefore from the outset have a closer link with the semantics. Thus, for example, the presence of different classes of group (which relate to the realization of semantic concepts such as **thing**, **quality**, etc.), or the difference between a clause (realizing the semantic notion of **situation**) and a nominal group, is already semantically significant.

A first important semantic distinction appears to be in terms of what Huddleston refers to as 'the standard of comparison'. In other words, we are comparing something (a certain measure of quality as an attribute of a **thing**) with a standard. The standard chosen is the measure against which a comparison can be made. It is not necessarily shared information between speaker and addressee, since if I say

(37) The plant is bigger than it was yesterday.

I do not presuppose that the addressee knows how big it was yesterday, but I am suggesting, in my use of a different time reference, that the plant has changed in size over time. Gradable qualities such as 'big' or 'heavy' are in a sense inherently comparative in any case, and even to state that someone is tall is to indicate that the person mentioned is taller than the height which culturally we associate with people. The essence of comparison, therefore, would seem to be to signal change or difference.

One very obvious way of indicating difference in comparison is to give as the standard a measurement. So that, assuming that the addressee is familiar with institutionalized scales of measurement (feet, pounds, kilometres, etc.), if we say, as in example (8), that someone is

(8) taller than five foot

we are providing the addressee with a quantification with which to construe the difference.

More often than not, however, we compare the **quantity** of quality in question (how tall, how pretty, etc.) with the **quantity** of quality 'possessed' by the same thing in a difference circumstance or by a different thing. In terms of features in a system network, therefore, an initial choice is available between stating the standard as a known and conventionalized measurement (with the syntactic structure that such measurements have, and which I have not dealt with here), or stating it by reference to a thing which itself 'possesses' it. It is, I would maintain, the reference to the thing which accounts for the various degrees of non-realization. If I say that something is

(38) taller than this one

it is implicit that *this one* has a quantity of tallness. A semantically strange utterance such as

(39) ?John is happier than a pen.

is difficult to interpret, precisely because degrees of happiness are not associated with pens and the comparison is therefore not a useful one.

Let us return now to the three types of clause structure which were identified in the last section and examine how they might correlate with and reflect semantic distinctions. Type I, exemplified by (10) appears to be used when the standard of comparison is the **same thing in a different situation** or a **different thing** either in the **same situation** or in **a different situation**. We might give further examples, like those below, to illustrate this.

(40) taller than John is
(41) taller than John was at his age

We should note that when it is a question of a different thing in same situation, that is, the same process, time reference, circumstance, etc., an alternative realizational choice is THAN + NOMINAL GROUP structure. In other words, the choice of this latter structure implies that the two situations are the same.

Type II, as we have seen, contains some kind of cognition process and degrees of complementation. Here the standard of comparison is no longer simply a thing in a different situation but someone's idea of the **quantity of quality** associated it. The thing in question differs in **quantity of quality** from the mental picture that had been built up of it. It is bigger, taller, etc., than we had wanted, expected, thought or were told. The 'mental image' is of the same **thing**, however, as we can observe from the anomalous example:

(42) *he's taller than I thought John was.

Once again, the common absence of the complementation of such clauses would seem to indicate that the process and quality are implicit. The only difference, and thus the recourse to comparison, is between the thing as observed and the idea that was held about it in someone's mind, and this difference is carried by the cognition process.

Type III appears to represent an appeal to a hypothetical thing with attributes which allows us to assess the quality of the thing under comparison. To elaborate on this, taking example (15), we are invoking a hypothetical thing in a given situation which indicates a standard against which to measure the thing under comparison. In the case here, we are invoking a thing or range of things which are characterized by having the height which would permit them to fit under the stairs. This situation therefore constitutes the standard of comparison, but not simply an alternative way of representing it, since presumably, if one were choosing a cupboard to buy, for example, and gauged its height in terms of its fitting under the stairs, it would be intended to go under the stairs. This is not always the case, however, as one might say of a car:

(43) it's longer than would go in my garage.

even though no one had ever intended to park it there. Yet, even here, one might understand, through pragmatic implicature, that the speaker meant that they could never have a car of that length because it would not fit in their garage. As we saw in the proposed syntactic analysis, the situation by which the hypothetical thing is characterized is represented as a relative clause filling the qualifier in a nominal group. And, given that it is the characterizing **situation** which serves essentially as the standard of comparison, the rest of the structure tends to be unrealized.

Now that we have teased out and made a tentative gloss of the meanings realized through the various structures, it is possible to attempt the drawing of the system network which represents the meaning potential in this kind of comparison. The proposed network is shown in Figure 7.6. Many of the options have already been discussed above, but several points need still to be made. Firstly, the central criterion for the arrangement of the network appears to be the ways in which we wish to present the standard of comparison. These include:

(i) A quantified measurement.
(ii) The same **thing** in a different **situation**.
(iii) A different **thing** in the same or different **situation**.
(iv) A mental (cognitive) image of the same **thing**).
(v) A hypothetical **thing** possessing the characteristics which indicate the standard.

The different syntactic structures allow the speaker to realize the standard in these various ways, through the nominal group alone or through the nominal group in a clause where the **situation** is important in clarifying the value of the standard. The proposed system network in Figure 7.6, as can be seen, allows for all these options, including options of whether to make certain aspects of the situation or thing explicit or leave them implicit.

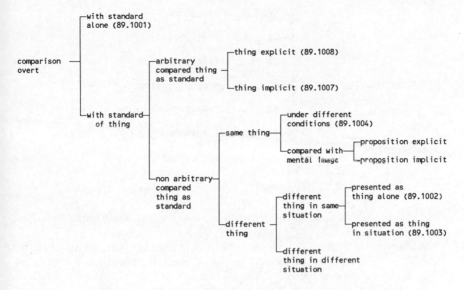

Figure 7.6 The Overt Comparison system network

7.5 REALIZATION

System networks, especially when they are semantically oriented, explain very little in generative terms unless they are accompanied by realization rules which provide the structural realization. Moreover the realization rules which need to be specified must, in a computational generative grammar, be implementable. This latter consideration highlights one of the methodological implications of computational grammars. As one develops the grammar, computational solutions are required to support the kinds of rules which are deemed necessary. But, as is inevitably the case, one cannot always predict from the outset the complete set of operations which might be required. An obvious solution to the grammar/computation interface would be to write the complete grammar of English, clarify all the types of rules and operations which are necessary for successful generation and *then* to specify them to the system designer. There are, however, clearly two disadvantages in such an approach. First, we are as yet unable to specify the whole of the grammar of English, and perhaps we never will be, and second, if we wait until we can, we cannot produce even a partial computational generator. GENESYS, the system which implements the COMMUNAL systemic functional grammar already permits an impressive amount of structural realization. As grammar writing proceeds, especially in relatively uncharted areas such as comparison, it is sometimes the case that the implementation system cannot support the kinds of syntactic operation required by the linguistic theory. This is not necessarily an insuperable problem, however, since if the kinds of operation are

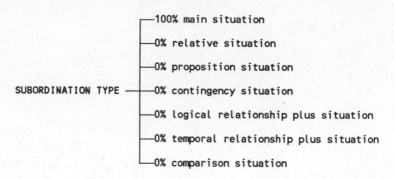

Figure 7.7 The system of clause subordination types

theoretically justified, then the implementation system may be modified to incorporate them.

Another related problem is that expansion of one area of the system network – in this case the **quality** network – often entails modification of other parts of the network. This is easily illustrated with the case of comparative constructions. As we have seen, *THAN* + CLAUSE STRUCTURE represents a type of 'subordinate clause' and this must be added to the range of options in the **situation** network (see Figure 7.7 for an illustration). The need for a feature [comparison situation] (realized as a subordinate clause with Binders such as *as* and *than*) may not be immediately evident, given that there are various types of subordinate clause structure, and clearly a single feature cannot be solely responsible for generating the necessary structure. Indeed, once an appropriate option in the 'comparison' network has been selected, the feature [comparison situation] must be **pre-selected**. In the normal generation of a matrix or main clause, [comparison situation] is not an option. What is important, however, is that the selection of other features – those which lead to the realization of the elements and exponents in such a subordinate clause – may themselves be dependent on the prior selection of [comparison situation], in the sense that it is an entry condition to the system in question. We should remember that we have the task of generating a clause with various degrees of non-realization; in none of the comparative clauses, for example, do we wish to generate the exponent of a Complement/Attribute, even though for reasons of interpretation we may wish to generate this element of structure in the clause. Furthermore, realization rules often have conditions attached to them, and these refer to the prior selection of features in the system network. Such conditions determine whether one realization or another is to be made.

Two of the most significant rules in the COMMUNAL grammar are the **re-entry rule** and the **preferences rule**. The former determines re-entry into a system network where a specific unit will be generated. If we wish to fill the Subject/Agent of a clause with a nominal group, for example, we must have a rule which effects re-entry into the **thing** network where the nominal group is generated. In the case of comparatives, where we are generating a quantity–quality group, as we need to generate a clause at finisher, then we must invoke re-entry into the **situation** network where a new (subordinate clause) can be generated. This rule, therefore, controls movement down the rank scale and allows for rank shift or embedding. The latter rule, on the other hand, controls the selection of features in the network to be re-entered. Any feature mentioned in a preferences rule will be automatically pre-selected if it is the only feature specified in a given system and if that system is entered during the traversal of the network.

Provided that the relevant features are present in a network, it is therefore possible to determine the syntactic structure which will be generated by that network. It is in such a way that we can ensure that from the choice of [comparison overt] only the types of nominal group and clause structure that can follow *than* are generated. One example of such rules will illustrate this procedure;

> 89.1003 : *presented as thing in situation* :
> *for 'f' re-enter at situation,*
> *for 'f' prefer [congruent situation,*
> *comparison sit, information, giver,*
> *relational, attributive, simple carrier at,*
> *carrier S theme presented, unmarked at,*
> *attribute as property of thing ca,*
> *as quality ca, quality recoverable].*

If we select the feature [presented as thing in situation] we are moving towards a clause of the type:

(12) . . . than it was yesterday

Naturally, aspects of temporal and spatial circumstances will be selected as required. In a complete system there will be a knowledge representation which will guide or determine these. In terms of the clause, however, we MUST select features such as [information] and [giver], since a comparative clause of this type cannot be 'imperative' or 'interrogative'. The final preferred features in the rule ensure realization of the appropriate relational process and the non-realization of the exponent of the Complement/Attribute through the feature [quality recoverable]. It may be argued that the selection of the relational process *be* may also be determined by reference to the knowledge representation of the situation, in which case it need not be specified or pre-selected. Its inclusion here, however, constrains the grammar to generating this and only this process type, hence not accepting as grammatical clauses such as:

(44) *taller than John has a book

which the grammar would otherwise generate. One would naturally expect the process *be* with this type of comparative and, if it is the only choice, it seems reasonable to constrain it within the grammar. The non-realization of the exponent of the Complement/Attribute, I would claim, must be handled by the grammar in the manner suggested above.

7.6 CONCLUSION AND IMPLICATIONS FOR OTHER FORMS OF COMPARATIVE

Quirk *et al.* (1985: 1134) identify seven different functions of the comparative item *more*, which in their terminology they list as: 'determinative', 'head of a noun phrase', 'subjunct', 'modifier of an adjective head', 'modifier of a premodifying adjective', 'modifier of an adverb' and 'modifier of a premodifying adverb'. Here I have dealt exclusively yet, I hope, extensively with comparison in terms of 'modifier of an adjective head'. Clearly, whilst suggesting possible general principles for the grammar of all the types listed, this discussion does not solve the problem of handling and generating them. Even with the closest type to the one discussed here, where the comparison is within the nominal group (see example (5)), other problems arise. The most significant is perhaps **discontinuity**; *more* accompanies the adjective at modifier, whereas the *than* clause follows the head of the nominal group, even though it belongs to the structure of the quantity–quality group. Another restriction of this type concerns the semantic relations that must hold between the sense realized by the head of the nominal group and that realized by the head of the nominal group in the comparative structure, as can be seen by the ill-formedness of examples such as:

(44) *A taller boy than Mary

It has yet to be seen whether the comparison network proposed on p. 161, if modified and expanded, would form the basis for the other types of comparison, or whether in each case a separate network will be necessary. In order to establish this, each type must be examined in detail, as has been attempted here. What is of significance, however, is that the grammar for the type discussed here provides a mechanism for ellipted and non-realized elements of structure which are a syntactic consequence of semantic choice. Such a mechanism can certainly be used with the whole range of comparative types and, indeed, in many other areas of the grammar.

NOTES

1 The distinction between **ellipsis** and **non-realization** is a necessary one. I take ellipsis to be the omission of some part of a structure that can be fully recovered. Ellipsis may also be the consequence of semantic choice. In the case of non-

realization the 'missing' elements are not clearly recoverable and the 'incomplete' structure tends to be determined by previous choices.
2 The nominal group construction following *than* in English is discussed in detail in Stassen (1985) and compared with a similar phenomenon in Dutch.

REFERENCES

Fawcett, R.P., 1980, *Cognitive Linguistics and Social Interaction: towards an Integrated Model of a Systemic Functional Grammar and the other Components of an Interacting Mind*, Heidelberg, Julius Groos, and Exeter University
Fawcett, R.P., and Tucker, G.H. (1990), 'Demonstration of GENESYS: a very large, semantically based systemic functional grammar', in *Proceedings of the Thirteenth International Conference on Computational Linguistics*, 1, pp. 47–9, Helsinki.
Halliday, M.A.K., and Hasan, Ruqaiya (1976), *Cohesion in English*, London, Longman.
Huddleston, Rodney (1967), 'More on the English comparative', *Journal of Linguistics* 3, 91–102.
Quirk, R., Greenbaum, S., Leech, G., and Svartvik, J. (1985), *A Comprehensive Grammar of the English Language*, London: Longman.
Stassen, Leon (1985), *Comparison and Universal Grammar*, Oxford, Blackwell.
Tucker, G.H. (1989), 'Natural language generation with a systemic functional grammar', in *Laboratorio degli studi linguistici, 1989/1*, Università degli studi di Camerino.
Veltman, Robert (1982), 'Comparison and intensification: an ideal but problematic domain for systemic functional theory', in James Benson and Willian Greaves, *Systemic Perspectives on Discourse*, 1, Norwood, N.J., Ablex.

ACKNOWLEDGEMENTS

The computational linguistics project that this work relates to is the COMMUNAL project at the University of Wales College of Cardiff, directed by Dr Robin Fawcett and funded by RSRE, Malvern. For accounts of the COMMUNAL natural language generator see Tucker (1989) and Fawcett and Tucker (1990).

Part IV. Functional Sentence Perspective and Theme

8 On some basic problems of Functional Sentence Perspective

Jan Firbas

8.1 INTRODUCTION

The co-founder of the linguistic school of Prague, Professor Vilém Mathesius, once said to his students that language is a fortress that must be attacked with all means and from all sides (Vachek 1972b: 69). I should like to concentrate on one of the attempts to attack this fortress or, to be exact, its part constituted by what has been termed 'functional sentence perspective' (FSP). I can only speak of an attempt, because the older I get the clearer it becomes to me what a formidable fortress we have to deal with – a fortress with a remarkable capacity to hold out.

My paper is based on my research into FSP, and will bring little new in comparison with what I have already written on FSP. In pointing out some of the most essential problems of FSP, I intend to offer an outline of the results of my research. I trust that such an outline will be found useful both by those who have already read some of my studies in FSP as well as by those who have not had the opportunity or time to acquaint themselves with them. Moreover the outline served as a framework for the FSP analysis of a text which I presented at the 1990 Workshop on Rheme in Nottingham. I should perhaps add that what I am going to offer is a fairly extensive abstract of a synthesis of my writings on FSP (Firbas forthcoming). But even an extensive abstract merely summarizes. For more detailed discussions of the problems raised I therefore beg those who are interested to refer to my previous writings or to the synthesis.

Let me start with a quotation concerning the term 'functional sentence perspective'. David Kilby (1984: 61) finds it to be a useful term – 'useful because, being a mistranslation from the Czech, it is totally meaningless and therefore unlikely to be misleading'. Believing myself to have been the first to use the term (in an English summary of a paper written in Czech, Firbas 1957: 171–3), I feel responsible for it and propose to demonstrate that it does convey some meaning after all. I hasten to add, however, that I am aware that I must not adorn myself with borrowed plumes. I must say that, in a private communication in 1956, the term was actually suggested to me by Professor Josef Vachek, prompted by Vilém Mathesius's (1929) use of the (unexpanded) German term *Satzperspektive*.

Let me first illustrate what I mean by FSP. In the spoken language, the different communicative perspectives in which a semantic and grammatical sentence structure can function are co-signalled by the different placements of its intonation centre (IC: the most prominent prosodic feature borne by the sentence structure); cf. *I flew to EDINBURGH yesterday, I FLEW to Edinburgh yesterday, I flew to Edinburgh YESTERDAY, I DID fly to Edinburgh yesterday* and *I* [IC bearer] *flew to Edinburgh yesterday*. The different placements of the IC point to a wide contextual applicability of the sentence structure in question, in other words, to its ability to serve different communicative purposes, and hence function in different perspectives.

The different placements of the IC reflect different developments of the communication. In the sentence structure under discussion, the IC co-signals the element that conveys the information towards which the development of the communication is oriented, i.e. perspectived. It co-signals the element that conveys the information completing the development of the communication and which in this respect is the most dynamic element within the sentence, carrying the highest degree of communicative dynamism (CD). It is important to note that the development of the communication need not necessarily coincide with the actual linear arrangement of the sentence elements.

By a degree of CD carried by a linguistic element (of any type or rank) I mean the relative extent to which the element contributes towards the further development of the communication. (On the hierarchy of elements as carriers of CD, see below.)

I intentionally speak of intonation co-signalling degrees of CD, for intonation does not operate independently of non-prosodic means. Intonation is not the only factor yielding signals of CD degrees. Also non-prosodic factors are in play: the contextual factor, linear modification and the semantic factor.

As intonation is a means of the spoken language, it does not operate in the written language. It is the interplay of the non-prosodic factors that determines the distribution of degrees of CD over the written sentence, i.e. its FSP. Intonation joins the interplay of FSP factors at the level of the spoken language. Before coming back to the role played by intonation in FSP, let me first concentrate on the written sentence and discuss the operation of each of the non-prosodic factors. As I shall demonstrate, an FSP factor is a formative power which in the development of the communication participates in modifying the communicative value of the semantic content of a linguistic element. It co-determines the place of this element in this development, in other words, its degree of CD.

At this point let me mention that I subscribe to the results of Vachek's extensive inquiries into the written language (e.g. 1989). They have established the written language and the spoken language as two language norms which 'differ not only materially (phonic *v.* graphic substance) but

. . . also functionally' (Vachek, 1989). Prosodic features (intonation) are absent from the written text and participate in signalling FSP only in the spoken language, i.e. also in the process of transposing written utterances into spoken utterances and vice versa. Haas (1970) aptly speaks of 'phonographic' translation.

8.2 THE CONTEXTUAL FACTOR

Context certainly presents a vexed question. For instance, Daneš regards the concept of context as vague, this – among other things – being due to the graded character of context (1974b: 109). According to Daneš, the concepts of old (given) information, known from the context, and of new (non-given) information, unknown from the context, are also vague (ibid.). Enkvist finds the concept of context to be an awkward notion to deal with (1980: 75). In discussing what she terms information structure Keijsper does not take context into consideration at all, holding that the differentiation between given and new serves no useful purpose and can therefore be abolished (1985: 73).

Nevertheless, an element conveying known information contributes less to the development of the communication than an element conveying unknown information, the former carrying a lower degree of CD than the latter. But what is to be regarded as known or unknown information in FSP? Let us look at the following two brief passages from Katherine Mansfield's short story *At the Bay*.

Beryl stepped over the window, crossed the veranda, ran down the grass to the gate.
[. . . and a very gay figure walked down the path to the gate.] It was Alice, the servant girl, dressed for her afternoon out.

The notions of 'the window', 'the veranda', 'the grass', 'the gate' and 'Alice, the servant girl' have all been mentioned in the preceding context. They are retrievable from it and in that sense dependent on it. They have become items of common knowledge shared by the writer (producer) and the reader (receiver), and in that sense old (given, known) information. However, at the moment the sentence is produced and/or perceived, i.e. in regard to the immediate communicative step to be taken, they convey new (non-given, unknown) information. They tell the reader the place Beryl ran to (the gate) and how she got there (over the window, across the veranda and down the grass), and who was just coming down the path (Alice). All this information is irretrievable from the immediately relevant context and is in this sense context-independent.

It follows that a piece of information may be retrievable from a wider context and in that sense dependent on it, but at the same time irretrievable from the immediately relevant context and in that sense independent of this narrow contextual sphere, which the language user (producer or receiver) is induced to regard as pertinent to the communicative step about to be taken. In the rest of the present paper it is in the latter, narrow sense that I use the terms 'retrievable' and 'irretrievable', and in consequence also 'context-dependent' and 'context-independent', without further specification of the contextual sphere.

All this naturally raises the question of how long a stretch of text a piece of information remains retrievable for (from the immediately relevant preceding context, that is) if not immediately re-expressed. In other words, what is the length of the retrievability span (in regard to the immediately relevant context, that is) of a piece of information?

Analysing an old English homily, Svoboda (1981) came to the conclusion that without re-expression a piece of information remained retrievable for a span not exceeding seven clauses. No statement of general validity has so far been offered concerning the exact limit to the number of clauses taking up the retrievability span. But Svoboda's observation can undoubtedly claim general validity in the sense that the retrievability span is very brief.

It is possible to approach the question of the length of the retrievability span from a different angle. One can set out to establish the distances between the items of co-referential strings in a text (going by a working definition of the co-referential string, according to which such a string is constituted by an opening item introducing a new piece of information into the text or reintroducing a piece of information after its longer absence from the text, and an item or items re-expressing such information).

Examining a chapter of a short story by Katherine Mansfield (see Firbas forthcoming) and a part of a chapter of a novel by Muriel Spark (Firbas 1989b), I found that the distances between the items of co-referential strings did not exceed three sentences (simple or complex). Distances of this extent certainly do not obliterate the retrievability of the information involved. It is worth noticing that in the texts examined the problem of the length of the retrievability span did not arise. The examination testified to the striking shortness of the retrievability spans existing in the texts.

Apart from the immediately relevant preceding verbal context, there is the immediately relevant situational context. It is constituted by two types of referent: (i) by objects that are of immediate concern both to the producer and to the receiver of the message, and (ii) by objects that in the ever changing situational context are permanently present irrespective of time and place.

(i) For instance, two friends see a ferocious dog, which naturally becomes the object of their immediate concern. 'I do hope he won't bite us,' one friend says to the other, making the pronoun *he* express a referent that is retrievable from the section of the situational context that has become immediately relevant.

(ii) Under this heading come the producer of the message (speaker or writer) and its receiver (listener or reader), people in general, nature in general and the given situation itself, conceived of in a general way. These referents are frequently expressed by such pronominal forms (pro-words) as

I, *you*, *one*, (G) *man*, (Fr) *on*, (impersonal) *it* and (existential) *there*. It is important to note that through these forms they are introduced into the text directly without pronominalizing any antecedents. The pronouns *I* and *us* in the 'dog' sentence above can serve as examples.

Cases coming under (i) are predominantly operative in the spoken language. In the written language, on the other hand, even the immediately relevant following context can be taken into account. (It can help the reader in the interpretation of the communicative purpose of a given sentence.)

Context is a very complex phenomenon. The immediately relevant context, verbal and situational, is embedded within the entire preceding context, equally consisting of a verbal part and a situational part accompanying it. In its turn, this sphere is embedded in a still wider sphere of common knowledge and experience shared by the producer and the receiver of the message. Eventually the entire contextual complex so far described is embedded within the wide context of human knowledge and experience. Needless to say, there are borderline spheres. It is the borderline sphere between the immediately relevant context and the rest of the context that is of particular importance to FSP. (See the discussion of the phenomenon of potentiality offered below.)

In regard to the immediately relevant context, the criterion of the context dependence or independence of a piece of information is the actual presence of that piece (or its referent) in, or its absence from, the immediately relevant preceding verbal context (or the immediately relevant situational context). This presence or absence is a signal of context dependence or independence. In this respect the contextual factor of FSP can be regarded as a signal-yielding force.

The narrow concept of context dependence/independence induces me to speak of cases of heterogeneity in regard to context dependence/independence. Such heterogeneity is displayed, for instance, by *'The Three Musketeers'* in *Give me 'The Three Musketeers'*, used in reply to *Which of the two books would you like to have, 'The Three Musketeers' or 'An Introduction to Metereology'?*, or by *me* in *Well, they've elected me*, used in reply to *Whom did they elect in the end?* Both *'The Three Musketeers'* and *me* convey context-dependent information, but at the same time they also convey information that is context–independent: they express the result of a choice, an irretrievable piece of information. On account of this information they become predominantly context–independent. In fact it is this piece of information towards which the communication is perspectived.

It is important that an entirely or predominantly context–dependent element carries a lower degree of CD than a context–independent element. This holds good irrespective of sentence position. Note the positions of the context–dependent *him/he* in *Why did they praise him so much?* and *He was much praised by everybody*. Note also the position of *er* in the following sentences. Provided *er* is the only context–dependent element present, it will carry the lowest degree of CD, irrespective of sentence position. The same would apply to a non-pronominal element, *Peter*, for instance, provided it is context–independent.

Er/Peter ist nach Edinburgh geflogen.
Nach Edinburgh ist er/Peter geflogen.
Geflogen ist er/Peter nach Edinburgh.
Ist er/Peter nach Edinburgh geflogen?
Nach Edinburgh flog er/Peter.

8.3 LINEAR MODIFICATION

The wording 'irrespective of sentence position' is important because linear modification must be taken into account as another important factor co-determining the distribution of degrees of CD. A clue to its operation is offered by Bolinger's observation on linear modification. He finds that 'gradation of position creates gradation of meaning when there are no interfering factors' (1952: 1125).

Inspired by Bolinger's observation, I started my inquiries into FSP on the hypothesis that linear modification gradually raises the degrees of CD in the direction from the beginning towards the end of the sentence provided it is not itself modified by other factors. I believe that this hypothesis has proved to be sound.

The operation of linear modification can be illustrated by the following triad of sentences.

Give me here John Baptist's head in a charger. (A.V.)
Give me here on a platter the head of John the Baptist. (R.V.)
Give me the head of John the Baptist here on a platter. (R.S.V.)

Under the circumstances the only element which works counter to linear modification is the contextual factor. The latter operates through the context–dependent *me*, which in the presence of context–independent elements carries the lowest degree of CD, even if it does not occupy the front position. As to the context–independent elements, in each case their linear arrangement shows a gradual rise in CD. For reasons to be given later, we are particularly interested here in the degrees of CD carried by *John Baptist's head/the head of John the Baptist, here* and *in a charger/on a platter.* It is the position (linear modification) that determines their degrees of CD. (For a detailed discussion of the FSP of these sentences see Firbas 1986b.)

Like the contextual factor, linear modification is a formative force in FSP. Unless something works counter to it, it signals degrees of CD through sentence positions. Like the contextual factor, it is a signal-yielding power.

8.4 THE SEMANTIC FACTOR

The third factor participating in the interplay of factors determining the distribution of degrees of CD over the written sentence, i.e. its FSP, is the semantic factor.

The character of the semantic content of an element, together with the character of the semantic relations into which this content enters, gives the element a certain communicative value. In the dynamics of the communication, this communicative value is necessarily modified in regard to the extent to which the element contributes to the further development of the communication, i.e. in regard to the degree of CD it carries.

If rendered context–dependent by the contextual factor, an element has the communicative value of its semantic content weakened to such an extent that irrespective of sentence position it does not exceed in CD any context–independent element.

If context–independent, then, in accordance with the character of its semantic content and the character of the semantic relations entered into, an element is either capable or incapable of working counter to linear modification. If capable of doing so, the communicative value of its semantic content is unaffected by linear modification. If it is incapable of doing so, linear modification will affect its communicative value. By way of illustration let me at least demonstrate how, on account of the character of its semantic content and the character of the semantic relations entered into, the verb participates in the development of the communication.

The verb shows a strong tendency not to complete the development of the communication if one or more of the following elements is present: a context–independent object, a context–independent subject complement, a context–independent object complement or a context–independent adverbial serving as a specification (see below); in fact, even in the absence of these context–independent elements, the verb tends to recede into the background in the presence of a context–independent subject. Needless to say, this behaviour of syntactic elements is due to the character of the semantic contents they convey and the character of the semantic relations into which they enter.

Considerations of space prevent me from dealing with the types of cases in which the strong tendency just outlined does not assert itself. A contribution to a discussion of such types has been offered, for instance, in Firbas (forthcoming).

Provided that in *Peter flew to Edinburgh yesterday* only *Peter* is context–dependent, the adverbial *to Edinburgh* exceeds the verb in CD. It does so because in expressing a context–independent notion of the goal of a motion it takes the development of the communication further than the verb, which expresses the motion itself. In this way it does not express a mere setting, i.e. mere background information, but performs the dynamic semantic function of conveying a specification (see below). It in fact completes the development of the communication and therefore carries the highest degree of CD. In regard to this development the context–

independent *to Edinburgh* proves to be a successful competitor of the verb. As long as *to Edinburgh* is context–independent, the verb cannot become the element completing the development of the communication.

Under the contextual conditions stipulated, context–independent *to Edinburgh* also acts as a successful competitor of the context–independent *yesterday* and context–dependent *Peter*. *Yesterday* expresses mere background information and therefore performs the dynamic semantic function of a setting. It performs this function as long as both *flew* and *to Edinburgh* are context–independent. It could become a successful competitor of *Peter*, *flew* and *to Edinburgh* and complete the development of the communication if all these elements were context–dependent. Under these circumstances, it would no longer act as a setting, but as a specification.

In regard to the development of the communication, competitorship is an important phenomenon testifying to the existence of various degrees of CD.

It is important that the categorial exponents of the verb should enter into competition as well. (By categorial exponents of the verb I mean the formal signals of such indications as those of person, number, tense, mood, aspect, voice, positive or negative polarity, etc. They are implemented as endings, suffixes, prefixes, auxiliaries – cf. *-s*, *-ing*, *ge-*, *-en*, *is*, *ist* in *he goes*, *She is going*, *Er ist gekommen* – or even as submorphemic features – cf. the vowel alteration in *sing*, *sang* and *sung*.) An indication conveyed by a categorial exponent completes the development of the communication if, together with all the non-verbal elements, even the notional component of the verb has been rendered context–dependent and thereby excluded from competitorship. For instance, in *He did fly to Edinburgh yesterday* the positive polarity conveyed by *did* becomes the piece of information towards which the communication is perspectived if the notional component of *fly* and the non-verbal elements both convey context–dependent information.

In regard to the development of the communication, the verb – or, rather, its notional component – performs one of two communicative roles, in other words, dynamic semantic functions: either the presentation function (Pr) or the quality function (Q).

If in *Then Peter came into the room* only *into the room* is context–dependent, the verb performs the Pr-function and perspectives the sentence to the subject *Peter*. The subject performs the dynamic semantic function of expressing a phenomenon to be presented (Ph). The adverbial performs the dynamic semantic function of expressing a setting (Set).

If in *Then Peter came into the room* only *Peter* is context–dependent, the verb perspectives the communication away from the phenomenon expressed by the subject. It assigns a quality (in the widest sense of the word) to that phenomenon. In this way it performs the Q-function and perspectives the sentence to the adverbial *into the room*. Under these circumstances the subject performs the dynamic semantic function of expressing the bearer of a quality (B) and the adverbial that of expressing a specification (Sp).

These observations point to two scales of dynamic semantic functions: the Presentation Scale (Set – Pr – Ph) and the Quality Scale (Set – B –

Q - Sp - F[urther]Sp). The two scales represent two perspectives in language. They can be fused into a Combined Scale (Set - Pr - Ph - B - Q - Sp - FSp).

In principle the scales reflect a gradual rise in degrees of CD as they are carried by context–independent elements. This interpretative arrangement in accordance with a gradual rise in CD may, but need not, coincide with the actual linear arrangement.

Through context dependence the contextual factor tends to neutralize the dynamic semantic functions, reducing their status to that of a setting. If rendered context–dependent, a dynamic semantic function may retain its original status provided that status is still distinctly signalled by the functions unaffected by context dependence. This applies especially to the B-function. A context–dependent function cannot naturally exceed in CD a context–independent function.

I trust that the usefulness of the concepts of the dynamic semantic functions and their scales have been borne out by analyses presented in Firbas (1975, 1981, 1986a, b, 1989a, b, forthcoming), as well as in Svoboda's writings (e.g. 1981, 1987). The scales occupy a central position within the system of language; peripheral cases as a rule allow of being interpreted against their background.

The strong tendency to permit the verb - or, rather, its notional component - to complete the communication only in the absence of successful competitors can be particularized as a tendency to induce the verb to mediate between elements carrying lower degrees of CD, on the one hand, and those carrying higher degrees of CD on the other. This mediatory role is invariably performed by the TMEs (temporal and modal exponents) of the verb. In terms of the development of the communication, reflected by the interpretive arrangement, they start building up the core of the message upon the foundation provided by elements carrying lower degrees of CD. The foundation-laying elements constitute the theme (Th); the core-constituting elements constitute the non-theme (non-Th).

Under the heading of thematic (foundation-laying) elements come all context–dependent elements, all elements (context–dependent or context-independent) performing the Set-function and all elements (context–dependent or context–independent) performing the B-function. The rest of the elements (all context–independent) constitute the non-Th.

Having become thematic, an element can perform different functions within the Th. It can serve as theme proper (ThPr), a ThPr oriented element, a diatheme-oriented element or a diatheme (DTh). (The arrangement used is interpretive, i.e. in accordance with a gradual rise in CD.) The credit for establishing these functions goes to Svoboda (1983). Considerations of space prevent me from discussing them in detail. A brief discussion of the following string of sentences will have to suffice.

And then Stanley appeared. He looked almost uncannily clean and brushed; he was going to town for the day. Dropping into his chair, he pulled out his watch.

[K. Mansfield; adapted]

According to Svoboda (1983), a thematic element conveying irretrievable information (*then*, *Dropping into his chair*) or information that in the immediately preceding context appeared in the non-theme (*He* of the second sentence) is to be regarded as diathematic. A piece of thematic information re-expressed in the next sentence (*he* of the third and *he* of the fourth sentence) serves as ThPr. ThPr always carries the lowest degree of CD within the Th, and hence within the entire sentence (clause). DTh always carries the highest degree of CD within the Th. A thematic element ranking between ThPr and DTh stands closer either to ThPr and is therefore regarded as ThPr-oriented or to the DTh and is therefore regarded as DTh-oriented.

In terms of the development of the communication, reflected by interpretative arrangement, the place taken up by the verb in this development and the significance of this place can be described as follows. Within the non-Th, the lowest degree of CD goes with the mediatory role of linking the non-Th on to the Th. As has been mentioned above, (in verbal clauses of any rank) this role is invariably performed by the TMEs. The competitorless element completing the development of the communication and carrying the highest degree of CD in the non-Th serves as rheme proper (RhPr). Between TrPr and RhPr rank the elements serving as TrPr-oriented elements, the rest of transition (Tr) and the rhematic elements not serving as RhPr. For a discussion of these functions, may I refer the reader, for instance, to Firbas (1986a, 1987a, 1989b, forthcoming)? Let me just point out that a context–independent notional component of a verb performing the Pr-function serves as Tr. Also transitional is a context-independent notional verbal component performing the Q-function in the presence of successful competitors. (In their absence, as has been shown, it completes the communication and becomes RhPr.)

Neither the thematic nor the non-thematic elements are invariably linked with sentence position. If in *Peter flew to London yesterday* only *Peter* is context–dependent (d), the following interpretation applies:

Peter		flew	to London	yesterday
d, b, Th	TrPr; Q, Tr		Sp, RhPr	Set, Th

The two contextual applications of *Then Peter came into the room* – with *into the room* as the only context–dependent element in the first application and with *Peter* as the only context–dependent element in the second – yield the following interpretations:

	Then	Peter	came	into the room
(1)	Set, Th	Ph, RhPr	TrPr; Pr, Tr	d, Set, Th
(2)	Set, Th	d, B, Th	TrPr; Q, Tr	Sp, RhPr

Note that in the following sentence, in which only *Du* and *mir* are assumed to be context–dependent, the notional component of the verb is transitional although occurring in the end position. The degrees of CD of the items of the string of specifications, however, are determined by linear modification (Firbas 1986b).

Du mußt	mir	sofort	auf einer Schlüssel	den Kopf des Täufers Johannes		geben
d, B, Th TrPr	d, Set, Th	Sp, Rh	FSp, Rh	FSp, RhPr	TrPr; Q, Tr	

The fact that in my approach neither the thematic nor the non-thematic elements are invariably linked with sentence positions necessitates a distinction between two starting points: one conceived of as the beginning of the actual linear arrangement and hence identical with the beginning of the sentence, and the other conceived of as the beginning of an interpretative arrangement reflecting a gradual rise in degrees of CD and hence the development of the communication. These are the interpretative arrangements yielded by the three sentences adduced above:

Peter	yesterday	flew	to London
Th	Th	TrPr;Tr	RhPr

into the room	then	came	Peter
Th	Th	TrPr; Tr	RhPr

Peter	then	came	into the room
Th	Th	TrPr; Tr	RhPr

Du	mir	mußt	geben	sofort	auf einer Schlüssel	den Kopf des Täufers Johannes
Th	Th	TrPr	TrPr;Tr	Rh	Rh	RhPr

Like the contextual factor and linear modification, the semantic factor is a formative power in FSP. The signals it yields are the character of the semantic contents and the character of their semantic relations.

In determining the functional perspective of a semantic and grammatical sentence structure, all the signals yielded by the interplay of FSP factors must be taken into account. For instance, the thematicity or rhematicity of *Peter*, as well as the FSP status of each of the other constituents of the first three sentences above, is due to different outcomes of the interplay of factors, each outcome yielding different complexes of signals. A simple FSP signal is, of course, yielded by the TMEs as implementers of TrPr. This function is performed by them invariably.

8.5 FACTORS, SIGNALS AND CARRIERS OF CD

At this point let me insert a note on the concepts of factor and signal. In examining the development of the communication, I have attempted to demonstrate what roles are played by context, linear modification, semantics, and in the spoken language also by intonation, in determining the extent to which a linguistic element contributes to the further development of the communication, i.e. the degree of CD carried by the element. Bringing about the distribution of degrees of CD over the sentence (i.e. its FSP), context, linear modification, semantics and in the spoken language also intonation act as formative forces or factors. They assert themselves through their specific means exemplified here and treated as signals.

It may be asked how many degrees of CD a sentence can show and whether every sentence has a theme and a non-theme. As long as a linguistic element of any type or rank conveys some meaning, it participates in the development of the communication and becomes a carrier of a degree of CD. Through grammatical structure the linguistic elements are ultimately organized into sentences, which in the act of communication serve as distributional fields of degrees of CD. Within these fields, the syntactic constituents subject, object, subject complement, object complement, adverbial element, as well as conjunction, serve as communicative units. A special case is presented by the verb. Its notional component and its categorial exponents are considered to act as two communicative units, mainly because the TMEs invariably serve as transition proper (cf. the interpretations of the finite verb forms in the preceding section).

Realizable by more than one element, a sentence constituent can carry more degrees of CD than one. It follows that every communicative unit is a carrier of CD, but not every carrier of CD necessarily acts as a communicative unit.

For instance, the sentence structure *He said that Peter had flown to Edinburgh* provides a distributional field of degrees of CD, within which the object clause serves as a communicative unit. In its turn, this communicative unit provides a distributional sub-field of degrees of CD. In this way, one communicative unit shows a greater number of degrees of CD. (At its lower level, the sub-field has its own communicative units, which are regarded as units of lower rank than those of the basic distributional field.)

In fact even a semantic feature without a formal implementation of its own in the written language is a 'linguistic element' and is therefore to be regarded as a carrier of CD: for example, the contrast implicit in *Peter stayed in Stirling and Paul decided to go to Edinburgh*. The contrast raises the degrees of CD carried by the two communicative units without itself becoming a communicative unit. The number of degrees of CD shown by a distributional field of CD need not necessarily coincide with the number of its communicative units, but may exceed it.

Viewed against the background of the operation of the two dynamic semantic scales, the Presentation and the Quality Scales, the question of whether every sentence has a Th and a non-Th can be answered as follows. The sentence need not invariably contain a Th. But in order to fulfil a communicative purpose it must contain an element towards which the communication can be perspectived. For instance, if *Rain is falling* conveys only context–independent information, it implements the Presentation Scale without realizing the thematic Set-function. This entails the following interpretative arrangement:

```
    is    -ing   fall-   rain
   TrPr   TrPr    Tr     RhPr
```

8.6 POTENTIALITY

It occasionally happens that the signals yielded by the interplay of factors do not determine FSP unequivocally, leaving room for more than one interpretation. Such situations create the phenomenon of potentiality, the possibility of more interpretations than one being potentially present. Out of the six clauses (Matt. 13.2, 27.17, 27.17, 13.2, 26.57, 27.1) quoted below, the last but one shows equivocalness. (1, 3, 5 and 6 are quotations from the Moffatt Bible, and 2 and 4 from the Good News Bible).

1. [but,] as great crowds gathered to him, [he entered a boat and sat down, while all the crowd stood on the beach.]
2. [At every Passover Festival the Roman governor was in the habit of setting free one prisoner the crowd asked for. . . . So] when the crowd gathered, [Pilate asked them, . . .]
3. [so] when they had gathered, [Pilate said to them, . . .]
4. The crowd that gathered round him was so large that he got into a boat and sat in it, while the crowd stood on the shore.
5. [but those who had seized Jesus took him away to the house of Caiaphas the high priest], where the scribes and elders had gathered.
6. When morning came, all the high priests and the elders took counsel against Jesus, so as to have him put to death.

In clause 1, *to him* is context–dependent, conveying information retrievable from the immediately relevant context. (The presence of the information in this contextual section is a signal yielded by the contextual factor.) The elements *great crowds* and *gathered* are context–independent. The irretrievability of 'great crowds' permits the non-generic indefinite article to act as a co-signal of context independence.

By way of experiment, let me replace *gathered* by *came*. The verb *come* explicitly expresses the meaning of appearing on the scene and under the contextual conditions stipulated performs the Pr-function, perspectiving the communication towards the subject *Great crowds*, which expresses the phenomenon to be presented. (The non-genericness of the indefinite article and the insufficient determination indicated by it, as well as the character of the semantic content of the notional component of the verb, are signals yielded by the semantic factor.)

The verb *gather*, actually used in clause 1, does not express appearance on the scene explicitly, but under the conditions stipulated it does so with sufficient implicitness. Like *come*, it performs the Pr-function and perspectives the sentence to the subject *great crowds*, which performs the Ph-function. The clause under examination implements the Presentation Scale. In the above examined interplay of FSP factors, linear modification cannot assert itself, because both the contextual factor and the semantic factor operate counter to linear modification.

In 2 *the crowd* is a context–dependent element. The context dependence of 'crowd' permits the deicticness of the definite article to act as co-signal of context dependence. (Not every definite article can co-signal context dependence; cf. the definite articles referring back beyond the immediately relevant preceding context, for instance those accompanying the nouns *window*, *veranda*, *grass*, *gate* and *girl* in the example sentences adduced in section 8.2.) The context dependence of the notion 'crowd' is further borne out by possible pronominalization; see *they* of 3. In the absence of successful competitors, the notional component of *gather*, performing the Q-function, expresses the piece of information towards which the clause is perspectived. Both 2 and 3 implement the Quality Scale.

In 4, *gather* appears in a clause attributed to *The crowd*. Within this clause it functions in the same way as in 2 and 3. *The crowd* is the head of an expanded subject, which in its entirety performs the B-function and is therefore thematic. *Crowd* is context–independent; the definite article linked with it does not refer back to the immediately relevant context. The notion of 'largeness' is expressed by a predicative adjective, which performs the Q-function and appears in the non-theme. Within it the notion of 'largeness' is brought together with the notions of its consequences. Sentence 4 implements the Quality Scale.

The interpretation of 5 is not so straightforward as those of 1, 2, 3 and 4. True enough, the subject conveys context–independent information, the definite article accompanying it not referring back to the immediately relevant context, but beyond it. This permits us to interpret 5 in the same way as 1.

But the definite article does not refer back to a distant section of the preceding context, only to the section adjacent to the immediately relevant context. The scribes and elders play an important role in the drama and have been mentioned in the borderline area between the immediately relevant preceding context and the rest of the preceding context. Under these circumstances *gather* may not express appearance on the scene with sufficient explicitness, which may induce the interpreter to perspective the communication away from the persons to the act of their assembling. According to this interpretation, 5 would implement the Quality scale.

Both interpretations are potentially present. Nevertheless, in view of the strong tendency which in the absence of other successful competitors induces a context–independent subject to exceed the verb in CD, the Ph-perspective is the more probable interpretation.

A French version (*La Bible de Jérusalem*) removes potentiality by giving full play to linear modification:

[Ceux qui avaient arrêté Jésus l'emmenèrent chez Caïphe le Grand Prêtre] où se réunirent les scribes et les anciens.

In 6 the subject *all the high priests and the elders of the people* unequivocally performs the B-function. The verb neither explicitly nor implicitly expresses appearance on the scene. The sentence is perspectived to *so as to have him put to death*; it implements the Quality Scale.

As for the spoken language, the interpretations offered require the IC to be put on the element towards which the given sentence is perspectived. Potentiality shown by 5 would be removed by the placement of the IC either on *gathered* or on *the scribes and elders*. (The problem of correspondence between the distribution of degrees of CD as determined by the interplay of the non-prosodic FSP factors and the distribution of degrees of prosodic prominence will be taken up in section 8.7.)

The study of cases of unequivocal interplay of FSP factors makes us aware of the necessity to distinguish between the interpretation of the producer, that of the receiver and that of the objective observer, a role to be taken up by the linguist.

Keijsper finds a theory of FSP that reckons with potentiality as inadequate, because it does not invariably offer straightforward solutions (1985: 64). But language is not a rigidly closed system. This cannot be disregarded by a theory striving at an adequate account of language. Contrary to Keijsper's view, I therefore find it necessary to reckon with potentiality. Further research may, of course, reduce the number of types of potentiality. Potentiality, however, is a fact that merits the linguist's attention.

8.7 INTONATION

In the spoken language the interplay of FSP factors is joined by intonation. The signals yielded by this factor are the various degrees of prominence shown by the prosodic features. A relationship between these degrees of prosodic prominence (PP) and the degrees of CD as determined by the interplay of non-prosodic FSP factors is indicated, for instance, by O'Connor and Arnold's observations (1973: 5).

Describing the tone unit, O'Connor and Arnold (pp. 31-6) distinguish between its salient and its non-salient parts. The salient part is constituted by the head and the nucleus, and the non-salient part by the prehead and the tail. The stresses within the head are regarded as accented and the stresses within the prehead and the tail as unaccented. All this suggests a gamut of degrees of salience – in other words, prosodic prominence (PP) – that are linked by O'Connor and Arnold with degrees of informativeness.

The basic gamut of degrees of PP is made up by absence of stress, unaccented stress, accented stress and nuclear stress. But this gamut must be extended if the operation of linear modification in the spoken language is taken into account. It is assumed that linear modification asserts itself in lending the second of any two successive prosodic features of the same rank (for instance, two unstressed elements, two nucleus bearers) a higher degree of PP. The most important modification of this observation is necessitated by a low rise occurring after a fall within one distribution field of PP (provided by a sentence, subclause, semiclause or noun phrase). Such a low rise is regarded as prosodically less prominent than the preceding fall (cf., e.g., Halliday 1970: 38; O'Connor and Arnold 1973: 82; Quirk *et al.* 1985: 1601).

I `like ʻchocolate.

[O'Connor and Arnold 1973: 83]

It must be remembered that what has been termed a communicative unit can bear more prosodic features than one. But, in determining the mutual relations of the communicative units in regard to PP, it is their representative features that are relevant. (By a representative prosodic feature of a communicative unit I understand the most prominent prosodic feature borne by it.)

Examining the relationship between the distribution of degrees of CD as determined by the interplay of the non-prosodic FSP factors (non-prosodic CD distribution) and the distribution of degrees of PP (PP distribution), I have come to the following conclusions.

The basic type of relationship between the two distributions is their perfect correspondence. (The example sentence is taken from Arnold and Tooley 1972: 5.)

He'   ll   'come round with   `Marjory,   he   ₀says
(Th   TrPr   'TrPr;Tr   `'RhPr)RhPr Th   ₀TrPr;Tr

The PP distribution perfectly reflects the non-prosodic CD distribution. A rise in PP reflects a rise in CD. The interpretative arrangement is the following.

Th ₀TrPr;Tr   (Th TrPr   'TrPr;Tr   `RhPr)RhPr

Against the background of perfect correspondence between the two distributions, we can speak of the following types of prosodic intensification of the non-prosodic CD distribution:

1. Non-re-evaluating prosodic intensification:

    (a) Non selective.
    (b) Selective.

2. Re-evaluating prosodic intensification.

Example sentences (taken from Arnold and Tooley 1972; 59, 25, 39) follow.

(1a). He   's   'such a per^fectionist
       Th   TrPr;Tr   '^RhPr

The PP distribution reflects the relations within the non-prosodic CD distribution. None of the communicative units deviates from this perfect correspondence. But the rise–fall is marked. Its use prosodically intensifies RhPr The markedness of the nucleus conveys additional attitudinal information – the speaker's wish specially to emphasize his friend's perfectionism. In consequence, it raises the degree of CD carried by RhPr. Not affecting the Th–Rh relationship, this prosodic intensification is classified as non-re-evaluating. It will become evident from the comments on (1b) why it is also classified as non-selective.

(1b). `All this 'travelling      makes   me   `ravenous
       '^Th   TrPr;Tr   Th   `RhPr

Once again, the Th–Rh relation remains unaffected. In this respect the two distributions are in perfect correspondence. There is, however, now deviation from perfect correspondence between the two distributions: the transitional *makes* is prosodically weaker than the thematic *All this travelling*. The latter has been prosodically intensified; in other words, it has been selected for prosodic intensification. (No such deviation is shown by sentence (1a), whose prosodic intensification has therefore been classified as non-selective.) The prosodic intensification of (1b) is selective but non-re-evaluating.

It is worth noticing that in an overwhelming majority of cases it is the most dynamic element of the Th (i.e. the one carrying the highest degree of CD in the Th) that is selected for intensification at the expense of the transitional verb, or merely its TMEs.

PP distribution does not obliterate the non-prosodic CD distribution. The TMEs, frequently together with the notional component of the verb, start building up the non-Th upon the foundation provided by the Th. Prosodic intensification may raise the CD of the Th, but the further development of the communication, taken up by TrPr, starts at a CD level higher than that of the Th.

(2)   [`Robert's $_o$coming.] 'He   mustn't $_o$see   it   yet.
       Th   TrPr;Rh   TrPr;Rh   Th   TrPro >
       'RhPr   TrPr;Th $_o$TrPr;Th   Th   Th

Provided only *He* is context–dependent, the non-prosodic CD distribution perspectives the sentence to *n't* and ultimately to *see*. But the PP distribution places the IC on *He*. In this way it strikingly deviates from perfect correspondence between the two distributions by affecting the Th–Rh relationship as determined by the non-prosodic FSP factors. This deviation is highly functional, serving a special communicative purpose. Under the circumstances, it effectively underlines the speaker's concern that the very person not to see the object is Robert.

Without obliterating the non-prosodic CD distribution, intonation adds a new dimension to the message, re-perspectiving it to *He*. This element becomes the main bearer of the additional heavy emotional information. On account of it, *He* becomes predominantly context–independent and carries the highest degree of CD. In this way the Th–Rh relationship as determined by the interplay of the non-prosodic FSP factors has been re-evaluated by intonation. The symbol >, placed at the end of the line offering the interpretation of the non-prosodic CD distribution, indicates and introduces this re-evaluation. (For a more detailed treatment of re-evaluating prosodic intensification see Firbas 1985, 1987b, forthcoming.) Let me add that the TMEs are regarded as continuing to serve as TrPr. (For further examples, more detailed discussions and analyses of texts see Firbas 1985, 1987b, 1989a, forthcoming.)

It follows that, in regard to perfect correspondence between the non-prosodic CD distribution and the PP distribution, intonation acts as a mere reflecter of the non-prosodic CD distribution, or as its intensifier, which either leaves unaffected the Th–Rh relationship as determined by the non-prosodic CD distribution or re-evaluates it.

But, like the spoken language, the written language is not a rigidly closed system. A peripheral feature *sui generis* is the inattentive interpreter's automatic placement of the IC on the last stressed word of the sentence. Such an automatic placement cannot obliterate the non-prosodic CD distribution but will more or less blur it. An instance of such a placement would be the occurrence of an IC on *gathered* in *as great crowds gathered to him*, discussed here in section 8.6 (see example (1)).

As a factor of FSP intonation does not operate independently of the non-prosodic FSP factors. It is not the only factor determining the place of an element in the development of the communication, i.e. its degree of CD. On the other hand, being an FSP factor, intonation is of course capable of raising the degrees of CD. Seen in this light, the concept of CD cannot be identified with that of PP.

As I have attempted to demonstrate, the distribution of degrees of CD over the elements of a sentence constitutes FSP. The CD distribution is determined by an interplay of factors: the contextual factor, linear modification, the semantic factor and – in the spoken language – also intonation. The way these factors operate bears out that FSP is a system, one of the systems that constitute the system of language (cf. Vachek's view of language as a system of systems, 1958).

Recalling Mathesius's dictum that language is a fortress that must be attacked from all sides, let me add that my approach, or my attempt at an attack, if you like, is not identical with Halliday's. A special comparison of the two approaches would be necessary to establish the similarities and the differences. A few notes towards such a comparison have been offered in Firbas (1987a), where I have emphasized that 'any functional approach to language – even if not following the same paths – can benefit from the investigations concerning the beginning of the sentence carried out by M.A.K. Halliday' (1987a: 44). Needless to say, it is not only for these inquiries that Halliday's approach has had a world-wide impact on linguistic thought.

8.8 CONCLUSION

Coming to the close of my paper, let me recall that I have set out to justify the usefulness of the term 'functional sentence perspective '. I have attempted to demonstrate that in the act of communication a semantic and grammatical sentence structure indeed functions in a definite perspective, being oriented through the distribution of degrees of CD towards the element carrying the highest CD degree. 'Functional' stresses the immediate relevance to the act of communication, in which a sentence structure functions in order to fulfil a communicative purpose; it stresses the dynamic character of the perspective involved. (Perspective can be conceived of in a static, non-functional way, cf., for example, the active or passive perspective of a sentence, viewed out of context, either of which can appear in different functional perspectives when employed in the act of communication.)

SELECTIVE REFERENCE LIST OF ABBREVIATIONS AND COMMENTS ON SOME TERMS

B	Bearer of a quality.
B-function	Function of expressing a bearer of a quality.
d	Context-dependent (abbreviation used in diagrammatic interpretations).
DTh	Diatheme.
FSp	Further Specification.
IC	Intonation centre.
non-prosodic FSP factors	Factors the interplay of which determines the non-prosodic CD distribution.
non-Th	Non-theme (all elements OTHER THAN theme elements, i.e. all context-dependent elements, all elements (context-dependent or context-independent) fulfilling the Set(ting) function and all elements performing the B(earer)- function); also referred to as the core of the message.
non-thematic	Core-constituting (an explanatory synonym for non-thematic).

Ph	Phenomenon to be presented.
Ph-function	The function of expressing the phenomenon to be presented.
PP	Prosodic prominence.
PP distribution	Distribution of prosodic prominence.
Pr	Presentation.
Pr-function	The function of presentation, i.e. of introducing into the communication the phenomenon to be presented.
Q	Quality.
Q-function	Function of expressing a quality.
RhPr	Rheme proper (the element carrying the highest degree of CD within the rheme). Such an element completes the development of the communication; it is the element towards which the communication is perspectived; in this sense it deserves the designation 'proper'. Other rhematic elements may, but need not, be present. If present, they do not complete the communication in the narrow sense of the word indicated.
Scales	Presentation Scale: Set – Pr – Ph 　　Quality Scale: Set　　　　　– B – Sp – F[urther]Sp 　　Combined Scale: Set – Pr – Ph – B – Sp – FSp.
Set	Setting.
Sp	Specification.
Th	Theme (all context-dependent elements, all elements (context-dependent or context-independent) fulfilling the Set(ting) function and all elements (context-dependent or context-independent) performing the B(earer)-function).
theme	Foundation (an explanatory synonym for theme).
thematic	Foundation-laying.
ThPr	Theme proper (an element that if present performs a thematic function which is always linked with the lowest degree of CD within the theme, and in consequence also within the entire sentence).
TMEs	Temporal and modal exponents (of the verb).
TrPr	Transition proper (the carrier of the lowest degree of CD within the non-theme; it links the non-theme on to the theme).

REFERENCES

Arnold, G.F., and Tooley, O.M. (1972), *Say it with Rhythm* 3, London, Longman.
Bolinger, D.L. (1952), 'Linear modification', *PMLA* 42, 1117–47.
Breivik, L.E., (ed.) (1989), *Essays on English Language in Honour of Bertil Sundby*, Oslo, Novus.
Cooper, C., and Greenbaum, S. (eds) (1986), *Studying Writing: Linguistic Approaches*, Beverly Hills, Sage.
Daneš, F. (ed.) (1974a), *Papers on Functional Sentence Perspective*, Prague, Academia.
—— (1974b), 'Functional sentence perspective and the organization of the text', in Daneš (1974a), 106–28.
Enkvist, N. E. (1980), 'Categories of situational context from the perspective of stylistics', *Language Teaching and Linguistics*, 1980, 75–94.
Firbas, J. (1957), 'K otázce nezákladových podmetu v soucasné anglictine' (On the problem of non-thematic subjects in contemporary English), *Casopis pro moderní filologii* 39, 22–42, 165–73. See also Firbas (1966).
—— (1966), 'Non-thematic subjects in contemporary English', *Travaux linguistiques de Prague* 2, 239–56. An abridged English version of Firbas (1957).
—— (1975), 'On the thematic and the non-thematic section of the sentence', in Ringbom (1975), 317–34.
—— (1981), 'Scene and perspective', *Brno Studies in English* 14, 37–79.
—— (1985), 'Thoughts on functional sentence perspective, intonation and emotiveness', *Brno Studies in English* 16, 11–48.
—— (1986a), 'On the dynamics of written communication', in Cooper and Greenbaum (1986), 40–71.
—— (1986b), 'A case study in the dynamics of written communication', in Kastovsky and Szwedek (1986), 859–76.
—— (1987a), 'On two starting points of communication', in Steele and Threadgold (1987), vol. 1, 23–46.
—— (1987b), 'Thoughts on functional sentence perspective, intonation and emotiveness', 2, *Brno Studies in English* 17, 9–49.
—— (1989a), 'Interpreting Psalm 91 from the point of view of functional sentence perspective', in Breivik (1989), 107–16.
—— (1989b), 'Degree of communicative dynamism and degrees of prosodic prominence', *Brno Studies in English* 18, 21–66.
—— (forthcoming), *Functional Sentence Perspective in Written and Spoken Communication*.
Haas, W. (1970), *Phono-graphic Translation*, Manchester, Manchester University Press.
Halliday, M.A.K. (1970), *A Course in Spoken English: Intonation*, London, Oxford University Press.
Kastovsky, D., and Szwedek, A. (eds) (1986), *Linguistics across Historical and Geographical Boundaries* 1, Berlin, Mouton de Gruyter.
Keijsper, C.E. (1985), *Information Structure*, Amsterdam, Rodopi.
Kilby, D. (1984), *Descriptive Syntax and the English Verb*, London, Croom Helm.
Mathesius, V. (1929), 'Zur Satzperspektive im modernen Englisch', *Archiv für das Studium der neueren Sprachen und Literaturen* 84. 155, 202–10.
O'Connor, J.D., and Arnold, G.F. (1973), *Intonation of Colloquial English*, 2nd ed., London, Longman.
Quirk, R., Greenbaum, S., Leech, G., and Svartvik, J. (1985), *A Comprehensive Grammar of the English Language*, Harlow, Longman.

Ringbom, H. (ed,) (1975), *Style and Text: Studies presented to Nils Erik Enkvist*, Stockholm, Skriptor.
Steele, R., and Threadgold, T. (eds) (1987), *Language Topics: Essays in Honour of Michael Halliday*, Amsterdam, Benjamins.
Svoboda, A. (1981), *Diatheme*, Brno, Masaryk University.
—— (1983), 'Thematic elements', *Brno Studies in English* 15, 49–85.
—— (1987), 'Functional perspective of the noun phrase', *Brno Studies in English* 17, 61–86.
Vachek, J. (1958), 'Some notes on the development of language seen as a system of systems', *Proceedings of the Eighth International Congress of Linguists*, pp. 418–19, Oslo, Oslo University Press.
—— (ed.) (1972a), *Z klasického období prazské školy* (From the classical period of the Prague School), Prague, Academia.
—— (1972b), 'Epilogue', in Vachek (1972a), 67–73.
—— (1989), *Written Language Revisited*, Amsterdam, Benjamins.

ACKNOWLEDGEMENTS

My sincere thanks are due to Martin Davies and Peter Fries for all their valuable suggestions about the final version of this paper.

9 Towards an understanding of the notion of Theme: an example from Dari

Linda Stump Rashidi

9.1 INTRODUCTION

An area that has been attracting much attention lately within systemic linguistics is the notion of Theme. Research on how Theme functions in English is flourishing. Yet the concept of Theme is still loosely defined and tightly tied to its realization in English. Most recent work on expository English (in particular that of Berry,[1] Fries and Jordan) assumes, following Halliday (1967, 1985), that the topical Theme is the first ideational element in the clause and proceeds to analyse Theme from that given. If we are going to come to any kind of functional understanding of the concept of Theme, we must investigate message structure in languages other than English and attempt to separate the IDEA of Theme from its REALIZATION. I would like to take a step in this direction by investigating the Theme/Rheme structure of a Dari (Afghan Persian) narrative. In order to establish a foundation from which to work, I will first explore the concept of Theme and attempt to set up a substantive operational definition. I will then analyse the message structure of a section of an oral Dari narrative. From this analysis I will discuss what I perceive to be the thematic and rhematic elements of the clauses and how they contribute to the flow of the discourse.

9.2 BACKGROUND

The earliest notions of Theme were quite semantically based. Most of our current understanding of Theme within systemic linguistics arises from the work of V. Mathesius, the founder of the Prague school, and later F. Trávníček's exposition and criticism of the ideas of Mathesius (Firbas 1966a). Mathesius's notion of Theme is tied to the criterion of known/unknown information from the decoder's point of view, or, probably more accurately, from the encoder's assessment of the decoder's point of view. But this concept of known is a broad one, including what is accessible from the text, either anaphorically or cataphorically, the context of situation, or even the gnostology[2] of the decoder. Trávniček objected to the inclusion of this broad concept of known as a criterion for themehood. He narrows but delineates the concept of Theme to 'the sentence element that links up directly with the object of thought, proceeds from it and opens the sentence thereby' (Firbas 1966a: 269).

Jan Firbas, in an effort both to replace the known/unknown criterion and to establish a more precise working definition of Theme, proposed the criterion of communicative dynamism (CD) (Firbas 1966a, b, and chapter 8 above). CD is a relational concept. The degree of CD carried by a sentence element is the extent to which it pushes the communication forward. Theme is the sentence element that carries the lowest degree of CD within the sentence. As such, Theme need not necessarily contain known information; a sentence may, in fact, contain only unknown information, in which case the unknown element with the least CD is Theme.

Firbas does not use either the known/unknown dichotomy of the early Prague school or Halliday's Given/New. Instead, he speaks of context-dependency or -independency. A sentence constituent is context-dependent if it is retrievable from the immediate context, either verbal or situational (Firbas 1987). Context-dependency is a complex and graded phenomenon; an item, such as a pronoun, that is retrievable from the immediate situation contributes more to CD than a textually given item but less than a context-independent item. So while for Firbas known/unknown is not part of the essential definition of Theme, it is not irrelevant. This is still a notion of Theme that is highly semantic and inextricably linked to the notion of known/unknown.

For Firbas, and Mathesius and Trávniček before him, Theme is essentially, in Hallidayan terms, ideational and highly content-based. It is also a notion that has firm psychological underpinnings. In the normal course of conveying information, human speech works to produce a linear string of elements, and these elements follow each other in ascending order of the degree of CD contained, provided there is no overriding interference such as contrast or marked intonation. So the usual order is *theme–transition–rheme*. (Firbas posits a unit of message structure between Theme and Rheme which he calls Transition.) The order, however, may vary. Different linear arrangements can produce different orientations, but do not necessarily do so (Firbas 1987: 40). Unlike Halliday, Firbas does not tie the recognition of Theme to sentence-initial position. Firbas would not, for example, distinguish between the following (Firbas 1966b: 243):

A fly / settled / on his hair.
Rheme   Theme

On his hair/   a fly / settled.
Theme   Rheme

(The verb *settled* adds little beyond the mere fact of 'appearance on the scene' and thus lacks CD altogether.) Thus Firbas determines CD, and therefore Theme, by considering the interplay of various factors, including linear arrangement, intonation (in spoken language), context-dependency/independency and semantic content.

Theme, in the early Prague school sense of sentence-level Theme, seems to receive little attention outside systemic and functional linguistics. Most not immediately connected with Hallidayan linguistics equate Halliday's concept of Theme with Topic. For example, Chafe (1976) discusses the various packaging statuses that a noun may have. He uses Halliday extensively but in the end treats Topic and Theme as synonymous terms (p. 49). It is interesting to note that Topic is the only packaging device that Chafe discusses that has varying definitions cross-linguistically. For him, Topic in a topic-prominent language such as Chinese is a different notion from Topic in a subject-prominent language such as English. He states that what the term topic means 'seems to differ from language to language' (1976: 55). And none of these notions of Topic is the same as the notion of Theme, as we are defining it here.

Analysing case in Persian, Ali Asghar Aghbar (1981) also uses Halliday's conceptualization of Theme in discussing 'topicalization'. Like Chafe, Aghbar makes use of the notion of 'psychological subject'. He restates Halliday's definition of Theme as 'that part of the clause about which a message has been asserted and which usually occurs in sentence-initial position' (p. 179). He adds that he will call this notion Topic and proceeds to discuss topicalization, not thematization. Aghbar's points on topicalization in Persian are valid and interesting but they may or may not be pertinent to thematization in Persian.

9.3 A DEFINITION OF THEME

In trying to come to some kind of understanding of this elusive notion, several parameters of Halliday's Theme have surfaced. First of all, Theme is encoder-oriented; it is 'what I, the speaker, choose to take as my point of departure' (Halliday 1985: 278). Second, thematic structure is what 'gives the clause its character as a message' (1985: 38). Theme is what the clause is about; 'it is that with which the clause is concerned' (ibid.). Third, 'Theme is the element which serves as the point of departure of the message' (ibid.). Halliday has made a number of assertions here: (i) Theme takes a speaker point of view rather than a hearer point of view; (ii) Theme is a psychological notion, not just a packaging strategy; (iii) Theme is essentially a clausal element represented by a single constituent.

These parameters distinguish Theme from other related notions. First, Theme is not to be equated with Given (or Known), which is decoder-oriented as opposed to encoder-oriented. The two notions, of course, often coincide and are realized by the same element, and, as Halliday points out, both are speaker-selected (1985: 278). But unlike the early Prague School notion of Theme, Given is not a definitional aspect of Theme.

Given for Halliday is a broad notion, including not only that which is retrievable from the text or the context of situation but also 'something that is not around at all but that the speaker wants to present as Given for rhetorical purposes' (Halliday 1985: 277). Given will be defined here as that which is already in the mind of the hearer.

Second, Theme is not the same as Subject. Halliday distinguishes the two concepts by relating Theme to the late nineteenth-century concept of the psychological subject and Subject to the notion of the grammatical subject of the same period (1985: 33–4). Subject is more intimately tied to surface features of grammaticality than is Theme. Chafe describes Subject as 'the hitching post for the new knowledge' (1976: 44). The primary result of hearing the assertion is that you know something new about the Subject. This is different from 'point of departure of message' which is more textually oriented and more intimately linked with discourse flow.

Third, Theme is not synonymous with Topic in the usual grammatical sense in which that term is understood. As Halliday points out, as well as others (see Chafe), Topic has taken on many guises and is used in too many ways to be understood in any universal sense. But several common aspects of Topic emerge. (i) Topic is a sentence-level constituent, not a clause-level constituent. It often does not participate in case frame relations. (ii) Topics, like Themes, but unlike Subjects, are highly discourse-oriented. (iii) Topics are not selectionally related to the verb (Li and Thompson 1976: 466). Chafe says that Topic is 'the frame within which the sentence holds' (1976: 51). Topic seems to set up a frame of reference for the predication.

With this in mind, perhaps we can set up a working definition of Theme that is cognitive and substantive. Theme is the clause-level constituent that the encoder uses as the starting point of the message, the constituent that begins moving the decoder towards the core of the communication. Theme is the essential ideational jumping-off point directing the decoder's attention to the ultimate goal of the communication, the kernel of the message, the Rheme. We will treat Theme as a universal and as obligatory. Theme is also a discrete element. In other words, for the time being we will assume that all clauses have a Theme and only one Theme (we will ignore here textual and interpersonal Theme), and all languages have the notion of Theme encoded in one way or another. Theme may be mapped on to the same constituent as Subject, Topic or Given. In fact all four notions may be realized by the same clausal element.

9.4 THE STRUCTURE OF DARI

Having set up a framework for analysis, I would like to investigate the concept of Theme by analysing a short story. The language for this analysis is Afghan Persian, or Dari. The text is an oral narrative told informally to me by a native speaker. It has been transcribed morphophonemically and divided into clause and sentence-level units. I will not go into the details of the analysis here, but the criteria for word, clause and sentence division were both grammatical and phonological. Like most oral discourse, the narrative does not always divide neatly into clause-level units, and some units lack predicates. Though the entire narrative was analysed, only the first seven sentences have been included here.

Before looking at the text it is necessary to make a few comments about the structure of Dari if we are to understand the choices made by the narrator in textually arranging the constituents. Persian, in general, is what Joseph Greenberg (1963) calls a rigid verb-final language. For the most part in Dari the verb comes at the end of the clause. Verbs are obligatorily marked for person and number. Third person singular is usually realized as zero. As a result, subject pronouns are not necessarily overtly present, and the form of their realization is context-dependent. Dari has (except for its verb-final status), in theory, relatively free word order. Grammatically this is true. Contextually there is less freedom of choice. Thus normal unmarked word order in Dari is (SUBJECT) – OBJECT/COMPLEMENT–VERB, i.e. an optional Subject, an Object or Complement, followed by a verb; but variations from this are common.

In addition, there appears to be a distinct sentence-level topic–comment structure, plus a clause-level subject-prominent structure. Because of the flexibility of word order and the restricted use of the so-called passive construction (Moyne 1974), topicalization (in the broad sense of placing the Topic at the beginning of the sentence) is common in Persian in general (Aghbar 1981: 179–81). Because a pronominal grammatical subject is not normally present in the surface structure, the status of a topicalized element as a clausal constituent is sometimes ambiguous. Thus the following sentence (S20 in the narrative) could be translated either:

1. Ebrahim, he broke his [someone else's] good leg;

or

2. Ebrahim broke his [someone else's] good leg.

S20.   ebrahim   poi-i   xub-iš-ra   šikast-and
       Ebrahim   leg-i   good-his-D.O.   broke-3s

In contrast to the clause, the nominal group (or noun phrase in traditional terms) has a relatively rigid word order (Rashidi 1989). Nominal groups have their head first, with the modifiers connected to the head (or the preceding modifier) by the clitic -i, referred to as the 'ezafe' or 'izafet' in literature on Persian and Arabic. This particle is phonologically attached to the preceding element but is semantically part of the modifier. At times the ezafe can be translated 'of', but for the most part -i simply serves to attach a modifier to a preceding element. In rare instances where a modifier precedes a head it does so for emphasis and is clearly a marked construction. Because of the ezafe connectors, nominal groups are easily distinguished as single clausal constituents as opposed to, say, a subject noun plus an adjective complement. In reality the latter construction never occurs in Dari; instead the language is rife with single-participant existential processes.

Though it would seem that intonation should play an important role in the identification of Theme and Rheme in spoken text, in fact intonation plays a far less significant role in Dari than it does in English. Dari stress patterns are highly predictable (Bing 1980) and stress in general is less distinct than for English. A Dari speaker is more likely to use word order for prominence than to use stress. In the narrative under analysis, intonation contours were all unmarked, there being no marked tonic prominence.

The text that will be analysed here has been reproduced with an English gloss and translation in the appendix. The English translation was done in order to present a cohesive storyline. It is interesting to note the way in which the various clauses are textually presented in English, as opposed to Dari, and how the various clausal constituents have been arranged for a cohesive presentation in English. It is a clear indication that the two languages offer different options in terms of the textual arrangement of concepts. These contrasts will be discussed as we proceed.

9.5 ANALYSIS OF A DARI NARRATIVE

What is happening in the Dari text? How does the narrator textually arrange the various constituents for a coherent flow of ideas? A detailed look at the first section of the narrative will give some understanding of the message structure of this text.

S1. ma o ebrahim\ senf-i awal-i fakulte-i enjiniri\ bud-im
    I and Ebrahim class first school engineering was-1p
    Ebrahim and I were in the first year of the School of Engineering.

Sentence 1 (S1) has three clause constituent elements: (i) *ma o ebrahim*, (ii) *senf-i awal-i faculte-i enjiniri*, and (iii) *bud-im*. The first constituent is new information in terms of the text, of course, but the audience for this story-telling knew both the characters (and *ma*, the narrator, is physically present), and thus the participants needed no introduction. The second element is a single nominal group, as can be seen by the ezafe connectors between the head, *senf*, and the modifiers that follow. The free translation is misleading; to indicate the grammatical function of this second element better, a truer translation might be 'Ebrahim and I were engineering freshmen,' as *senf-i awal-i fakulte-i enjiniri* is a nominal group acting as Complement, not a prepositional phrase. The verb, *bud-im*, is the past tense of the copula. This sentence is in normal, unmarked word order, SUBJECT–COMPLEMENT–VERB. The narrator introduces the two major participants in the story by placing them in a time frame, their freshman year in college.

S2. ba xal-m\   sol-i nozda sod o   pinjaa o   no\ bud
    in opinion-my   year 19   100 and   50   and   9   was
    I think the year was 1959.

The second sentence is almost an aside, where the narrator tries to give us an exact year. He begins with the interpersonal *ba xal-m*, literally 'in my opinion', or 'as I recall', and then states the date as a single nominal group. This is the standard obligatory way in which dates are stated. In English we might say, 'It was 1959 (nineteen-fifty-nine),' but one cannot do that in Dari. First of all, there is no 'dummy' subject construction. Second, one cannot just say 'nineteen-fifty-nine'; one must say 'year' followed by the full number. So we have, literally, 'in my opinion, year nineteen hundred and fifty and nine was'. This is an existential clause with a single participant. This kind of clausal construction is very common in Dari. What would be a two-participant identifying clause in English ('the year was 1959') is usually a one-participant existential process in Dari, realized as a single nominal group, with the head connected to the modifiers by the ezafe connector -*i*.

S3. ebrahim\   waxt\   dar kampani-i   gošo-i   japan\   partaim   kor   mekard
    Ebrahim   time   in company   Gosho   Japan   part-time   work   did
    Ebrahim at that time was working part-time in the Japanese company Gosho.

Sentence 3 has four constituents. The initial element is *ebrahim*, followed directly by *waxt*, 'time', with no pause or intonational variation. It is the element *waxt* that connects the hearer back to the previous sentence. *waxt*, 'time', is directly anaphoric to *sol-i nozda sod o pinjaa o no*, 'the year 1959'. *ebrahim*, however, appears first, and there is a reason: discourse-wise, Ebrahim must be introduced as a new participant. He has appeared earlier as part of the unit *ma o ebrahim* but not as an individual participant. If the story had begun *ebrahim* instead of *ma o ebrahim*, sentence 3 might well have left out *ebrahim* altogether. This fronting of the agent, however, is very typical of Dari, and while *ebrahim* is probably the grammatical subject of the clause, agency is often simply a topicalized sentence element that does not participate grammatically as a clausal argument.

S4. pul-i   ke   zaxira   karda   bud\   yak motirsikel\   xarid
    money that   savings did   was   one motorcycle   bought
    With the money that he had saved he bought a motorcycle.

The first constituent in sentence 4 again illustrates the tendency of Dari toward a topic–comment structure. The best English translation that I can come up with is: 'With the money that he had saved, he bought a motorcycle.' Dari does not require the overt realization of a separate subject pronoun, and none is needed in this sentence in either the dependent *ke* clause or the main clause. The English statement of this idea requires the preposition 'with' for the expression of instrumentality, but Dari does not.

And 'money' cannot be Subject of 'bought' in Dari; *xarid* requires a human Subject. As in English, 'buy' in Dari requires three arguments: Actor, Instrument and Goal. All three are realized here, though Actor is realized only as a verbal suffix. Instrument is fronted in order to tie this sentence to the previous sentence. *pul-i ke zaxira karda bud*, 'the money that he had saved', is the only constituent with given information.

> S5. motirsikel-i   jawa-i   čekoslavakia\   bud
>   motorcycle   Jawa   Czechoslovakia   was
>   *The motorcycle was a Czechoslovakian Jawa.*

Sentence 5 is, like S2, a single-participant clause. Semantically, however, the process is one of attribution. Clearly, what the narrator is telling us is that this motorcycle, which was just mentioned in the previous clause, is a Czechoslovakian Jawa; he is describing it for us. We already know that the motorcycle exists. But, as is common in Dari, the attributes are connected to the thing in a single nominal group, so that both the thing and its attributes are realized by the same constituent. In fact the narrator has no other options for the realization of this particular message except very marked ones. Note that my free English translation fronts *the motorcycle*, thus retaining it as the point of departure of the message but separating it grammatically from its attributives. A closer translation of this sentence would be 'It was a Czechoslovakian Jawa motorcycle'; this translation retains both the single constituency nature of the Dari and the cohesive flow of the narrative.

> S6. kalon motirsikel\   čor silandar\   besior kawi
>   large motorcycle   four-cylinder   very powerful
>   *A large motorcycle, four cylinder, very powerful.*

Sentence 6 is not a 'grammatically correct' Dari clause. It would probably appear only in casual oral discourse. First of all, there is no overt predicate. This kind of elision is far more common in Dari than in English because of the verb-final nature of clauses. It is very common with the third person singular present tense copula, which is simply -*s*; elision is less common for the past tense *bud* as here. Nonetheless, S6 is perceived as a clause and this is reinforced intonationally. Second, the modifier *kalon*, 'large', has been fronted from its normal post-head position (but it does not receive tonic prominence). Such transposition in Dari is very unusual. The narrator's reason for doing it is not entirely clear. The clause as a whole seems to be a further expansion of his description of the motorcycle. Perhaps he wants to make sure that his audience recognizes Jawas as big machines. The powerfulness of the motorcycle will play a prominent role as the tale unfolds. *kalon* is most likely new information, though *motirsikel* is given information. If this is the case, *kalon motirsikel*, taken as a single constituent, is New.[3] It is, of course, possible that the narrator expected the audience to be familiar with Jawas and, thus, extract 'largeness' from the previous sentence. In that case, *kalon motirsikel* would be Given. Either way, the other two constituents tell us more about the size of the motorcycle and are definitely new information.

S7. dar hudud-i yak maa\   praktis kard   o   amoxt\
    about   one month   practice did   and learned

    ke   motirsikel-a   draiv kon-a
    that   motorcycle-DO   drive did-3s
    For about one month he practised and learned to drive the motorcycle.

The final sentence (S7) in this section begins with a time phrase of duration, *dar hudud-i yak maa*, 'for about one month'. Though formally a circumstantial element, the phrase adds new information and semantic content that is an integral part of the process of the clause, not just a narrative device that moves the story. The narrator has put this constituent in clause-initial position because it is the only viable alternative he has here. This is a compound sentence, the two halves connected by *o*, 'and'. 'He' is Ebrahim, realized only as the verbal suffix, which here is zero (see p. 193). I think that English would reinsert the name, *Ebrahim*, here, instead of using the pronoun 'he'. This narrator has done neither, leaving the subject slot empty. The second clause also lacks an overt subject but it is again 'he', realized as the null verbal suffix. The verb *amoxt*, 'learned', is followed by a dependent *ke* clause. S7 seems to be a transition sentence between the opening section, where the major story participants are introduced, and the actual relating of the event itself.

9.6 THEME

Starting from our working definition of Theme, and keeping in the forefront that we wish to understand the notion of Theme better from a functional point of view, how is Theme realized in Dari and how do we recognize it? If Theme is the constituent that is the jumping-off point for the message, then some overt and external criteria for the recognition of Theme can be set up.

The essential criterion for recognizing Theme is semantic content. Here it will be useful to define Rheme and set up the Theme/Rheme interplay of message structure. Following Firbas, Rheme will be taken as the clausal constituent that contains the core idea that the encoder is trying to impart; it is the essential purport towards which the communication is developing. If such is the case, then Theme is the constituent that orients the decoder, paving the way to the core of the communication. This semantic criterion will be the foundation for recognizing Theme and will involve, of course, identifying Rheme.

But are there some more overt signals that might be used? Four other considerations, while not definitional criteria, will be weighed in determining the

Theme of a clause: (i) linear position; (ii) information structure; (iii) grammatical structure; and (iv) discourse flow and cohesive ties.

Linear position should correlate with Theme/Rheme structure. In the normal course of producing a sentence one element follows another. From a cognitive standpoint this is significant, especially for spoken text. It would seem natural that the orienting part of the communication should appear early in the linear sequence and before the core idea. While intonation markedness may act to counterbalance this tendency, in general Theme should appear before Rheme and will probably be the first ideational element in the clause. This may be particularly true of Dari, where word order is relatively flexible from a grammatical standpoint and intonation is highly predictable and plays a minor role in marking prominence.

A second correlate with Theme is givenness. While the Rheme of a clause will always be news (or the speaker would not be mentioning it), the Theme will probably, but not necessarily, NOT be news. We are most likely to orient our listeners to our message by a piece of content that is already in the consciousness of the listener, i.e. has been activated either linguistically or extralinguistically. In other words, Theme is most likely to be Given.

The third correlate lies in the grammatical structure of the clause. It would seem reasonable, given Chafe's definition of Subject as 'the hitching post', that the Subject of a clause should have a tendency to be Theme. As we have seen in the data above, however, Dari does not have obligatory overt subjects, and overt subject pronouns only occur markedly. This makes the linking of Subject with Theme less attractive in Dari than it would be in English. However, the grammatical status of a constituent will be an additional factor in looking at Theme.

Finally, discourse flow will play a part in Thematic structure. Sentences do not occur in isolation but are connected, both semantically and structurally, to the surrounding text. The encoder of text forms clauses in relation to what came before and what will follow. Theme, since it is the orienter, will be likely to have cohesive ties with preceding text in particular. This is, of course, intimately bound up with the notion of Given, but the two are not synonymous.

While all these correlates will reinforce the identification of Theme, the essential criterion for recognizing Theme in the following text will be semantic content and the function of the constituent as paving the way to the core of the communication, the Rheme.

9.7 IDENTIFICATION OF THEME

In S1 Theme is *ma o ebrahim* and Rheme is *senf-i awal-i fakulte-i enjiniri*. The narrator focuses our attention by announcing the participants, and then he identifies the time setting. This time frame is the core of the message of this clause (the Rheme), when the story will take place; it is news. *ma o ebrahim* is new information in terms of the immediate context but is part of the common gnostology of the speaker and hearers and, therefore, not entirely news. It is the grammatical Subject and the Carrier of the attribute, *senf-i awal-i fakulte-i enjiniri*.

In S2 *ba xal-m* is an interpersonal Theme, not an ideational one. The copula *bud* adds nothing in the way of pushing the communication forward, to use a Firbas concept. The only other clausal element is *sol-i nozda sod o pinjaa o no*, 'the year 1959'. It cannot be both Theme and Rheme. I see three possible solutions. The first is to call *sol-i*, 'year', Theme and '1959' Rheme, but this would require splitting a single idiomatically indivisible clause constituent. The second solution would be to call the entire nominal group Theme, but then the clause would have no rhematic development. A third interpretation would be to call *sol-i nozda sod o pinjaa o no* Rheme, leaving the clause with only an interpersonal Theme. This does not seem untenable to me and would be in line with a Firbas interpretation of the clause.[4]

S3 is rather complicated. Semantically, *waxt* seems to be the point of departure of the message. Discoursewise, *ebrahim* must come first but does little to move the communication forward. Though the character Ebrahim is the Actor in the process, the element *ebrahim* may or may not be the Subject and, therefore, may or may not be a clausal constituent; it is quite possible that the Subject of *kor mekard* is 'he' realized only as a verbal suffix. Both *waxt* and *ebrahim* are Given. The rest of the sentence is New. I posit *waxt* as Theme of this clause.

S4 seems straightforward. The narrator is introducing into the story a major participant, *yak motirsikel*. This is the core of the message. *pul-i ke zaxira bud*, 'the money that he had saved', has cohesive ties back to the previous sentence and is clearly the point of departure of this sentence. It is the only constituent with given information. This initial nominal group, then, is Theme; *yak motirsikel* is Rheme.

S5 is another single-participant clause, like S2. It is quite clear here, however, that *motirsikel* is given information and the point of departure of the message, and *jawa-i čekoslavakia* is 'more about the motorcycle' or rhematic development. Though Dari structures both bits of information as a single constituent, it makes sense to split this nominal group into Theme and Rheme.

S6 is a very marked sentence and problematic. *motirsikel* is Given, but *kalon* is New. As a unit, *kalon motirsikel* is considered New; nonetheless, it seems to be the point of departure of the clause, and, therefore, Theme. The other two elements, 'four cylinders' and 'very powerful', are clearly development of the idea of 'large motorcycle'. The clause builds gradually towards the notion of powerful. This is reinforced intonationally; the narrator makes a long pause before the final element and puts tonic prominence on the last word, *kawi*, 'powerful'.

S7 is a transition sentence, having, typically for a narrative, a time phrase as Theme; the rest is Rheme. The only given information in this sentence is the motorcycle, which appears in a dependent *ke* clause.

The text develops, then, by making thematic first the two main characters, then the time frame; next the narrator elaborately introduces the instrument around which the tale revolves, the motorcycle. The motorcycle is Rheme first. Then it is the Theme of the next two sentences. Thematically we move from the two main characters, through the setting of time, to the means of acquiring the motorcycle (the money), to the motorcycle itself, and back to a time reference. This seems a fairly usual thematic line for a narrative. Rheme develops the thematic line by first identifying the characters as college freshmen, then describing how Ebrahim earned money and what he did with the money; finally the narrator describes the motorcycle, establishing its powerfulness, and puts the characters on this large machine ready to ride out to their tale of woe.

We can tell from this initial section that Ebrahim, not the narrator, is the main character. We also know that the motorcycle is going to figure prominently in the story and that its power will be crucial to the plot.

Chart of Theme identification
(Theme is underlined, Rheme is in bold face)

S1. ma o ebrahim/   **senf-i awal-i fakulte-i enjiniri/**   bud-im
I and
Ebrahim   class first   school   engineering was-1p

S2. ba xal-m/   **sol-i nozda sod o   pinjaa o   no/**   bud
in opinion-my   year 19   100 and 50   and   9 was

S3. ebrahim/ waxt/ dar kampani-i gošo-i   japan/ **partaim kor mekard**
Ebrahim time in company Gosho   Japan part-time work did

S4. pul-i ke   zaxira karda bud/ **yak motirsikel/** xarid
money that savings did was one motorcycle bought

S5. motirsikel-i **jawa-i čekoslavakia/**   bud
motorcycle Jawa Czechoslovakia   was

S6. kalon motirsikel/ čor silandar/   **besior kawi**
large motorcycle four-cylinder   very powerful

S7. dar hudud-i yak maa/ **praktis kard**   o   **amoxt**
about   1 month practice did   and   learned

Table 9.1 Realization of Theme

Sentence	Subject	Information structure	First	Rheme
1	Subject	New	First	–
2	Circ.	New	–	–
3	Circ.	Given	Second	Rheme – 1
4	Circ.	New	First	Rheme – 1
5	Subject	Given	First	Rheme – 1
6	Subject	New	First	Rheme – 1
7	Circ.	New	First	–

Key: Circ., Circumstantial element. First, First ideational element. Rheme – 1, Rheme minus one; anaphoric to Rheme of previous sentence.

Theme	*Rheme*
S1. characters	time frame
S2. interpersonal	time frame
S3. time frame	source of money
S4. money	motor cycle (result of money)
S5. motor cycle	type of motor cycle (size?)
S6. large	powerful
S7. time	use of motor cycle

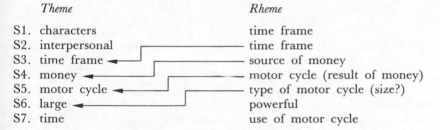

Theme is realized as in Table 9.1.

9.8 DISCUSSION

In Dari narrative the realization of Theme seems to pattern along several interacting parameters. First, Theme is connected with linear development. It is most often the initial sentence element and usually the first ideational element, though in S2 Theme is not an ideational element and in S3 Theme is the second ideational element in the sentence and probably in the clause as well. In this text Theme always precedes Rheme, though I suspect exceptions to this would be found in a larger corpus.

Thematic correlation with information structure varies in this text. Though it appears from the chart that Theme is most often New, this is misleading. As was seen in the analysis of the narrative, an element formally labelled New may in fact contain some given information and, therefore, not be entirely news. By contrast, Rheme is always New and always news.

As anticipated, Theme does not correlate highly with Subject; in only three of the seven sentences is Theme the Subject of the clause. In at least two sentences, S4 and S7, and maybe a third, S3, there is no overt realization of Subject. In S2 there is only one ideational element, and that we have designated Rheme for reasons stated above. If Theme is not the Subject of the clause, it is a circumstantial element of one kind or another, not a participant element.

Finally, Theme/Rheme structure does seem to be linked with discourse flow. Though Theme is often called the thread of discourse, in this narrative it is the Rheme that is the core of the storyline. The Rheme development in this opening section sets up the narrative, introducing the major participants in the story and establishing the centrality of the motorcycle and the importance of its powerfulness. The four middle sentences in this section (S3–S6) follow Daneš's 'zigzag' pattern of Theme/Rheme progression where the Rheme of one sentence becomes the Theme of the next (Daneš 1974: 118–19). Theme in this section is usually directly anaphoric to the Rheme of the preceding sentence.

9.9 CONCLUSION

Halliday at least implies (1985: 38) that a language, if it has Theme/Rheme structure, signals Theme in some consistent overt manner (e.g., in English, sentence-initial position; in Japanese, the particle -*wa*). In Dari it is not so obvious that Theme has a consistent structural realization. Though there is a tendency to linear development of the message, Theme does not necessarily coincide with first position, nor does it necessarily coincide with Subject or Given. If we are to define Theme as 'the point of departure of the message', then Theme will be realized not only in different ways in different languages but also in different ways within a single language.

APPENDIX

S1. ma o ebrahim/ senf-i awal-i fakulte-i enjiniri/   bud-im
    I and Ebrahim class first   school   engineering was-1p
    Ebrahim and I were in the first year at the School of Engineering.

S2. ba xal-m/   sol-i nozda sod o   pinjaa o   no/   bud
    in opinion-my   year 19   100 and 50 and 9   was
    I think the year was 1959.

S3. ebrahim/ waxt/ dar kampani-i gošo-i japan/ partaim   kor mekard
    Ebrahim time in   company Gosho Japan part-time work did
    Ebrahim at that time was working part-time in the Japanese company Gosho.

S4. pul-i   ke   zaxira   karda bud/ yak motirsikel/   xarid
    money that   savings did   was one motorcycle   bought
    With the money that he saved he bought a motorcycle.

S5. motirsikel-i jawa-i čekoslavakia/   bud
    motorcycle Jawa Czechoslovakia was
    The motorcycle was a Czechoslovakian Jawa.

S6. kalon motirsikel/ čor silandar/   besior kawi
    large motorcycle four-cylinder   very powerful
    A large motorcycle, four cylinders, very powerful.

S7. dar hudud-i yak maa/   praktis kard o   amoxt
    about   one month practice did and   learned

    ke   motirsikel-a   diaiv kon-a
    that   motorcycle-DO   drive did-3s
    For about one month he practised and learned to drive the motorcycle.

NOTES

1 Margaret Berry is at present examining the relationship between thematic choice
   and degree of success in the written texts of children. In addition Berry has
   several students in the Department of English Studies at the University of
   Nottingham working on projects in which a thematic framework is being used to
   investigate the problem of what makes a text a successful instance of a genre.
2 The term 'gnostology' is used here following Michael Gregory. Gregory uses the
   term to refer to the knowledge base of the encoder/decoder. For his latest exposition see Gregory (1988).
3 Firbas feels that, if a part of a constituent is irretrievable, the whole constituent
   is considered irretrievable (from discussion in the final session of the Second
   Nottingham International Systemic Workshop (on Rheme). I would agree with
   Firbas on this.
4 I would like to express my debt to Jan Firbas for insights in the analysis of these
   data and of this clause in particular.

REFERENCES

Aghbar, A.A. (1981), 'Case Grammar and Persian Verbs', Ph.D. dissertation,
    Georgetown University.
Berry, M. (1990), 'Thematic analysis and stylistic preferences', paper presented at
    the Seventeenth International Systemic Congress, University of Stirling.
Bing, J.M. (1980), 'Linguistic rhythm and grammatical structure in Afghan
    Persian', *Linguistic Inquiry* 11.3, 437–63.
Chafe, W. (1976), 'Givenness, contrastiveness, definiteness, subjects, topics, and
    point of view', in Charles N. Li (ed.), *Subject and Topic*, pp. 25–56, New York,
    Academic Press.
Daneš, F. (1974), 'Functional sentence perspective and the organization of the
    text', in Frantisek Daneš (ed.), *Papers on functional sentence perspective*, pp. 106–
    28, The Hague, Mouton.
Firbas, J. (1966a), 'On defining the theme in functional sentence analysis', in Josef
    Vachek (ed.), *Travaux Linguistiques de Prague* 1, pp. 267–80, University, University
    of Alabama Press.

——— (1966b), 'Non-thematic subjects in contemporary English', in Josef Vachek (ed.), *Travaux Linguistiques de Prague* 2, pp. 239–56, University, University of Alabama Press.

——— (1987), 'On two starting points of communication', in R. Steele and T. Threadgold (eds), *Language Topics: Essays in Honour of Michael Halliday*, 1, pp. 23–46, Amsterdam, Benjamins.

Fries, P.H. (1983), 'On the status of Theme in English: arguments from discourse', in Janos S. Petöfi and Emel Sozer (eds), *Micro and Macro Connexity of Texts*, pp. 116–52, Hamburg, Buske.

——— (forthcoming), 'Patterns of information in initial position in English', in P.H. Fries and M. Gregory (eds), *Discourse in Society: Functional Perspectives*, Norwood, N.J., Ablex.

Greenberg, J.H. (1963), 'Some universals of grammar with particular reference to the order of meaningful elements', in J.H. Greenberg (ed.), *Universals of Language*, 2nd ed, pp. 73–113, Cambridge, Mass., MIT Press.

Gregory, M. (1988), 'Generic situation and register: a functional view of communication', in J.D. Benson, M.J. Cummings and W.S. Greaves (eds), *Linguistics in a Systemic Perspective*, pp. 301–30, Current Issues in Linguistic Theory 39, Philadelphia, Benjamins.

Halliday, M.A.K. (1967), 'Notes on transitivity and theme in English', *Journal of Linguistics* 3.1, 37–81; 3.2, 199–244; 4.2, 179–215.

——— (1985), *An Introduction to Functional Grammar*, London, Edward Arnold.

Jordan, M.P. (1985), 'Non-Thematic re-entry: an introduction to and extension of the system of nominal group reference/substitution in everyday English use', in J. Benson and W. Greaves (eds), *Systemic Perspectives on Discourse* 1, pp. 322–32, Norwood, N.J., Ablex.

Li, C.N. and Thompson, S.A. (1976), 'Subject and topic: a new typology of language', in Charles N. Li (ed.), *Subject and Topic*, pp. 457–89, New York, Academic Press.

Moyne, J.A. (1974), 'The so-called passive in Persian', *Foundations of Language* 12, 249–67.

Rashidi, L.S. (1989), 'The experiential structure of the Dari nominal group', paper presented at the 16th International Systemic Congress, Helsinki.

Part V. Text Studies

10 The notion of technicality in register: a case study from the language of bridge

James D. Benson and William S. Greaves

10.1 INTRODUCTION

In a number of papers J.R. Martin and colleagues (Martin forthcoming; Wignell *et al.* 1987; Martin *et al.* 1988) have investigated the nature and function of technical language in the discourses of a number of disciplines encountered by students in secondary school. There is obviously much to be gained both theoretically and practically from such register-specific analyses. The theoretical distinction between technicality in the field of geography and abstraction in the field of history (Martin *et al.* 1988: 149–64), for example, makes it possible not only to see how these two types of nominalization are privileged, but also to intervene pedagogically to enable all students to gain access to the registers of geography and history. Our own study seeks to extend this work by focusing on another well-defined register, that of bridge, which resembles geography in being technical but which differs from it in not being scientific. We shall be using the treatment of geography in Wignell *et al.* (1987) as a base line for our discussion of the similarities and differences between the two registers. Our data show that the most significant difference between the two arises from the function of technicality in bridge.

Like Wignell *et al.* (1987), we are looking for realizations of technicality in lexicogrammatical function structures, but instead of making comprehensive analyses of short passages of text, in their case from a secondary school textbook, we analyse a data set produced from collocations in an entire text, an introductory instructional book, *The Joy of Bridge*. Narrow-span collocations (Benson and Greaves 1989) of frequently occurring lexis, such as *hand*, *suit*, *bid*, and the verb forms *is* and *are*, produced by the CLOC computer program (Reed 1977, 1984), yield tokens of grammatical types in nominal group and clause structure. An example of CLOC output can be seen in Table 10.1, in which the collocation *is like* yields information about clause structure. The first line of output means that the orthographic word-token *is* is being treated as a node, and occurs 1,056 times in the text as a whole. The second line means that the

Table 10.1 Example of CLOC output

---

node **is** occurs 1056 times
collocate **like** occurs 29 times
node-collocate pair occurs 4 times

1 a process called BIDDING. Bridge bidding **is like** an AUCTION. The bidding
4 with eight or more combined trumps **is like** magic. Experience has shown that
6 The Sign-off Bid   A SIGN-OFF BID **is like** the warning on a stop
6 The Forcing Bid   A FORCING BID **is like** the green signal on a

---

orthographic word-token *like* is being treated as a collocation, and occurs
twenty-nine times in the text as a whole. CLOC has been instructed to
search for narrow-span collocations (in this case the span is one to the right
of the node), and the third line shows that node and collocate co-occur four
times in the text as a whole. CLOC is actually looking for orthographic
word-tokens of orthographic word-types, but in doing so has in effect
captured four grammatical tokens of a grammatical type, in this case a
relational circumstantial attributive clause with Carrier and Attribute (as
Circumstance). The occurrences in the text are indexed by chapter
numbers, which appear at the left edge of each citation. In this study we
have not looked at any node-collocate pairs which occur fewer than five
times. Many occur much more frequently. For example, node *is* with
collocate *the* (forming part of Token Value structure) occurs fifty-seven
times. These collocations are displayed in Table 10.13.

We begin with an overview of the analysis of geography and how it
compares with bridge. Wignell *et al.* (1987: 57) say that geography
OBSERVES the experiential world by introducing and defining technical
terms, ORDERS the world by arranging the technical terms into
taxonomies, and EXPLAINS the world through IMPLICATION SEQUENCES of
cause and effect (which we could think of as 'the laws of nature'). This
technicalizing principally involves the grammatical resources of Token–
Value structures to introduce and define terms, Carrier–Attribute structures and Classifier–Thing structures to create taxonomies, and Token–
Value structures together with clause complexes to construct implication
sequences. Like geography, bridge observes the world by introducing and
defining technical terms, orders this world by arranging the terms into
taxonomies, and explains it through implication sequences. In so doing,
bridge makes use of the same grammatical resources as geography. In
addition, however, bridge taxonomy technicalizes probability and evaluation with adjectival Attributes at the clause rank, and with Epithet–Thing
structures at the nominal group rank. Bridge also differs from geography
in that implication sequences explaining why things are as they are, i.e.
the 'rules of the game', involve human agency. Bridge is even more unlike
geography when it technicalizes decision-making, which is a central part of
the 'rules of the game', through Token–Value structures.

10.2 INTRODUCING AND DEFINING TECHNICAL TERMS
(RELATIONAL INTENSIVE IDENTIFYING CLAUSES)

As Wignell *et al.* (1987: 47) point out, technical terms must be introduced and defined before they can be taxonomically organized. One way in which technical terms are introduced is through relational intensive identifying clauses with an encoding direction. In our text many, but by no means all, of the technical terms of bridge can be found in IS/ARE CALLED collocations, such as *these six tricks are called the BOOK*. Table 10.2 shows technical terms in bridge that are introduced and defined simultaneously in Value-Token structures. We have preserved the orthographical convention by which the technical term is printed in capitals. In all cases the technical term is a Token. In chapter 4, for example, *The partner of the opening bidder* is a Value, and *the RESPONDER* is a Token. The Value of *being the partner of the opening bid* is made 'recognizable' by the Token, which is the technical term RESPONDER. At the same time, the Value is the definition of the technical term, so the term RESPONDER is being defined as well as introduced.

There are many other technical terms in the text besides these, but the Tokens in Table 10.2 identify a great many of the crucial Things of Bridge: roles played in the exchange of bidding messages (e.g. *responder*), decisions (e.g. *how high?*), kinds of bids (e.g. *marathon bids*), the play of the hand (e.g. *finesse*) and scoring (e.g. *penalty double*). We would also expect to find definitions of terms in the opposite coding direction, i.e. with Tokens identified by Values. If we look at the *is the* collocations of just the first chapter displayed in Table 10.3, there is one definition with a decoding direction, (1.1) *THE ACE* (Token) *is THE HIGHEST-RANKING CARD* (Value), but two with an encoding direction: (1.3) *THE HIGHEST-RANKING CARD IN THE CUT* (Value) *is THE DEALER* (Token), and (1.6) *OTHER MEMBER OF THE OFFENSIVE TEAM* (Value) *is THE DUMMY* (Token).

The remaining Token-Value structures, however, do not **define** technical terms, in the sense of assigning them a permanent and stable meaning; rather they **redefine** them on an *ad hoc* basis. In (1.2), for example, *THE ACE OF DIAMONDS* (Token) is redefined as *THE HIGHEST CARD PLAYED* (Value), i.e. as having this meaning under a particular set of circumstances. Similarly, in (1.5) *WEST* (Token) is temporarily redefined as *DEALER* (Value), and in (1.4) *THE DECLARER* (Token) is temporarily redefined by an example *HEARTS FIRST FOR THE OFFENSIVE TEAM* (Value). The remaining identifying clauses (1.7–11) ask the reader to supply Tokens for Values. (1.8) *WHAT* (Token) *is THE HIGHEST-RANKING CARD IN THE DECK?* (Value) and (1.9) *WHAT* (Token) *is THE LOWEST-RANKING CARD?* (Value) ask for canonical definitions of terms like the one in (1.1), whereas (1.7) *Which player is the dealer*, (1.10) *What is the maximum number of tricks* and (1.11) *What is the lowest bid you can make?* ask for *ad hoc* redefinitions like those in (1.2), (1.4) and (1.5). This suggests, quite unlike geography, that the reader or player is involved in a continuous redefinition of 'terms' depending on the circumstances.

Table 10.2 Technical terms introduced and defined in Value–Token Structures

---

node **are** occurs 422 times
collocate **called** occurs 39 times
node-collocate pair occurs 5 times

  1 taken for granted. These six tricks **are called** the BOOK. The one-level, then
  3 those for tricks bid and made **are called** BONUSES. Bonuses are awarded for
  6 Game level is reached. Such bids **are called** MARATHON BIDS because the
  7 partner bid the suit first), these **are called** DUMMY POINTS. To illustrate
     the
23 three-level or higher in a suit **are called** PRE-EMPTIVE OPENING BIDS or

node **is** occurs 1056 times
collocate **called** occurs 39 times
node-collocate pair occurs 29 times

  1 any card from another suit. This **is called** DISCARDING. The trick is won
  1 a trump can be played. This **is called** TRUMPING or RUFFING the trick
  1 first player to open the bidding **is called** the OPENING BIDDER or
     OPENER
  1 trump suit of the final contract **is called** the DECLARER. For example, if
  1 on the table: this face-up hand **is called** the DUMMY. Declarer's partner is
  3 which is worth less than 100 points **is called** a PART-GAME (PART-
     SCORE). For
  4 The partner of the opening bidder **is called** the RESPONDER . . . he
     RESPONDS to
  4 partnership contracts to take; this decision **is called**: HOW HIGH? – How
     high
  4 that the partnership chooses; this decision **is called**: WHERE? – Where should
  4 more cards in the combined hands **is called** a MAGIC FIT. How does
  5 one that says, 'Please Pass, partner', **is called** a SIGN-OFF BID. Here are
  5 a five-card Major suit. Three Spades **is called** a FORCING BID because it
  7 higher than necessary. Such a response **is called** a JUMP SHIFT and alerts
  8 of opener's hand. Opener's second bid **is called** OPENER'S REBID. When
     making
  8 'shifting' to a new suit, this **is called** a JUMP SHIFT. For example
  8 the describer and your second bid **is called** OPENER'S REBID. You can
     determine
11 Spades? Responder's bid at this point **is called** RESPONDER'S REBID.
11 any of his other suits. This **is called** GIVING PREFERENCE to opener's first
12 of choosing between opener's two suits **is called** PREFERENCE. The '5-4'
13 Using the double in this way **is called** making a PENALTY DOUBLE.
     Another
14 bid) over the opponent's bid, this **is called** an OVERCALL. Opening bid
     'One
17 in this manner, the double **is called** a TAKE-OUT DOUBLE because you
18 the opponent's suit! Such a bid **is called** a CUE BID of the
20 artificial or CONVENTIONAL bid. It **is called** the STAYMAN
     CONVENTION.
21 at the two-level in a suit **is called** a STRONG TWO-BID. This is
23 Marathon bid). Bidding the opponent's suit **is called** a CUE BID. Let's look
23 suit at the three-level or higher **is called** a PRE-EMPTIVE OPENING BID.
     The
24 higher card. This kind of play **is called** a FINESSE. In a finesse
25 exhausting the opponents of their trumps **is called** DRAWING TRUMPS. In
     this

Table 10.3 Token–**Value** definitions and redefinitions of terms in chapter 1

1.1	RANK OF THE CARDS. The Ace is the highest-ranking card, followed by the
1.2	trick since the Ace of Diamonds is **the highest card played**. South leads
1.3	**the highest-ranking card in the cut** is the DEALER (if there was no
1.4	**Hearts first for the offensive team** is the declarer. Here is an example
1.5	Pass Pass Pass West is **the dealer** and says Pass. North
1.6	**other member of the offensive team** is the Dummy. The player on the
1.7	Which players are partners? Which player is **the dealer**? (2) What is the
1.8	Which player is the dealer? (2) What is **the highest-ranking card in the deck?**
1.9	highest-ranking card in the deck? What is **the lowest-ranking card?** (3) What
1.10	What is the lowest-ranking card? (3) What is **the maximum number of tricks**
1.11	your right bids Three Spades. What is **the lowest bid you can make?**

The reader/player is in fact overtly technicalized, and is represented in the text as a Token defined by a Value. Table 10.4 displays *you are the* collocations. *You* as reader/player is defined at any one time by the various roles possible in the game. *You are South and the bidding proceeds*, another variation of this terminology, occurs six times but is not displayed. In the activity of bridge, then, even the reader/player is treated as a technical term whose role meaning changes depending on the circumstances.

Table 10.4 Technicalizing reader/player: Token–**Value**

2	is discussed in chapter 21. Exercises (1) You are **the dealer** and therefore
2	not enough to overcall) Exercises (1) You are **the dealer**. What would you bid
3	way to score POINTS. If you are **the offensive team**, you score points
3	to make your contract. If you are **the defensive team**, you score points
21	Let's look at some examples. You are **the opening bidder**. What do you
23	Let's look at some examples: You are **the opening bidder**. What would you
5	partner opens One No-Trump and you are **the responder**. Your hand is: S
8	a second bid. As opener, you are **the describer** and your second bid
5	for your side, Two Spades. You are **the captain** so opener will say
5	opens the bidding One No-Trump, you are **the captain** and must determine HOW
23	your own. Bid Three No-Trump. You are **the captain**, so opener will accept
26	leads the Two from dummy. You are **the second player to the trick**
26	plays the Two from dummy. You are **the third player to the trick**

10.3 TAXONOMIZING

Once technical terms have been defined, they can be organized into taxonomies. In geography the principal means of doing this are Carrier–

Table 10.5 Taxonomy: bid, suit, scoring (representative examples): Carrier–
Attribute

(i) *Bid taxonomy*

'Raising partner's Minor to the three-level is	**an invitational bid** and shows'
'The Jump Shift is	**a marathon bid**'
'you cannot pass since partner's rebid is	**marathon**'
'a new suit at the two-level is	**a forcing bid**'
'doubles are	**forcing bids**'
'Since Three Hearts is	**forcing**, responder will bid Four Hearts'
Three No-Trump is	**a sign-off bid**'

(ii) *Suit taxonomy*

'If your second suit	is **lower-ranking**	**than your first suit**'
'suit at the two-level if it	is **higher-ranking**	**than his first suit**'

(iii) *Scoring taxonomy*

'Your opponents are	**vulnerable** and bid to a contract'
'You are	**not vulnerable** and bid to a'
'Neither side is	**vulnerable** during the first hand of'
'are higher than if your side is	**not vulnerable**'

Attribute structures at clause rank and Classifier–Thing structures at nominal group rank (Wignell *et al.* 1987: 47–9). Collocational analysis allows us to show how these and additional structures create the semantics of the world of bridge.

10.3.1 Relational processes of attribution: superordination

Table 10.5 shows three simple taxonomies: (i) the types of messages exchanged (i.e. types of bids), (ii) the comparative ranking of suits, and (iii) a factor in the scoring of points. This and subsequent tables display representative selections from the data set. For example, the nine co-occurrences of *is an invitational bid* are represented by the string '*Raising partner's Minor to the three-level is an invitational bid and shows . . .*'. As was the case with the Values of Tokens in the preceding section, the Attribute categories are stable but the Carriers are variable. For example, both *a new suit at the two-level* and *Three Hearts* are categorized as *forcing bids*. The *bid* Attributes, of course, can be further decomposed as Classifier–Thing structures, as shown in Table 10.8.

Unlike geography, Bridge taxonomizes (i) probability and (ii) evaluation, as can be seen in Table 10.6. This involves the technicalization of Interpersonal rather than of Ideational meaning. Estimating the chance of success in any particular game of bridge is a matter of opinion, but opinion

Table 10.6 Probability and evaluation taxonomy (representative examples): Carrier–**Attribute**

(i) *Probability taxonomy*

Low probability:
'Game is **very unlikely** so stop at the'
'Game is **unlikely** so settle for Part-Game'
'Sometimes it is **possible** to build extra tricks using'

Median probability:
'the Game, if there is one, is **likely** to be in No-Trump'

(ii) *Evaluation taxonomy*

'With 23 points, you are **strong enough** to open at the'
'Some levels are **more attractive than others**'
'Responder chooses whichever bid is **more descriptive**'
'Still, a 50% chance is **better than none**'

---

becomes technical when it is that of an expert rather than that of a layman. In this case the expert's opinion is ideationally based on the quantification of the combined point values of the partners' hands. The taxonomy of probability and evaluation is developed further in Epithet–Thing structures, discussed in more detail in section 10.3.3.2.

10.3.2 Relational processes of possession (realizing meronymy) or circumstance

These structures do not play as important a role in bridge as they do in geography. There is, of course, some meronymy, e.g. *A TRICK consists of four cards*, and *A round of bridge consists of four deals (or hands), each player dealing once in turn*, but these are the only two occurrences of *consists* in the entire text. Instead we find through *is/are in/at* collocations that circumstances of location are taxonomized as shown in Table 10.7. These locations are a reflection of the technical term *how high*, which refers to the increasing number of tricks required to achieve *part-game*, *game*, *slam* and *grand slam*, which in turn has implications for scoring.

Table 10.7 Location taxonomy (representative examples): Carrier **Circumstance** as **Attribute**

'You are **in a contract of One No–Trump**'
'Since you are **already in a Game contract**'
'Neither defender is **in a similar position**'
'Since the bidding is **already at One No–Trump**, a glance'
'to be in Game if responder is **at the top of his range**'

Table 10.8 Classifier **Thing**: hand, suit, bid (representative examples)

(i) 'balanced **hand**' (× 62)
(× 62)

'Since opener has shown a balanced **hand**, he must have
at least two Spades'

'unbalanced **hand**'
(× 15)

'With an unbalanced **hand**, he should bid an old suit at
the three-level'

'invitational **hand**'
(× 6)

'That would show an invitational **hand**'

'following **hand**'
(× 214)

'Suppose you hold the following **hand**'

(ii) 'higher-ranking **suit**'
(× 14)

'With a choice of two five-card suits, bid the
higher-ranking **suit**, Two Spades'

'lower-ranking **suit**'
(× 9)

'Why should he bid One Diamond, the lower-ranking **suit**,
rather than One Spade, the higher-ranking suit?'

'trump **suit**' (× 53)

'In each case, Spades are the trump **suit**'

'spade **suit**' (× 22)

'No, you don't have a four-card Spade **suit**'

'heart **suit**' (× 22)

'You have a potential loser in the Heart **suit**'

'diamond **suit**' (× 11)

'The Diamond **suit** represents your best choice'

'club **suit**' (× 13)

'The Club **suit** seems to offer the best possibility'

'major **suit**'
(× 213)

'Remember, you either play Game in a MAGIC MAJOR **SUIT**
FIT or in No-Trump'

'minor **suit**'
(× 75)

'You have too many points to raise opener's minor **suit**
to the three-level'

'new **suit**' (× 206)

'Can you bid a new **suit** at the one-level?'

'old **suit**' (× 28)

'With an unbalanced hand, he should bid an old **suit**
at the three-level'

'unbid suit' (× 11)

(iii) 'sign-off bid' (× 12)
'invitational bid' (× 27)
'forcing bid' (× 18)
'marathon bid' (× 28)
'opening bid' (× 110)
'cue bid' (× 11)
'substitute bid' (× 5)

'You should have at least three-card support for any unbid suit'

'In both examples, responder's rebid is a sign-off bid.'
'When a player makes an invitational bid, partner may Pass if he is satisfied with the contract'
'While a forcing bid tells partner that he must bid again at his next turn'
'After a marathon bid, HOW HIGH has been determined . . . Game . . . and the'
'As you will see in later chapters, the opening bid is just the start of the auction'
'Partner's cue bid forces you to bid'
'With eleven or more points, find a suitable substitute bid if necessary'

Table 10.9 Epithet **Thing**: hand, suit (representative examples)

(i)	'strong **hand**' (× 12)	'If responder has a strong **hand**, he will be able to carry on to a game contract'
	'weak **hand**' (× 66)	'Do you have a weak **hand**?'
	'short **hand**' (× 5)	'Take your tricks in the short **hand** first'
	'minimum **hand**' (× 112)	'Do I have a minimum **hand**?'
	'medium **hand**' (× 48)	'Opener has shown a medium **hand**'
	'maximum **hand**' (× 51)	'Four Spades is a possible game if partner has a maximum **hand**'
(ii)	'longest **suit**' (× 29)	'Bid your longest **suit** first, Two Spades'
	'longer **suit**' (× 31)	'With a four-card or longer **suit** bid three No-Trump'
	'long **suit**' (× 12)	'You have a good, long **suit** and only ten points'
	'short **suit**' (× 8)	'Lead a short **suit** (other than the trump suit)'
	'best **suit**' (× 7)	'On this hand, the opponent has bid your best **suit**
	'good **suit**' (× 5)	'You will have to overcall Two Clubs to show your good **suit**'

10.3.3 Nominal group structure

10.3.3.1 Classifier–Thing structures realizing superordination

Table 10.8 displays the sub-classifications of three of the most frequently occurring Things of bridge, (i) *hand*, (ii) *suit* and (iii) *bid*, with typical examples. Collocational frequencies are given in parentheses. Here we observe Classifers ranging from those that are Thing-oriented, such as *spade suit*, to those which have nominalized processes, such as *invitational bid*.

10.3.3.2 Epithet–Thing structures realizing superordination

The Epithets in the Epithet–Thing structures displayed in Table 10.9 function very like Classifiers, because they clearly develop the evaluation taxonomy realized at clause rank shown previously in Table 10.6. In this case they have an experiential rather than an attitudinal orientation. We would normally think of the Epithet *strong* as being attitudinal, but in *If responder has a strong hand, he will be able to carry on to a game contract*, *strong* has experiential meaning within the field of bridge: 'it is defining . . .

Table 10.10 Possessive Deictic **Thing** (representative examples)

'opener's **suit**' (× 6)	'a minimum rebid of opener's **suit**'
'partner's **suit**' (× 22)	'you do this by raising partner's **suit** to the appropriate level'
'opponent's **suit**' (× 33)	'You could bid the opponent's **suit**'
'responder's **bid**' (× 7)	'After hearing responder's **bid**, opener can make a second bid which tells responder'
'opponent's **bid**' (× 7)	'If the opponent's **bid** has interfered with your normal response, try to find'

relative to some norm' (Halliday 1985: 163). The norm in this case is the number of tricks required for game (v. part-game or slam) which in turn can be estimated by calculating the point values of the cards in the partners' combined hands.

Since the categories *strong, weak, longest, longer, long, short, maximum, medium,* and *minimum* are all derived from the point value of the cards, they have a precise technical meaning and behave like Classifiers. They remain Epithets, of course, because they can accommodate intensification and comparison.

10.3.3.3 Possessive Deictic Thing structures (not realizing meronymy)

In geography meronymy is realized at the group rank by Possessive Deictic Thing structures, for example 'the rainforest's canopy' (Wignell *et al.* 1987: 48). The Possessive–Deictic–Thing structures displayed in Table 10.10, however, do not realize meronymy. In *you do this by raising partner's suit to the appropriate level,* for example, *suit* is of course not part of the *partner*; instead *partner's suit* is a term in a taxonomy contrasting with *opponent's suit.*

10.4 EXPLAINING THE WORLD OF BRIDGE (THE 'RULES OF THE GAME')

10.4.1 Implication sequences

In addition to defining and ordering technical terms, geography explains the experiential world through IMPLICATION SEQUENCES of cause and effect. Some technical terms are 'defined by a relational identifying clause where the Value is an anaphoric referent for a preceding descriptive sequence of text' (Wignell *et al.* 1987: 51) in which the focus is on Participants and Processes rather than on Things. Other technical terms which have already been defined are 'arranged in a sequence of events in which each event implies the one or ones before it' (Wignell *et al.* 1987:

53). Such implication sequences, which are realized as clause complexes, could be thought of as the 'laws of nature'.

Implication sequences also explain the world of bridge – they are the 'rules of the game'. *DISCARDING*, for example, is a technical term for a Value [which] is an anaphoric referent for a preceding descriptive sequence of text:

> The play to each trick follows some rules: One of the players LEADS to the trick by placing any card he wishes face-up on the table. The other three players play a card, one at a time, in clockwise rotation. Players FOLLOW SUIT to the card led by playing a card in the same suit where possible. If a player cannot follow suit, he plays any card from another suit. This is called DISCARDING. The trick is won by the highest card played in the suit that was led.

At the same time, the whole text is an implication sequence: you cannot 'discard' unless 'following suit' is a rule of the game, and you cannot even play if you do not play in clockwise rotation after someone has initially led to the trick. So the definition of 'discarding' emphasizes 'things in action' rather than 'things in place', as is the case with taxonomy (Wignell *et al.* 1987: 52). Unlike geography, this particular implication sequence is less a matter of cause and effect than of the constraints on behaviour within a temporal ordering. Although 'discarding' does not easily fit into a taxonomy, it could quite comfortably be modelled as a system network with entry conditions leading to choices rather than as the transition networks suggested for modelling change of state in geography (Wignell *et al.* 1987: 53–6).

10.4.2 Decision-making

Not all the rules of the game, however, are expressed through implication sequences. The activity of bridge entails continuous decision-making, and the resource of relational identifying clauses comes into play as this crucial aspect of the world of bridge is explained. These relational identifying clauses foreground the defining of objectives. Table 10.11 ('is/to' collocations) displays definitions of objectives both global (e.g. *1 The object of the PLAY is to win as many tricks as*) and local (e.g. *2 The first step in bidding is to learn how to value your*). Objectives imply strategies for achieving them, so sub-goals are defined as well in terms of choices and options, as in *2 Your second choice is to open ONE OF A SUIT*.

The connection between decision-making and the rules of the game is made particularly clear in the dialogue the reader/player must have with himself/herself to answer the questions *how high?* and *where?*, as shown in Table 10.12. The effect of treating *the first question*, for example, as a Token with the Value *1. CAN I RAISE MY PARTNER'S MAJOR?* is to define *the first question* as a technical term with a field specific meaning. Similarly, *answer* is technicalized, and, depending on which question is being

Table 10.11 Defining Objectives and Strategies: Token **Value**

---

 1 Trick The object of the PLAY is **to win as many tricks as**
 2 hand. The first step in bidding is **to learn how to value your**
 2 No-Trump opening bid. Your second choice is **to open ONE OF A SUIT**
 2 search for your side's longest suit is **to tell partner which is your**
 3 OBJECTIVES The object of the game is **to win as many tricks as**
 3 Summary The object of the game is **to score more points than your**
 5 way for him to do this is **to use his point count**
 7 questions. Question One Responder's first priority is **to try and uncover a**
    MAGIC
 8 question. Question Four The fourth question is **to help you decide whether**
11 best Part-Game. WHERE: Diamonds. Your choice is **to Pass or to bid an**
11 these two cases? Responder's general approach is **to treat them as though**
12 has eighteen points. The more conservative view is **to assume the contract**
    should
14 you do? One of your choices is **to go ahead and bid your**
14 in Three Clubs. Their other option is **to let you play in Two**
15 hand. . . you have nine points. Your choice is **to raise partner's Minor suit**
    or
17 Minor suit(s). The 'ideal' distribution is **to have four-card support for all**
18 SUIT FIT so your first priority is **to bid a four-card or longer**
19 but the safer course of action is **to Pass**. Here's some examples after
19 convenient bid available, the best tactic is **to Pass**. You will hear again
20 do? The way around this dilemma is **to start off by bidding Two**
22 so many possibilities, your first task is **to look for the appropriate**
22 play the contract. The first step is **to apply responder's usual questions**
22 many Aces the partnership has. This is **to avoid getting to a Slam**
23 purpose of a pre-emptive opening bid is **to take bidding space away from**
24 Play Declarer's objective during the play is **to make his contract by taking**
24 his side contracted. The defenders' objective is **to take enough tricks to**
24 Suits Another way to build tricks is **to use your long suits to**
24 to building extra tricks using trumps is **to trump in the hand with**
25 the opponents achieve their objective, which is **to take enough tricks to**

Table 10.12 Defining the Decision-Making Environment: Value **Token**

(× 9) 'So the first question is: 1. **CAN I RAISE PARTNER'S MAJOR?**'
(× 7) 'The second question is: 2. **DO I HAVE A WEAK HAND?**'
(× 26) 'If the answer is **NO**: Go on to the next'
(× 32) 'If the answer is **YES**: Play in a Game contract'

---

answered, particular paths through the bidding system are indicated. These too are part of the 'rules of the game'.

In this dialogue with himself/herself that the reader/player must enter into, whether reading the book or playing a game, the emphasis is ultimately on encoding, since the outcome of the cognition has to be a bidding message which in turn is decoded by the addressee. Table 10.13

Table 10.13 Encoding orientation of wh- questions: **Token** Value (nineteen of fifty-seven)

1	RANK OF THE CARDS. **The Ace** is the highest-ranking card, followed by the
1	the highest-ranking card in the cut is **the DEALER** (if there was no
1	trick since **the Ace of Diamonds** is the highest card played. South leads
1	Hears first for the offensive team is **the declarer**. Here is an example
1	Pass Pass Pass **West** is the dealer and says Pass. North
1	other member of the offensive team is **the DUMMY**. The player on the
1	Which players are partners? **Which player** is the dealer? (2) What is the
1	Which player is the dealer? (2) **What** is the highest-ranking card in the deck
1	highest-ranking card in the deck? **What** is the lowest-ranking card? (3) What
1	What is the lowest-ranking card? (3) **What** is the maximum number of tricks that
1	your right bids Three Spades. **What** is the lowest bid you can make
3	tricks as you can because **this** is the way to score POINTS. If
3	turn. **The end of a round** is the natural breaking point in the
3	in excess of book) when **it** is the offensive team . . . the team that
4	to responder, the captain. Thus: **OPENER** IS THE DESCRIBER The opening bid is
4	IS THE DESCRIBER **The opening bid** is the first step in this process
4	**The decision on the final contract** is the responsibility of the CAPTAIN,
4	Q J 4 D. J 7 6 5 C. 7 4 3 **What** is the minimum number of combined points
4	you and your partner hold? **What** is the maximum number? HOW HIGH should
4	D. K J 7 6 C. K 6 **What** is the minimum number of Hearts in
4	opens the bidding One Spade, **what** is the minimum number of Spades you
4	opens the bidding One No-Trump, **what** is the minimum number of Hearts you
5	Responder (You) 'Three No-Trump' Since **responder** is the captain, it is up
5	by saying Pass. **One No trump** is the final contract. There is one
5	in No-Trump, the only bid available is **the specialized Two Club response**.
6	Four Hearts and Four Spades? (3) **What** is the invitational bid after a One
7	The aim of the bidding conversation is the same: **to discover whether the**
7	AT THE ONE-LEVEL One Spade NONE. **Spades** is the highest-ranking suit. One
7	This response is invitational. **Three No–Trump** is the most likely Game when
8	to place the final contract . . . **that** is the captain's job. By rebidding Two
9	new suit at the one-level. **Opener** is the describer. Responder's bid of a
11	chooses **whichever of the above bids** is the safest Part-Game. For example:
11	the three-level Responder chooses **whichever bid** is the most descriptive.
11	the three-level. Responder chooses **whichever bid** is the most descriptive.
11	to opener. Summary When **your partner** is the opening bidder and makes a
17	and bid his best suit. **It** is the perfect bid to get across
17	if you want to compete, **this** is the chance you must take. Maybe
18	strength . . . eight HCPs. **Your only four-card suit** is the one bid by the opponents
18	unbid suits, you are uncertain **what** is the best Game contract. Partner
19	One Heart One Spade Two Hearts? **What** is the effect of your right-hand
20	the bidding One No-Trump: **Two Clubs** is the Stayman convention Two Hearts

Table 10.13 contd.

21	partnership to the Slam level. **What** is the solution? Strong hands of 22 or
21	showing a five-card suit **Three Clubs** is the Stayman Convention You can use
21	no points, bids Two No-Trump. **This** is the conventional response to keep the
21	a four-card suit. However, since **this** is the exception rather than the rule
22	one or two tricks. The first is **the BLACKWOOD CONVENTION**, named after its
22	the Blackwood convention. The second tool is **the GERBER CONVENTION**, named
23	Pass and hope that **Three No-Trump** is the best contract, (2) FOUR SPADES.
24	keep two things in mind: **Experience** is the best teacher . . . especially when
24	be able to tell if **this** the case. If both opponents follow
24	one trick in the suit. **What** is the difference between this example and
24	win the trick by trumping. **That** is the advantage of playing in a
24	A K Q J 7 3 (You) (2) **What** is the maximum number of tricks you
25	do to build tricks. If **this** is the case, you should generally not
26	declarer trumping your winning tricks. **What** is the longest suit in your
26	your hand and hope that **it** is the longest suit in the combined

---

shows that nineteen *WH*-questions are seeking Tokens rather than Values, the precise and recognizable shapes and forms into which meanings are coded. That is to say, the key thing is to be able to deal in Tokens. It would in fact be quite natural in this text to find, for example, in chapter 4 *WHAT* (Token) *is* THE FIRST STEP IN THIS PROCESS (Value)? rather than *THE OPENING BID* (Token) *is* THE FIRST STEP IN THIS PROCESS (Value). Similarly in Table 10.14 it would be equally natural to find 'What is the most specific opening contract' rather than 'The most specific is One No-Trump'.

Table 10.14 Encoding orientation of bids: Value **Token**

(× 11)	'What is your trick score?'
(× 12)	'Your hand is worth **seventeen points** (thirteen HCPs plus three points for'
(× 6)	'The most specific opening contract is **One No-Trump**'
(× 5)	'The final contract is **Two Hearts** and the declarer is'
(× 5)	'Instead, your response is **Three No-Trump**, telling opener'

10.5 THE FUNCTION OF TECHNICALITY

Is technicality a necessary and benign shorthand or is it obscurantist and exclusive jargon? Wignell *et al.* (1987: 59) concluded that it would be wrong to stigmatize technical terms in geography as jargon, because 'attaching a Token to a Value is giving the term a VALEUR in the system within that field', but that the popular view of technical terms as shorthand was well founded linguistically, since technical terms distil meanings. Both these conclusions are as valid for bridge as they are for geography.

Technicality in bridge functions in much the same way as it does in geography. Technical terms are introduced and defined in relational intensive identifying clauses. Then these terms are taxonomized as field-specific systems of Valeur, such as types of bid and kinds of suit, although bridge has taxonomies of probablility and evaluation as well. The activity of bridge is 'explained' by the rules of the game. In 'explaining' bridge, however, technicality functions somewhat differently from the way it does in geography, since it enables the 'doing' of bridge as well as the 'knowing about' of bridge. At the same time, 'knowing about' and 'doing' are very interdependent. Bridge is primarily a cognitive activity, and the intensive identifying clauses turned up in this study force the reader/player to think very precisely and in a defining way about roles, objectives, strategies and choices in order to make decisions which are ultimately encoded as bidding messages which must in turn be decoded in an equally precise way. Fuzzy thinking will lead to losing, whereas precise thinking will lead to winning. So the 'rules of the game' involve much more than simply playing 'according to Hoyle'.

REFERENCES

Benson, J.D., and Greaves, W.S. (1989), 'Using narrow-span collocations in parsing lexicogrammatical output of field in a natural language text', paper presented at the 16th International Systemic Workshop, Helsinki.

Grant, A., and Rodwell, E. (1984), *The Joy of Bridge*, Toronto, Prentice-Hall.

Halliday, M.A.K. (1985), *An Introduction to Functional Grammar*, London, Edward Arnold.

Martin, J.R. (forthcoming), 'Life as a noun: arresting the universe in science and humanities', in E. Ventola (ed.), *Selected Theoretical Papers from the 16th International Systemic Congress*, Amsterdam, John Benjamins.

Martin, J.R., Wignell, P., Eggins, S., and Rothery, J. (1988), 'Secret English: discourse technology in a junior secondary school', in L. Gerot, J. Oldenburg and T. Van Leeuwen (eds), *Language and Socialisation: Home and School: Proceedings from the Working Conference on Language in Education*, Sydney, Macquarie University.

Reed, A. (1977), 'CLOC: a collocation package', *ALLC Bulletin* 5, 168–73.

—— (1984), 'Anatomy of a text analysis package', *Computer Language* 9.2, 89–96.

Wignell, P., Martin, J.R., and Eggins, S. (1987), 'The discourse of geography: ordering and explaining the experiential world', in S. Eggins, J.R. Martin and P. Wignell, *Working Papers in Linguistics* 5, *Writing Project Report*, Sydney, University of Sydney Linguistics Department.

11 Splitting the referent: an introduction to narrative enactors

Catherine Emmott

11.1 LOCATING THE FICTIONAL REFERENT

The characters in a fictional narrative have no existence in the real world and yet for the reader they seem to have an interest over and above that of mere names on a page. This apparent anomaly can be explained by the fact that as we read we collect information from the text about each character, remembering details about their appearance, personality, actions and background. We build an 'image' of a character in our mind and with every subsequent mention of the individual we not only add to this MENTAL REPRESENTATION (Brown and Yule 1983) but utilize it. At each step the information that has already been stored away casts light on the character's current actions and situation and enables us to view that character as a rounded individual with whom we can empathize.

If we incorporate these notions into a theory of reference, then in fiction the mental representation becomes the referent. So the referent, although constructed from the text, is located not in the text or in the real world but in the mind. Brown and Yule (1983: 202) provide linguistic evidence for mental representations from their example:

Kill an active, plump chicken. Prepare it for the oven. . .

Brown and Yule criticize linguists who view the referent of the pronoun *it* as being in the text in the form of the nominal *an active, plump chicken*. Brown and Yule argue that the referent is a mental representation of a dead plump chicken built by fusing information from the earlier sentence.

The position that Brown and Yule are criticizing is adopted by Halliday and Hasan (1976)[1] throughout much[2] of *Cohesion in English*. The following statements describe a referent that is located in the text: '*he* refers back to *Henry*' (Halliday and Hasan 1976: 14, their italics); 'a third person form typically refers anaphorically to a preceding item in the text' (p. 48). Halliday and Hasan nevertheless argue that reference is more than straight substitution, stressing repeatedly that whilst substitution is a lexicogrammatical

relation (because in such cases the pronoun must retain the same grammatical form as the antecedent), reference is a semantic relation (because
there is then no such restriction). A semantic relation should, however,
provide a key to meaning. Halliday and Hasan's reference ties are
supposed to indicate that a pronoun has the same meaning as its antecedent (although, as Brown and Yule demonstrate, the meaning is often not
quite the same), but they do not tell us what that meaning is. Halliday and
Hasan claim that *he* refers anaphorically to *Henry* but this does not tell us
anything about Henry. The reason is that Halliday and Hasan's model of
reference is designed to distinguish between text and non-text rather than
to account for the reader's processing of a text. As they point out, 'Cohesion does not concern what a text means; it concerns how the text is
constructed as a semantic edifice' (p. 26).

If we regard referents in fiction as existing in the mind in the form of
mental representations, then both pronouns and nouns refer ultimately to
these representations, unlocking the information within these stores and
giving the pronouns and nouns real meaning. Additional arguments for
mental representations are provided in Brown and Yule (1983) and
Emmott (1989). The main purpose of this chapter is to go one stage
further and look at the structure of mental representations, considering
how the information within them is stored. A psychologist doing this would
generally question or test a human subject in an attempt to reveal how the
mind works. A linguist, on the other hand,[3] examines text and infers
from it what must be happening in the mind if a reader is to understand
the text at a basic propositional level.[4] In this particular study we shall be
considering texts involving narrative flashback, arguing that in order to
account for how these texts are processed we must postulate mental
representations in which the information is stored in distinct compartments
and accessed selectively by the reader. An examination of ambiguity in
narrative text provides support for this proposal.

11.2 DIFFERENT FORMS OF AMBIGUITY

Ambiguity occurs only if there are two or more possibilities to choose from.
Normally when we talk of personal pronoun ambiguity in narrative we
mean that we are uncertain about which character is being referred to. In
such cases the choice is between two or more different mental representations. Since the mental representations that we have set up for the
characters are our referents, we will term this REFERENT AMBIGUITY.

Let us suppose, however, that it is still possible to have ambiguity even
when we are clear about which character is being referred to. If we have
identified the character we must already have selected one particular
mental representation. Ambiguity in such cases can be explained as a
choice between two or more different aspects or compartments of the
mental representation. Compartments are necessary for keeping information distinct about different ENACTORS. Narrative enactors are created

when a single referent has distinct roles in the narrative, such as when one referent coexists in narrative present and in flashback. This second type of ambiguity can, therefore, be termed ENACTOR AMBIGUITY.

Example 1, from Doris Lessing's *The Four-gated City*, will be used to explain the difference between referent ambiguity and enactor ambiguity. The analysis is given after the example to allow an unbiased reading of the text.

Example 1

A modest brown door had *Baxter's* on it – just the word, nothing more. There was a window completely covered by white muslin that needed washing. Martha stood outside for a moment, holding this delicious moment known only to newcomers in a city: behind this door, which was just like so many others, *what will there be?* A southern courtyard with a lemon-tree beside a fountain and a masked Negro lute-player asleep? [. . .] Why not? Since what actually does appear is so improbable. Last week she had opened a door by mistake on a staircase in Bayswater and a woman in a tight black waspwaisted corset, pearls lolling between two great naked breasts, stood by a cage made of gold wire the size of a fourposter bed, in which were a dozen or so brilliantly fringed and tinted birds. Martha said: 'I'm sorry.' The woman said: 'If you are looking for Mr. Pelham, he's in Venice this week.'

She went in. A man in shabby dinner clothes and sleeked-down dandruffy hair came forward . . .

[1972: 34; Lessing's italics]

Let us focus on the sentence *She went in* at the beginning of the second paragraph. On first reading this novel, the pronoun *She* seemed to me clearly to denote Martha, Martha being the only one of the two women to be outside and hence the only one who could be said to 'go in'. If all other readers respond to the text in the same way then there is no referent ambiguity here.[5] Referent ambiguity would arise only if a reader were unable to choose between the mental representations of the two characters, Martha and the woman wearing the corset, or if two different readers made opposing choices.

Enactor ambiguity is quite different. Even if we are sure that it is Martha who is 'going in', there may still be uncertainty or a lack of consensus about whether it is the Martha of the flashback going into the Bayswater room, or the Martha of the present going into Baxter's, a London restaurant. The verb form cannot be taken as a signal of a shift to the present here, for the flashback has itself already reverted from the far past (e.g. *she had opened*) to the simple past (e.g. *Martha said*). Neither does the paragraph boundary offer any proof of a switch, as narrative flashbacks often extend beyond the paragraph.[6]

Those readers who think that there is a switch to the present at this point will have their interpretation reinforced, for we are subsequently told that *the man in shabby dinner clothes* is a waiter, indicating that we have entered the restaurant. Readers who assume that there has been no forward time shift will be forced to employ a repair strategy at this later mention of the waiter, scanning back through the text for a point where such a shift might be assumed to have taken place. Other readers may be aware of these different possibilities on meeting the sentence *She went in* and may withhold judgement until further clues are supplied. Whatever our reading of the text, the choice that is being made now is not between mental representations, for we are assuming that we have already selected Martha, but between compartments within the one mental representation, the enactors of Martha.

11.3 THE STRUCTURE OF THE MENTAL REPRESENTATION

It could be argued that the ambiguity of the sentence *She went in* lies not in which Martha (past or present) is performing the action but simply in her whereabouts. If this were the case there would be no need to postulate enactors. There are, however, often differences between a character-in-the-present and a character-in-flashback other than their different locations. The enactors will be of different ages and may be different in appearance, be of different states of mind and have different intentions. The further back in time the flashback takes us, the more marked the differences are likely to be. We need to know the distinctive features of our particular enactor in order to make sense of the text. If one enactor is old and the other young, or if one is mad and the other sane, then the reader needs to be able to make the distinction.[7] So enactors need to be kept distinct in the text, and to achieve this the information needs to be stored separately.

Let us now consider the nature of enactors and the structure of the mental representation in more detail. In discussing example 1 we have assumed that there is just one present enactor and one past enactor. It could be argued that when we know a great deal about a character's past history our mind stores enactors from all these past periods. Enactors are, however, more concrete than that. They are formed only when the text actually refers to a character at a particular point in time. Enactors retain their status as enactors only whilst the text continues to refer to them or whilst there is the expectation that the text will shortly resume making reference to them. So, as we read the flashback in example 1, although we cease to refer to the present enactor, we nevertheless keep that enactor 'on hold', for we anticipate a return to the present.

For the purposes of filling the pronoun slot in the sentence *She went in* we need only decide between the two enactors, Martha of the present and Martha of the week before. Although we may have BACKGROUND BIOGRAPHICAL INFORMATION about Martha at other periods in her life from which we could in theory construct enactors, the text has not recently referred to these other periods and so we have not set up enactors from them. There seems little possibility that a reader could interpret *She went in* as meaning a Martha of, say, fifteen years ago when no flashback to that period has been signalled.

Background biographical information does, however, give us a complete picture of our selected enactor. In Lessing's *The Four-gated City* information about Martha's childhood in Africa explains her present political views and her relations with her mother. Such information is NON-CURRENT (Martha no longer lives in Africa) but it is still RELEVANT to our understanding of the enactor. The mental representation must, therefore, have a compartment for such background biographical information as well as compartments for enactors. When we select an enactor we foreground (bring to the forefront of consciousness) the information about that enactor against both background biographical information and information about the other enactor.

11.4 SIGNALLING THE APPROPRIATE ENACTOR

The way in which the selection of enactors and referents is signalled may also differ. For referents, a pronoun can eliminate from consideration a referent that is not of the same sex as the pronoun. A pronoun cannot, however, favour one enactor over another because both enactors, being the same person, are of the same sex. Moreover, referents can generally be distinguished because they have quite different names or because only a part of the name is common to them. Enactors, on the other hand, will usually have the same personal name(s) and family name, as is the case in example 1.

To select an enactor we will, therefore, often have to draw on additional clues in the text, both DESCRIPTIVE and CONTEXTUAL. A DESCRIPTIVE CLUE replicates information stored away in the mental representation of the character, such as information about the character's appearance. A clue can foreground the appropriate enactor only if the clue is DISTINCTIVE. So the information that the character is wearing red will identify one particular enactor only if that enactor is the only one who is wearing red. If both enactors are wearing red, then the clue is SHARED and cannot distinguish one from the other. Once a distinctive clue has been given, all the information stored about that enactor can be foregrounded.

Descriptive clues, such as information about clothes or hairstyle, are often used to distinguish between enactors in film. Since film is a visual medium, some descriptive information is normally given every time we see a character. In reading narrative text we never see the character (except perhaps in accompanying illustrations), so descriptive information can be presented only by means of the written word. To describe a character repeatedly can become verbose and can detract from the actions that the character is performing. Written narrative therefore frequently makes use of CONTEXTUAL CLUES to distinguish between enactors. A contextual[8] clue is a piece of information not about the enactor but about the

FRAME[9] (Emmott 1989, forthcoming) in which the enactor is present. Frames are mental stores which monitor a particular location at a particular time together with details of all the people and objects in that location. Shared contextual clues, like shared descriptive clues, cannot isolate an enactor. The information that Martha *went in* was insufficient to tell us whether this was Martha-in-flashback or Martha-in-the-present, because both Marthas were standing by doors. Distinctive contextual clues, however, can isolate an enactor. In the following example, from Doris Lessing's *A Man and two Women*, the mention of the car, in the last line, serves as a distinctive contextual clue.

Example 2

> *They* [Jack and Stella] *were walking to the car,* parked under a tree.
> 'How's the baby?'
> 'Little bleeder never sleeps, he's wearing us out, but he's fine.'
> The baby was six weeks old. Having the baby was a definite achievement: getting it safely conceived and born had taken a couple of years. Dorothy, like most independent women, had had divided thoughts about a baby. . . . Dorothy would talk, while she was pregnant, in a soft staccato voice: Perhaps I don't really want a baby at all? Perhaps I'm not fitted to be a mother? Perhaps . . . and if so . . . and how . . .
> She said: 'Until recently Jack and I were always with people who took it for granted that getting pregnant was a disaster, and now suddenly all the people we know have young children and baby-sitters and . . . perhaps . . . if . . .'
> Jack said: 'You'll feel better when it's born.'
> Once Stella had heard him say, after one of Dorothy's long-troubled dialogues with herself: 'Now that's enough, that's enough Dorothy.' He had silenced her, taking the responsibility.
> *They reached the car, got in.*
>
> [1965: 91–2, my italics]

The present enactors of Jack and Stella are put 'on hold' as they walk towards the car. They are still enactors, capable of filling unmarked pronoun slots, but remain unselected during the course of the flashback. The proximity of the car is a piece of contextual information which is stored away whilst we read the flashback. Subsequently, with the words *They reached the car, got in*, the mention of the car serves as a contextual clue which we can use to interpret the pronoun *They*. Since it is Jack and Stella who are near a car, *They* can be taken to refer to Jack and Stella. This in spite of the fact that in the previous sentence, *He had silenced her, taking the responsibility*, the referents were not Jack and Stella but Jack and Dorothy. Moreover, *They* foregrounds the present enactors of Jack and Stella even though the last mention of these characters was as flashback enactors. Contextual information, such as the proximity to a car, is generally of little interest to the reader once the action moves on. Such information can be temporarily significant, however, because it can function in place of an antecedent when we interpret a pronoun, allowing us to select a referent and to foreground the appropriate enactor.

11.5 CONCLUSION

If we accept the idea of mental representations we then view the antecedent of a pronoun not as the referent but as the key to the referent, the mental representation. This chapter leads us to question further the role of the antecedent. Cases where the referent(s) of a pronoun can be determined even though there is no adequate antecedent, as in example 2, may be rare but they do nevertheless need to be accounted for in a comprehensive model of reference. Cases where the antecedent gives no clue to the enactor(s) are more common and also need to be accounted for. When there is no adequate antecedent, the suggestion is that contextual clues may be used to help identify both referent and enactor. Contextual clues can recall a complete frame, with the appropriate enactors in the appropriate location at the appropriate time.

These frames are mental representations of fictional context. The term 'mental representation' has been used in this paper to mean a store of information about a particular character, in line with Brown and Yule (1983). CHARACTER (or ENTITY) CONSTRUCT is a more appropriate term for Brown and Yule's 'mental representation' once we begin to postulate other types of mental store such as the frame. A character construct is a mental representation which can function as a referent in narrative. A frame is a mental representation which can give access to this referent, help foreground the appropriate enactor, and recall an earlier fictional setting.

NOTES

1 *Cohesion in English* is not, of course, the only work in which Halliday and Hasan discuss reference theory, but it is probably their most influential statement on the subject.
2 Elsewhere in *Cohesion in English* Halliday and Hasan tell us that a pronoun, rather than referring to a noun, is co-referential with a noun, as both 'refer to the same thing' (1976: 3). The term REFERENCE is being used by Halliday and Hasan in two quite distinct ways in the same work.
3 These different methodologies are used by researchers with different types of expertise and should be viewed as complementary rather than competing.
4 This is the approach used by Brown and Yule (1983). They, however, restrict themselves either to made-up texts or to short, real texts, as opposed to the full-length real narratives examined here.
5 Although the woman wearing the corset is already inside, the sentence *She went in* could perhaps be taken to mean that the woman leaves the doorway and goes back into the room. This would need to be tested empirically, for ambiguity can be said to exist only when readers are undecided or make different choices, not

when text analysts argue for conflicting interpretations. True readers are those who are in the process of reading the entire novel for the first time, not those who just read extracts like example 1.

6 Emmott (1989: 180–4, 207–10) provides a more detailed discussion of this example.

7 Goffman (1979: 519–22) and Quirk (1986: 64) also postulate past and present realizations of a single referent.

8 I am using the term 'context' here in a fairly restricted way to mean features of the fictional setting in a narrative, i.e. fictional context.

9 Goffman's (1979) frames are a parallel notion in sociology. The term 'frame' is used in a rather different way by Minsky (1977), for Minsky's interest is in general knowledge schemata rather than the mental representations built from a specific text. (See Emmott 1989; forthcoming)

REFERENCES

Brown, G. and Yule, G. (1983), *Discourse Analysis*, Cambridge, Cambridge University Press.

Emmott, C. (1989), 'Reading between the Lines: Building a Comprehensive Model of Participant Reference in Real Narrative', unpublished Ph.D. thesis, University of Birmingham.

——— (forthcoming), 'Frames of reference: contextual monitoring and the interpretation of narrative', in R.M. Coulthard (ed.), *Papers in Text Analysis*, London, Routledge.

Goffman, E. (1975), *Frame Analysis: an Essay on the Organization of Experience*, Harmondsworth, Penguin.

Halliday, M.A.K., and Hasan, R. (1976), *Cohesion in English*, London: Longman.

Lessing, D. (1965), 'A man and two women' in D. Lessing, *A Man and two Women*, pp. 88–107, London, Grafton Books.

——— (1972), *The Four-gated City*, London, Grafton Books.

Minsky, M. (1977), 'Frame-system theory' in P.N. Johnson-Laird and P.C. Wason (eds), *Thinking: Readings in Cognitive Science*, pp. 421–32, Cambridge, Cambridge University Press.

Quirk, R. (1986), *Words at Work: Lectures on Textual Structure*, London, Longman.

ACKNOWLEDGEMENTS

Cambridge University Press, Cambridge, for an extract from *Discourse Analysis* by G. Brown and G. Yule (1983); Longman Group U.K., Harlow, for extracts from *Cohesion in English* by M.A.K. Halliday and R. Hasan (1976); HarperCollins Publishers, London, and Alfred A. Knopf Inc., New York, for an extract from *The Four-Gated City* by Doris Lessing (first published 1969); HarperCollins Publishers, London, and Jonathan Clowes Ltd., London, for an extract from 'A man and two women' in *A Man and Two Women* by Doris Lessing (first published 1963).

12 The uses of passivity: supressing agency in *Nineteen eighty-four*
Daniel Kies

12.1 INTRODUCTION

The linguistic criticism of *Nineteen Eighty-Four* has focused primarily on Newspeak as a language (Flammia 1987: 28–33; Harris 1987: 113–19) and on Orwell's ideas about the relationship between language and thought (Kress and Hodge 1979: 144–50). It has largely ignored, however, the literary language Orwell used in writing *Nineteen Eighty-Four*. Indeed, the few critical remarks about Orwell's use of language have generally been negative, sometimes attributing the dull, monotonous, dry writing style to Orwell's career as a journalist (Ringbom 1973: 11–12; Petro 1982: 95; Bloom 1987: 1–2) or to the phlegmatic topic of his novel. Irving Howe (1982: 321), for example, writes that

> the style of *1984*, which many readers take to be drab or uninspired or 'sweaty,' would have been appreciated by someone like Defoe, since Defoe would have immediately understood how the pressures of Orwell's subject, like the pressures of his own, demand a gritty and hammering factuality. The style of *1984* is the style of a man whose commitment to a dreadful vision is at war with the nausea to which that vision reduces him. So acute is this conflict that delicacies of phrasing or displays of rhetoric come to seem frivolous – *he has no time, he must get it all down.* Those who fail to see this, I am convinced, have succumbed to the pleasant tyrannies of estheticism; they have allowed their fondness for a cultivated style to blind them to the urgencies of prophetic expression. The last thing Orwell cared about when he wrote *1984*, the last thing he should have cared about, was literature.

Those critical responses to Orwell – including Howe's defence of his style – are wrong. Orwell asserted that one of his primary motives for writing was

> Aesthetic enthusiasm. Perception of beauty in the external world, or, on

the other hand, in words and their right arrangement. Pleasure in the impact of one sound on another, in the firmness of good prose or the rhythm of a good story. Desire to share an experience which one feels is valuable and ought not to be missed. The aesthetic motive is very feeble in a lot of writers, but even a pamphleteer or a writer of textbooks will have pet words and phrases which appeal to him for non-utilitarian reasons; or he may feel strongly about typography, width of margins, etc. Above the level of a railway guide, no book is quite free from aesthetic considerations.

[*Collected Essays* 1: 3–4[1]]

The Orwell who wrote that

What I have most wanted to do throughout the past ten years is to make political writing into an art. . . . I could not do the work of writing a book, or even a long magazine article, if it were not also an aesthetic experience.

[*Collected Essays* 1: 6]

could not have been indifferent to literary artistry, including literary style. In fact Orwell's writing style is a carefully constructed complex of various linguistic devices that contribute importantly to the central themes of *Nineteen Eighty-Four*.

One of those themes is the powerlessness of the individual under a totalitarian government. Orwell illustrated that futility through the fate of Winston Smith; however, it is not at the level of plot that the reader can best appreciate that powerlessness. Rather, it is through the language that Orwell used to describe Winston, to narrate his actions and to develop his character that the reader perceives not only the futility of struggle but also Orwell's sensitivity to both the use and the meaning of language. Specifically, Orwell manipulated the expression of AGENCY so that Winston Smith is never seen as active or in control of any situation.

AGENCY is one of the most widely used techniques to control a literary theme in a text (Cluysenaar 1975: 63–5; Dillon 1978: 9–21; Empson 1963: 1–47; Enkvist 1973: 115–18; Halliday 1971: 330–65; Leech and Short 1981: 189–91). It can be expressed (or suppressed) by a number of syntactic constructions, and Orwell employed them all to establish the complete abolition of human freedom. Many of the examples below come from one scene in the novel, the end of Part Two, Section III, in which Winston and Julia feel some satisfaction in their lives, in their physical relationship, and in their loving protection of each other. It is interesting to note that, just at the one point in the novel when the reader might expect these characters to be active and in control, Orwell used language that continually undercuts any sense of Winston or Julia as an agent, a conscious initiator of an action. Central among the linguistic features that undercut agency is passive voice.

Orwell was keenly aware of the potential that passive voice held for manipulating a hearer/reader: it allows the speaker/writer to hide the agent by neglecting to mention the agentive *by*-phrase. Orwell's fourth rule for clear writing was 'Never use the passive where you can use the active' (*Collected Essays* 4: 139). Yet just two years after writing that rule Orwell seemed to revise his thinking. In 'Politics and the English language' he was acutely aware of the subtleties of meaning afforded by changes in syntax; but in *Nineteen Eighty-Four* he seemed to incorporate the thematic, informational flexibility afforded by passive voice syntax into his writing. (This was not the only reversal in Orwell's thinking about language. Orwell came to realize that the Anglo-Saxon word stock that he had championed in 'Politics and the English language' might supply the vocabulary for Newspeak whereas Latinate English allowed greater scope for linguistic [and thereby human] freedom.)

12.2 ANALYSIS

In total Orwell exploited fourteen syntactic devices to undercut agency throughout the novel.

12.2.1 Passives

1. Bill hit John.
   [Active voice, grammatical subject clearly expressing the agent.]
2. John was hit (by Bill).
   [Passive voice, grammatical subject does not express agency; the agent is expressed through a prepositional phrase with *by*, if it is expressed at all.]

Passives are among the most common grammatical devices to undercut agency in English, allowing the agentive noun phrase to occur out of thematic, sentence-initial position in an optional agentive *by*-phrase at the end of the sentence (Curme 1931: 443-7; Quirk *et al.* 1985: 159-71). By writing in the passive voice, eliminating the agentive *by*-phrase, Orwell was able to suggest that his characters are not conscious initiators of action:

She described to him, almost as if she had seen or felt it, the stiffening of Katharine's body as soon as he touched her, the way in which she still seemed to be pushing him from her with all her strength, even when her arms WERE CLASPED tightly round him.

[*1984*, 110]

The instrument (the telescreen, it WAS CALLED) could BE DIMMED, but there was no way of shutting it off completely.

[p. 6]

Orwell does not use the active voice here as in these paraphrases of the examples above: *Katharine clasped her arms tightly round him*, or *People called it the telescreen*, or *Smith could dim the instrument*. The characters would appear far too agentive, too active, too much in control.

12.2.2 Nominalizations

1. Free radicals oxidize cell membranes quickly.
2. The oxidation of cell membranes (by free radicals) was quick.
   [Nominalization of the verb *oxidize*.]

Nominalized verbs undercut agency in that they can occur without any overt mention of agency (again supplied through the optional presence of an agentive *by*-phrase); see, for example, Kies (1985: 300–1). Orwell was able to describe Katharine's reaction to Winston's touch almost as if her stiffening were a physical process beyond Katharine's conscious control:

> She described to him, almost as if she had seen or felt it, the STIFFEN-ING of Katharine's body as soon as he touched her . . . .
>
> [p. 110]

To write that *Katharine stiffened her body* would make Katharine conscious and agentive. The nominalized verb *stiffening* robs Katharine of consciousness and thus agency. Notice also how Winston has a *sensation* (rather than *senses*) in this description of drinking Victory Gin:

> The stuff was like nitric acid, and moreover, in swallowing it, one had the SENSATION of being hit on the back of the head with a rubber club.
>
> [p. 8]

For Orwell to write *Winston sensed being hit on the back of the head* would make Winston too active, too conscious, too much the agent.

12.2.3 Intransitives

1. John opened the door.
   [Transitive pattern, agent clearly identified in the clause.]
2. The door opened.
   [Intransitive pattern, agent uncertain and thus suspense builds.]

Intransitive uses of verbs allow a writer to suggest that events arise or occur in the story beyond the control of characters by suppressing any explicit mention of human agents, as is usually required by the transitive use of verbs. (See Austin 1986 for an interesting discussion of the syntactic and thematic tension that can arise through the manipulation of transitivity patterns in the language of literature.) Orwell seems to strip Winston of control over his own thoughts by using an intransitive verb in the main clause:

Actually THE IDEA HAD FIRST FLOATED INTO HIS HEAD in the form of a vision, of a glass paperweight mirrored by the surface of the gateleg.

[p. 114]

The possible transitive paraphrases, for example *Winston floated the idea in the form of a vision of a glass paperweight*, present an agentive Winston.

12.2.4 PATIENTS as subjects

1. John sent a package.
   [Grammatical subject is agent, consciously initiates the action described in the predication.]
2. John got a package.
   [Grammatical subject is patient, the goal of the predication.]

Verbs like *get, see* and *hear* (as opposed to *send, look* and *listen*) undercut agency in that they imply that the grammatical subject of the sentence is not the initiator of the activity described by the verb, but is rather a patient affected by that activity. Notice Orwell's undercutting of Winston's agency in the following sentence, which also demonstrates the use of an atypical passive construction:

. . . the rule was not strictly kept, because there were various things such as shoelaces and razor blades which it was impossible TO GET HOLD OF . . . .

[p. 9]

The old man had grown noticeably more cheerful after RECEIVING the four dollars. Winston realized that he WOULD HAVE ACCEPTED three or even two.

[p. 81]

. . . look, I got a little packet of tea as well.

[p. 117]

You will receive orders, and you will obey them . . . .

[p. 144]

If you're happy inside yourself, why should you GET excited about Big Brother and the Three-Year Plans and the Two Minute Hate and all the rest of their bloody rot?

[p. 111]

Paraphrases like *why should you become excited about* or *take excitement in Big Brother* all present an agentive *you* as subject, where excitement builds from within the individual. However, the more passive *you* of the original passage must 'get' excitement from outside him- or herself.

12.2.5 Depersonalization

1. John spoke.
2. John's voice spoke.
   A voice spoke.
   [Both sentences in (2) represent a depersonalizing/dehumanizing metonymy.]

Depersonalization depends on metonymy, where a part of a person (often a voice or a thought – the least physical and hence least agentive features of a person) is used to represent, figuratively, the whole person:

HIS THIN DARK FACE had become animated, HIS EYES had lost their mocking expression and grown almost dreamy.

[*1984*, 45]

. . . and it was possible that HIS FEATURES had not been perfectly under control.

[p. 54]

A HAND fell lightly on his shoulder.

[p. 99]

THE YOUTHFUL BODY was strained against his own, THE MASS OF DARK HAIR was against his face . . . HER YOUTH AND PRETTINESS had frightened him . . . THE GIRL picked herself up and pulled a bluebell out of her hair.

[p. 100]

And THE THOUGHT struck him . . . .

[p. 112]

HIS MOTHER'S ANXIOUS EYES were fixed on his face.

[p. 135]

THE TELESCREEN barked at him to keep still.

[p. 191]

. . . A YELL from the telescreen bade them be silent.

[p. 191]

HIS FROGLIKE FACE grew calmer . . . [where the face is metonymical for the whole person]

[p. 192]

'Smith!' yelled THE VOICE from the telescreen.

[p. 193]

12.2.6 Perfect aspect

1. John wants to go.
   [Present tense expression of agent's desire.]
   John wanted to go.
   [Past tense, but still agent's desire is relevant.]
2. John had wanted to go.
   [Perfect aspect, agent's desire no longer relevant to the present.]

The perfect aspect of the verb suggests completed activity, that all action was finished in the remote past, undercutting any sense of action – even past action – that might have any relevance to the activity of the present. Orwell shifted to the perfect aspect to underscore the characters' sense of powerlessness and impotence:

. . . and it was possible that his features HAD not BEEN perfectly under control.

[p. 54]

Katharine, in any case, HAD long CEASED to be a painful memory and BECOME merely a distasteful one.

[p. 110]

Unlike Winston, she HAD GRASPED the inner meaning of the Party's sexual puritanism.

[p. 110]

She HAD CLASPED her arms around his neck, she was calling him darling, precious one, loved one. He HAD PULLED her down on to the ground, she was utterly unresisting . . .

[p. 100]

12.2.7 Negation

1. John hit Bill.
   [Positive assertion of agency.]
2. John didn't hit Bill.
   [Negated assertion undercuts agency.]

Negation undercuts agency most directly, highlighting the agent's limited abilities:

. . . so long as he stayed in his present position he could NOT be seen.

[*1984*, 9]

Unfortunately, he could NOT remember whether she had already been at that table when he arrived . . . .

[p. 54]

. . . and it was possible that his features had NOT been perfectly under control.

[p. 54]

He still had NOT the courage to approach her.

[p. 99]

In this game we're playing, we caN'T win.

[p. 112]

He stopped, but he did NOT come back.

[p. 135]

12.2.8 Stative verbs/resultative verbs

1. John stopped.
   [Ordinary intransitive verb.]
2. John was stopped.
   [Statal passive suggests an outside agency stopped John.]

Verbs that suggest the existence of a state or a result of some other action can also undercut any sense of immediate agency on the part of its associated grammatical subject. In the following example even cognitive activities such as remembering (in themselves suggesting less agency than physical activities) seem static rather than dynamic processes for Winston:

Katharine, in any case, HAD LONG CEASED TO BE A PAINFUL MEMORY AND BECOME MERELY A DISTASTEFUL ONE.

[p. 110]

There had been times when consciousness . . . HAD STOPPED DEAD
. . . .

[p. 198]

12.2.9 Presentational *there* structures

1. A man with a briefcase sat down.
   [Agentive subject.]
2. There sat down a man with a briefcase.
   [Agentive subject is de-emphasized in sentence-medial position.]

Michael Halliday (1985: 38–67) illustrates the significance of the sentence-initial position in organizing the clause as message. The sentence-initial position is significant, he reminds us, because it serves to introduce the 'theme' of discourse. Similarly, Quirk *et al.* (1985: 1356–7) highlight the significance of sentence-final position in organizing the information structure of a clause. The sentence-final position becomes important in English since it serves as the locus of 'new' information in the clause (and discourse). Hence, if one wished to use sentence position alone to downplay the agency of a particular noun phrase, sentence-medial position would seem ideal since it keeps that particular noun phrase out of thematic or informationally prominent positions within the sentence. Sentences with presentational *there* subjects allow speakers and writers to de-emphasize agentive grammatical subjects by burying them in sentence-medial position, as Orwell did:

THERE was nobody of whom they could ask the way.

[p. 111]

Also notice Orwell's use of negation in the grammatical subject above to undercut further any sense of agency.

THERE was no evidence, only fleeting glimpses that might mean anything or nothing . . . .

[p. 18]

In a place like this, the danger that THERE was a hidden microphone was very small, and even if THERE was a microphone it would only pick up sounds.

[p. 112]

Presentational *there* undercuts agency above, since the agents, presumably Winston and the Thought Police, go unmentioned; compare *Winston found no evidence* or *the danger that the Thought Police hid microphones was small*.

12.2.10 Subjunctive mood

1. I became a millionaire.
   [Indicative mood: real-world activity with real world consequences.]
2. If I became a millionaire . . .
   [Subjunctive mood: possible world only with no necessary suggestion of action in the real world.]

The subjunctive mood allows us to discuss possible worlds, and any sense of agency is understood as only hypothetical. Consider Winston's musing over the possible actions that he 'would have' taken if his world had turned out differently. Orwell understood how the subjunctive mood would make Winston's bold assertions ring hollow, suggesting that Winston would likely fail in his struggle to gain some degree of empowerment:

And it was exactly at this moment that the significant thing happened – IF, indeed, it did happen.

[p. 18]

Some nosing zealot . . . MIGHT start wondering why he had been writing . . . .

[p. 27]

. . . and it was POSSIBLE that his features had not been perfectly under control.

[p. 54]

I would have [given Katharine a 'good shove' over the cliff], IF I'd been the same person then as I am now. Or PERHAPS I WOULD – I'm not certain.

[p. 112]

To this day he did not know with any certainty that his mother was dead. It was perfectly POSSIBLE that she had merely been sent to a forced-labour camp. As for his sister, she MIGHT have been removed, like Winston himself, to one of the colonies for homeless children . . . or she MIGHT have been sent to the labor camp along with his mother.

[p. 135]

12.2.11 Linking verbs like *seem*

1. John has broken the window.
   [Transitive verb with agentive subject.]
2. John seems to have broken the window.
   [Linking verb, casting doubt on the agency of the grammatical subject.]

Linking verbs like *seem* and *appear* add a hedge, a sense of doubt, to any assertion into which they are incorporated. Just when Orwell could have described the physical encounter between Winston and Julia as the dynamic, life-affirming act it was, he chose instead to undercut the assertion by using a linking verb:

All this he SEEMED to see in the large eyes of his mother and his sister
. . . .

[p. 29]

There was a roar that SEEMED to make the pavement heave . . . .

[p. 72]

Her body SEEMED to be pouring some of its youth and vigour into his.

[p. 113]

Compare, for example, the difference in agency between the example passage immediately above and this paraphrase without the linking verb: *Her body poured some of its youth and vigour into his.*

12.2.12 Impersonal *one* and point-of-view shifts

1. I now can conclude that . . . .
   [First-person personal pronoun clearly indicates agency and responsibility.]

2. One now can conclude that . . .
   [Impersonal third-person pronoun undercuts a clear sense of agency
   and responsibility for any conclusions.]

Orwell employed the third person singular personal pronouns *he* and *she*
and the impersonal pronoun *you* throughout most of the novel. The occasional point-of-view shift to the impersonal *one* allowed Orwell another
grammatical device with which to downplay any sense of his characters'
agency, as in this passage describing Winston's reaction to drinking
Victory Gin. Note how this device generalizes and dilutes the reader's
sense of any direct personal reaction on Winston's part:

Instantly his face turned scarlet and water ran out of his eyes. The stuff
was like nitric acid, and moreover, in swallowing it ONE had the sensation of being hit on the back of the head with a rubber club.

[p. 8]

The smell was already filling the room, a rich hot smell which seemed
like an emanation from his early childhood, but which ONE did occasionally meet with even now . . .

[p. 117]

Given this background, ONE could infer, if ONE did not know it
already, the general structure of Oceanic society.

[p. 171]

Note the same shift, with the same effect, in these passages describing the
torture of Winston. (These passages also exploit many of the stylistic
features discussed earlier: passive voice, nominalization, depersonalization,
perfect aspect, negation, subjunctive mood and the linking verb *seem*.)

Style features	*Passage*
DEPERSONALIZATION	WINSTON'S HEART SANK. . . He had
NOMINALIZATION	A FEELING of deadly helplessness.
SUBJUNCTIVE MOOD	IF he could
PERFECT ASPECT	HAVE BEEN certain that O'Brien
NEGATION	was lying, it would NOT
PERFECT ASPECT, *SEEM*	HAVE SEEMED to matter. But it was perfectly
PERFECT ASPECT	possible that O'Brien HAD really FORGOTTEN the
SUBJUNCTIVE MOOD	photograph. And IF so, then already he
PERFECT ASPECT	would HAVE FORGOTTEN
NOMINALIZATION	HIS DENIAL of
NOMINALIZATION	REMEMBERING it, and forgotten the act
NOMINALIZATION	of FORGETTING. How could
IMPERSONAL *ONE*	ONE be sure that it was simply trickery?

[p. 204]

	A needle slid into Winston's arm. Almost in the same
NOMINALIZATION	instant A BLISSFUL, HEALING WARMTH spread all
PASSIVE VOICE	through his body. The pain WAS already HALF-FORGOTTEN. He opened his eyes and looked up gratefully at O'Brien. At the sight of the heavy, lined
DEPERSONALIZATION	face, so ugly and so intelligent, HIS HEART
SEEM	SEEMED to turn
SUBJUNCTIVE MOOD	over. IF he could
PERFECT ASPECT	HAVE MOVED he would
PERFECT ASPECT	HAVE STRETCHED OUT a hand and
PERFECT ASPECT	LAID it on O'Brien's arm. He had
NEGATION	NEVER loved him so deeply as at this moment, and
PERFECT ASPECT	NOT merely because he HAD STOPPED the pain. The
NEGATION	old feeling, that at bottom it did NOT matter whether
PERFECT ASPECT	O'Brien was a friend or an enemy, HAD COME BACK.
PASSIVE	O'Brien was a person who could BE TALKED TO.
SUBJUNCTIVE, *ONE*	PERHAPS ONE did
NEGATION	NOT want to
PASSIVE VOICE	BE LOVED so much as
PASSIVE VOICE	BE UNDERSTOOD.

[p. 208]

By shifting to the impersonal *one* in the last sentence of each passage above, Orwell avoids the proper nouns (like *Winston* or *Smith*) and the personal pronouns (like *he* or *him*). The impersonal *one* distances Winston from his desire for certainty or understanding. Such desires are too agentive, as can be seen in these paraphrases: *How could Winston be sure that it was simply trickery?* and *Perhaps he did not want to be loved so much as be understood.*

12.2.13 Modality shifts

1. John slapped the table.
   [Ordinary, agentive transitive.]

2. John { would / should / could / ought to / needs to / might / tried to } slap the table.

[The modal or quasi-modal auxiliary undercuts the agency of the transitive verb.]

As with the judicious use of impersonal *one*, Orwell used the modal auxiliary carefully. Modals allowed him to hedge the assertions made by transitive verbs; modals suggest obligation, necessity, willingness or attempts (etc.) to act, but they do not necessarily imply successful completed action:

> He [Winston] TRIED TO squeeze out some childhood memory. . . . But it was no use, he COULD not remember.
>
> [p. 7]

> If he COULD have been certain that O'Brien was lying, it WOULD not have seemed to matter. But it was perfectly possible that O'Brien had really forgotten the photograph. And if so, then already he WOULD have forgotten his denial of remembering it, and forgotten the act of forgetting. How COULD one be sure that it was simply trickery?
>
> [p. 204]

The hedge provided by the modality shift provides Orwell with an excellent means of downplaying agency. Compare the first example with this paraphrase: *he squeezed out some childhood memory.* Or consider Orwell's use of *could* in the first and last clauses of the second example. The paraphrases without modals would read *If he had been certain that O'Brien was lying* and *How is one sure that it was simply trickery?* The two paraphrases seem to suggest that Winston had the means to ascertain O'Brien's lies and trickery. However, the original passage with the modals promotes the hopelessness of Winston's ever acquiring such knowledge.

12.2.14 Existential *it* and other cleft sentences

1. John mailed the letter yesterday.
   [Ordinary, agentive transitive.]
2. It was yesterday that John mailed the letter.
   It was the letter that John mailed yesterday.
   [A cleft sentence, using for example the existential *it* as grammatical subject in the main clause, allows an information focus on one constituent, e.g. *yesterday* or *the letter* in example 2, effectively undercutting the agency of the grammatical subject in the more usual, unmarked sentence pattern as in example 1.]

Orwell could, in essence, lessen the suggested agency of certain concord subjects by using a clefted sentence pattern. A cleft sentence focuses on some peripheral part of a clause, such as an adverbial or adjective, and thereby demotes the agentive element to a subordinate clause:

> When one knew that any document was due for destruction, or even when one saw a scrap of waste paper lying about, IT WAS AN AUTOMATIC ACTION TO LIFT THE FLAP of the nearest memory hole and drop it in . . . .   [p. 35]

WHAT WAS even worse than having to focus his mind on a series of niggling jobs was the need to conceal his agitation from the telescreen.

[p. 90]

. . . IT struck him for the first time that she was beautiful.

[p. 180]

THE FUNNY THING IS I made sure it was full.

[p. 180]

IT WAS TRUE that he had no memories of anything different.

[p. 52]

The example immediately above is a classic form of wordiness, according to a host of composition handbooks. The handbooks would advise Orwell to rewrite the sentence as *Truly, he had no memories of anything different.* But by comparing the two briefly one can see that the 'more concise' revision presents an agent who is more definite, more assured. There is a sense of uncertainty in the original that cannot be captured without the cleft sentence focusing on some peripheral part of the proposition.

12.3 DISCUSSION

In concert, these fourteen stylistic features allowed Orwell to establish a limited third person narrator whose MIND STYLE is restricted to Winston's point of view and Winston's perceptions. (See Leech and Short 1981: 187–208 for an extensive discussion of mind style.) Such limited narration takes the reader into Winston's mind without creating a first person narrative. A first person narrative would not effectively promote the theme of passivity, since first person narrators are (by nature) too agentive; they are always doing, saying and thinking. Conversely, an omniscient third person narrator could not adequately convey the terrifying uncertainty of living in a totalitarian society. With a limited third person narrator, Orwell effectively confines the reader's knowledge: the reader can know only what Winston knows. Therefore, Orwell's limited third person narrative style allows readers to experience how truly passive Winston is.

In his personal relationships Winston is rarely, if ever, the initiator of action. The sexual aggressors in *Nineteen Eighty-Four* are Katharine ('the frigid little ceremony that Katharine had forced him to go through on the same night every week', p. 110) and Julia. Although Winston is endlessly curious about the Brotherhood, he does little to learn about it on his own; rather, O'Brien has to initiate him: 'He knew that sooner or later he would obey O'Brien's summons. Perhaps tomorrow, perhaps after a long delay – he was not certain' (p. 132).

His passivity extends even into his relationships with minor characters. It is Parsons who approaches and converses with Winston; it is Mrs Parsons who must ask for neighbourly help (Winston does not offer it).

Syme approaches Winston in the canteen seeking a lunchtime companion. Finally, Winston does not take much initiative or imagination to his work. He does not give the fictitious Ogilvy the Order of Conspicuous Merit because of the necessary cross-referencing that it would entail. In other words, he has ideas, but he will not act on them unless invited or ordered to do so.

The novel does present at least two moments in which Winston seems strongly agentive: in his memories of his childhood and in his opening a diary. Nevertheless, those moments also are suffused with language that undercuts Winston's agency. Significantly, those two moments of agency are also moments at which Winston feels profoundly guilty, and the horrible guilt that Winston associates with those two moments of agency reveals perhaps the psychological source of his passivity. For example, Winston remembers such aggressive acts as fighting for more food or stealing chocolate as a youth. Orwell's narration, however, downplays Winston's agency through the use of subjunctive mood, depersonalization, modality shifts, passive voice, presentational *there*, nominalizations, patient subjects, negations and the perfect aspect all in one passage.

Style features	Passage
SUBJUNCTIVE MOOD	Suddenly, AS THOUGH HE WERE LISTENING TO SOMEONE ELSE,
PATIENT SUBJECT	WINSTON HEARD himself demanding in
DEPERSONALIZATION	A LOUD BOOMING VOICE that he
MODAL,	SHOULD
PASSIVE VOICE	BE GIVEN the whole piece. His mother told him
NEGATION	NOT to be greedy.
PRESENTATIONAL *THERE*	*THERE* was a long, nagging
NOMINALIZATION	ARGUMENT that went round and round, with
NOMINALIZATION	SHOUTS, WHINES, TEARS, REMONSTRANCES,
NOMINALIZATION	BARGAININGS. His tiny sister, clinging to her mother with both hands, exactly like a baby monkey, sat looking over her shoulders at him with large, mournful eyes. In the end his mother broke off three-quarters of the chocolate and gave it to Winston, giving the
PATIENT SUBJECT	other quarter to his sister. THE LITTLE GIRL took hold of
NEGATION	it and looked at it dully, perhaps NOT knowing what it was. Winston stood watching her for a moment. Then with a sudden swift spring he
PERFECT ASPECT	HAD SNATCHED the piece of chocolate out of
DEPERSONALIZATION	HIS SISTER'S HAND and was fleeing for the door.

[pp. 134–5]

Likewise, when Winston commits himself to opening a diary, Orwell's narration erases Winston's agency:

Style features	Passage
CLEFT SENTENCE	THE THING THAT HE WAS ABOUT TO DO WAS TO OPEN A DIARY.
PRESENTATIONAL *THERE*	This was not illegal (nothing was illegal, since *THERE*
NEGATION	were NO longer any laws), but
SUBJUNCTIVE MOOD	IF detected
EXISTENTIAL *IT*	IT WAS REASONABLY CERTAIN THAT
MODAL	it WOULD
PASSIVE VOICE	BE PUNISHED by death, or at least by twenty-five years in a forced-labor camp. Winston fitted a nib into a penholder and sucked it to get the grease off. The
PASSIVE VOICE	pen was an archaic instrument, seldom USED even for
PERFECT ASPECT	signatures, and he HAD PROCURED one, furtively and with
NOMINALIZATION	some difficulty, simply because of A FEELING that the
PASSIVE VOICE	beautiful creamy paper deserved to BE WRITTEN ON with
PASSIVE VOICE	a real nib instead of BEING SCRATCHED with an ink-
NEGATION	pencil. Actually he was NOT
PASSIVE VOICE	USED to writing by hand.

[pp. 9–10]

Indeed, the pivotal act that sets the whole plot in motion – Winston's purchasing of the blank book to use as a diary – seems involuntary:

Style features	Passage
PERFECT ASPECT,	He . . . HAD BEEN
PASSIVE VOICE	STRICKEN immediately by
NOMINALIZATION +	
DEPERSONALIZATION	AN OVERWHELMING DESIRE to possess it.
NEGATION	. . . At the time he was NOT conscious of wanting it for any particular purpose

[p. 9]

12.4 ANALYSIS AND DISCUSSION OF MANUSCRIPT REVISIONS

The facsimile edition of the manuscript of *Nineteen Eighty-Four* reveals how Orwell frequently revised his prose to enhance the passivity of his language. For example, he extensively reworked the passages above describing Winston's opening of a diary to include cleft sentences, presentational *there*, subjunctive mood, negation, nominalizations, depersonalization, modality shifts, perfect aspect and additional passive voice verbs. Compare the manuscript passage below with the same passage from the novel discussed in the section above; notice how each clause but one in his earlier draft contains agentive active voice verbs:

As soon as he set eyes on it he had known that in just such a book he could write the diary he dreamed of – a diary that should be simply a transcript of the interminable monologue that went on and on inside his skull . . . . He dipped his pen in the ink and began to write. No mark appeared on the paper: instead, next moment, a huge blob of ink flopped off the nib and ruined the front page. . . . The pen was an archaic instrument, seldom used even for signatures. Normally one either used an ink-pencil or dictated into the speakwrite. . . .

[*Facsimile*, 23]

Likewise, note Orwell's revisions in two very different sections of the novel, each revision reaching for greater passivity in language The manuscript clause 'Private ownership has given way to group ownership' (*Facsimile*, 211) in Goldstein's book is revised to employ a passive voice verb: 'Private property has been abolished' (ibid., 211). Orwell further enhanced the passive voice with nominalizations and depersonalization:

Style feature	Passage
PASSIVE VOICE	Wealth and privilege ARE most easily
PASSIVE VOICE	DEFENDED when they ARE POSSESSED
NOMINALIZATION	jointly. The so–called 'ABOLITION of private property'
	which took place in the middle years of the century
NOMINALIZATION	meant, in effect, the CONCENTRATION of
DEPERSONALIZATION	property IN FAR FEWER HANDS than before. . . .

[*1984*, 170]

Similarly, another passage describing Winston's experience in his cell at Miniluv originally read, '. . . whereas they [the Thought Police] ordered the political prisoners about like dogs' (*Facsimile*, 213). That passage was revised to eliminate the agency of *they ordered*: '. . . even when they were obliged to handle them roughly' (*1984*, 187).

Indeed, the whole of Oceania becomes such a regimented society that even the police have no agency. They follow orders ('are obliged to handle them roughly') and become as thoroughly passive as their victims.

12.5 CONCLUSION AND SOME REMARKS ON QUALITATIVE AND QUANTITATIVE STYLISTICS

In the introduction I presented the thesis that the critic's responses to Orwell's writing style undervalued the precision with which he constructed the literary language of *Nineteen Eighty-Four*. (The critics felt, remember, that its style was drab, uninspired, 'sweaty'.) To support my thesis, I have outlined a host of syntactic structures that form a constellation of stylistic features, a lexicogrammatical motif in the language of the novel, promoting the theme of hopelessness and creating the sense of powerlessness within Winston's character. I hypothesized that Orwell developed his themes and characters through a narrative style that systematically undercuts AGENCY as a phenomenon of the novel's language.

Howe (1982: 324), more than other critics, is sensitive to the thematic import of the loss of agency:

> Oceanic society may evolve through certain stages of economic development, but the life of its members is static, a given and measured quantity that can neither rise to tragedy nor tumble to comedy. Human personality, as we have come to grasp for it in a class society and hope for it in a classless society, is obliterated; man becomes a function of a process he is never allowed to understand or control.

I justified my claims about the critics' responses and Orwell's narrative style in that novel by comparing the fourteen stylistic features discussed above with their possible paraphrases and their draft manuscript correspondences. That kind of stylistic analysis I take to be **qualitative** stylistics, examining through close reading the patterns of linguistic features in a text that together evoke particular, identifiable responses in the readers. Like all stylistic analyses, **qualitative** stylistics is comparative, to be sure, but its comparisons are made using the linguistic system as a whole as the background. **Qualitative** stylistics takes a finite (and sometimes very small) text and compares the author's choices of sound, lexis, grammar (and so on) in that text against the linguistic system as a whole.

One goal of **qualitative** stylistics is illuminating the patterns of linguistic choices that make a literary experience: that is, readers often say that a story 'made me feel' sad/happy/angry, etc. In other words, literature is experienced, not simply read; the literary experience occurs through language; and it is the goal of **qualitative** stylistics to highlight the linguistic features that evoke those literary (and emotional) experiences for the readers. This essay itself is essentially qualitative, as one can see in sections 12.2–4 above, where I regularly invite the reader to compare Orwell's language in the novel with paraphrases available to him in the linguistic system that he could have used (and actually sometimes did use in drafts).

Quantitative stylistics, on the other hand, compares the frequency of linguistic features in a text against a norm. Those features that are significantly higher or lower in frequency than the norm become stylistic markers for that text. **Quantitative** stylistics is not in opposition to **qualitative** analyses, as is often assumed in some literary studies, which denigrate 'statistics' (read here: **quantitative** stylistics) and elevate 'intuition' (read here: **qualitative** stylistics). **Quantitative** analyses can corroborate **qualitative** stylistics and can serve as an instrument with which to hone intuitive insights into a text.

For example, Table 12.1 presents quantitative data which in large part support the qualitative analyses of Orwell's style in the novel.[2] Looking at those style features for which there is an established norm,[3] one can see that Orwell relies heavily on PASSIVES, PERFECT ASPECT,

Table 12.1 Occurrence of style features per 1,000 words of *Ninteen Eight-Four* and normative text

Style feature	NEF	norm	Citation for norm
FINITE PASSIVE	10.9	6.0	Francis and Kučera (1982: 554)
NON-FINITE PASSIVE	5.4		
ALL PASSIVE forms	16.3		
PERFECT ASPECT	16.8	10/14	Francis and Kučera (1982: 555); Ellegård (1978: 65)
NOT	9.8	10.0	Francis and Kučera (1982: 545), Ellegård (1978: 61)
NOT-CONTRACTION	1.4	1.5	Francis and Kučera (1982: 546)
PRESENTATIONAL *THERE*	6.0	2.0	Ellegård 1978: 40)
Subjunctive mood (total frequency of *if, perhaps, possible, possibly, probably, as though* and *whether*)	5.2	3.8	Francis and Kučera 1982: 209, 304, 316, 322, 415, 450)
MODALS (appearing in overt subjunctive)	2.2	0.0	Ellegård (1978: 67)
BE (appearing in overt subjunctive)	0.5	0.3	Ellegård (1978: 66)
LINKING VERB *SEEM*	2.2	0.8	Francis and Kučera (1982: 364)
IMPERSONAL *ONE*	0.9	0.6	Francis and Kučera (1982: 289)
All MODALS	16.0	15.0	Francis and Kučera (1982: 545), Ellegård (1978: 67)
EXISTENTIAL *IT*	5.4	2.0	Ellegård (1978: 36)

PRESENTATIONAL *THERE*, SUBJUNCTIVE MOOD,[4] LINKING VERB *SEEM*, IMPERSONAL *ONE* and EXISTENTIAL *IT*, just as the qualitative stylistic analyses earlier in this essay suggested.[5]

There are style features of which Orwell's usage does not appear significantly different from the established norm. The statistics for *not*, its contracted form, and all modals are nearly identical. However, Francis and Kučera (1982: 544–7) note that *not*, its contraction, and the modals occurred significantly more frequently in the Imaginative Groups of genres than it did in the Informative Group of genres, a fact which should draw those norms considerably closer to Orwell's usage. (Nor does the similarity of those statistics lessen the **meaning** of negation or modals, and part of their meaning in the linguistic system is their ability to deny or undercut agency by negating a proposition or attributing 'obligation' or 'necessity' without implying completed action.)[6]

Orwell's style, then, is not the dry language of a hurried work. Rather, it demonstrates the best in literary art, a merger of grammatical form with meaning and theme. Orwell was sensitive to this iconic merger of form with function in literature:

When I was sixteen I suddenly discovered the joy of mere words, i.e.

the sounds and associations of words. . . . I wanted to write enormous naturalistic novels with unhappy endings, full of detailed descriptions and arresting similes, and also full of purple passages in which words were used partly for the sake of their sound.

[*Collected Essays* 1: 1–2]

Orwell's revisions reflect a conscious attempt to create a particular syntactic stance. That stance enabled Orwell to progress systematically through several levels of passivity:

theme → plot → character development → narration → style

Orwell conveyed the horrifying futility of life under a totalitarian regime not only through the overt passivity that readers can readily discover in plot and dialogue, but also through the covert passivity of Winston's mind style, as reflected in Orwell's narration and character development.

NOTES

1 The following abbreviations are used throughout this chapter for textual references to George Orwell's work: *1984* (Orwell 1961); *Collected Essays* (Orwell 1968); *Facsimile* (Orwell 1984). Small capitals are often added to passages quoted from *Nineteen Eighty-Four* and the *Facsimile* in sections 12.2–4 to highlight particular syntactic constructions under discussion.

2 I have changed the expression of some of the statistics in the cited references so that all statistics are expressed as the frequency of occurrence per thousand words of text. Francis and Kučera (1982), in particular, often present their statistics as totals for the whole Brown University corpus or as percentages. I have converted those statistics to reveal the number of occurrences per thousand words of text for easier presentation and comparison.

3 The statistics listed in the 'norm' column are derived from two sources: Ellegård (1978) and Francis and Kučera (1982). From Ellegård (1978) I have chosen statistics from the Popular Fiction genre, selected from the Imaginative Group of genres in the Brown University corpus. From Francis and Kučera (1982) I have chosen statistics from the General Fiction genre or from the Imaginative Group of genres in the Brown University corpus whenever possible. The Popular and General Fiction genres specifically (and Imaginative Group of genres generally) provide a set of texts which most closely match the language of *Nineteen Eighty-Four*, establishing a reliable comparative norm.

4 The normative number for the SUBJUNCTIVE MOOD in Table 12.1 is inflated in several ways. First, I counted only clearly SUBJUNCTIVE occurrences of *possible*, *possibly*, *probably* and *as though* in the novel. However, the frequency data in my normative reference (Francis and Kučera 1982) did not distinguish between SUBJUNCTIVE and non-SUBJUNCTIVE uses of those words; I simply counted all occurrences in the reference, knowing that would inflate the normative SUBJUNCTIVE MOOD statistic. Further, the cited reference has no data on AS THOUGH as a conjunction; therefore I included all occurrences of THOUGH in the statistics, assuming that I would capture all occurrences of AS THOUGH in the corpus (but

many non-SUBJUNCTIVE occurrences of THOUGH as well).

5 The statistics for *Nineteen Eighty-Four* in Table 12.1 were collected from approximately 10,000 words of the novel chosen at random. Each page holds approximately 400 words, 400 words per page × twenty-five pages = 10,000 words, and I chose the twenty-five pages randomly by counting the stylistic features of every nth page, where n = 9. The number 9 was drawn by lot. The pages in the statistics, therefore, were 9, 18, 27, 36, 45, 54, 63, 72, 81, 90, 99, 108, 117, 126, 135, 144, 153, 162, 171, 180, 189, 198, 207, 216, and 225.

6 See Ringbom (1973) for an interesting comparison between Orwell the novelist in *Nineteen Eighty-Four* and Orwell the essayist. Ringbom (1973: 28–36, 45–8), too, finds frequent use of IF, WOULD, impersonal ONE and negatives in the style of Orwell the essayist, attributing those features to Orwell's fondness for hypothetical cases and contrast in argumentation.

REFERENCES

Austin, T. (1986), '(In)transitives: some thoughts on ambiguity in poetic texts', *Journal of Literary Semantics*, 16, 23–38.

Bloom, H. (1987), 'Introduction', in H. Bloom (ed.), *George Orwell: Modern Critical Views*, pp. 1–7, New York, Chelsea House.

Cluysenaar, A. (1975), *Aspects of Literary Stylistics*, New York, St Martin's Press.

Curme, G. (1931), *A Grammar of the English Language 2, Syntax*, Essex, Conn., Verbatim.

Dillon, G. (1978), *Language Processing and the Reading of Literature*, Bloomington, Indiana University Press.

Ellegård, A. (1978), *The Syntactic Structure of English Texts: a Computer-based Study of Four Kinds of Text in the Brown University Corpus*, Göteborg, Acta Universitatis Gothoburgensis.

Empson, W. (1963), *Seven Types of Ambiguity*, 3rd ed., London, Chatto & Windus.

Enkvist, N. (1973), *Linguistic Stylistics*, The Hague, Mouton.

Flammia, M. (1987), 'Beyond Orwell: clarity and the English language', in C. Wemyss and A. Ugrinsky (eds) *George Orwell*, pp. 27–33, Westport, Conn., Greenwood Press.

Francis, W.N., and Kučera, H. (1982), *Frequency Analysis of English Usage: Lexicon and Grammar*, Boston, Mass., Houghton Mifflin.

Halliday, M.A.K. (1971), 'Linguistic function and literary style', in S. Chatman (ed.) *Literary Style: a Symposium*, pp. 330–65, London, Oxford University Press.

———— (1985), *An Introduction to Functional Grammar*, London, Edward Arnold.

Harris, R. (1987), 'The misunderstanding of Newspeak', in H. Bloom (ed.), *George Orwell: Modern Critical Views*, pp. 113–19, New York, Chelsea House.

Howe, I. (1982), '*1984*: history as nightmare', in I. Howe (ed.), *Orwell's Nineteen Eighty-Four: Text, Sources, Criticism*, pp. 320–32, 2nd ed., New York, Harcourt Brace Jovanovich.

Kies, D. (1985), 'Some stylistic features of business and technical writing: nominalization, passive voice and agency', *Journal of Technical Writing and Communication* 25, 299–308.

Kress, G., and Hodge, R. (1979), *Language as Ideology*, London, Routledge.

Leech, G., and Short, M.H. (1981), *Style in Fiction: a Linguistic Introduction to English Fictional Prose*, London, Longman.

Orwell, G. (1961), *Nineteen Eighty-Four*, New York, New American Library.

—————— (1968), *Collected Essays, Journalism, and Letters of George Orwell*, 1–4, S. Orwell and I. Angus (eds), New York, Harcourt, Brace & World.

—————— (1984), *Nineteen Eighty-Four: the Facsimile of the Extant Manuscript*, P. Davison (ed.), London, Secker & Warburg.

Petro, P. (1982), *Modern Satire: Four Studies*, Berlin, Mouton.

Quirk, R., Greenbaum, S., Leech, G., and Svartvik, J. (1985), *A Comprehensive Grammar of the English Language*, London, Longman.

Ringbom, H. (1973), *George Orwell as Essayist: a Stylistic Study*, Acta Akademia Aboensis, series A, vol. 44, No. 2, Åbo, Finland.

ACKNOWLEDGEMENTS

This chapter began as a paper presented at the seventeenth International Systemic Congress, 3–7 July, at the University of Stirling. I wish to thank Jonathan Rose both for his helpful comments and for his patient reading of several drafts of this essay. I also wish to thank Louise Ravelli and Martin Davies for their helpful insights into several issues. All errors, of course, are solely my responsibility.

The estate of the late Sonia Brownell Orwell and Martin Secker & Warburg Ltd are acknowledged for permission to include extracts from *Nineteen Eighty-Four* by George Orwell.

Index